Oppenheim Toy Portfolio
Award Rating System

Our rating system for quick reference!

ooooo An outstanding product, not to be missed.

oooo A very good worth-the-money product.

ooo Good, not fantastic. Will have limited appeal, but not for everyone.

oo Good idea, poorly executed; or great execution, terrible idea.

o Thumbs down, or "What were they thinking?"

What They Win

ooooo **Oppenheim Toy Portfolio Platinum Award.** These represent the most innovative, engaging new products of the year. See the 2006 Platinum Award List.

oooo **Oppenheim Toy Portfolio Gold Award.** Given to outstanding new products that enhance the lives of children.

ooo–o Nothing.

Other Notable Awards

 Oppenheim Toy Portfolio Blue Chip Classic Award—Reserved for classic products that should not be missed just because they weren't invented yesterday. Products must be in the marketplace for five years to be considered for this award.

 Oppenheim Toy Portfolio SNAP Award—Given to products that can be used by or easily adapted for children with special needs.

Applauding Manufacturers. We applaud the manufacturers that submitted products to our review knowing that we write about the good, bad, and otherwise. Unlike many other toy testers, we don't charge fees to submit products. We don't take ad dollars. We don't sell any products. Our editorial independence means we can say what works and what doesn't. No manufacturer refused to send us products for review. (We will keep you posted if that changes!)

Praise for

OPPENHEIM
TOY PORTFOLIO

As seen on NBC's TODAY Show, Oprah, and CNN

If thoughts of holiday shopping have you fretting about what to buy for the little ones, help is on the way... the Oppenheim Toy Portfolio is just out... recognizing the year's best new toys.

—*USA Today*

...cuts through the confusion and offers the consumer sound information about what's good—and not so good.

—*Associated Press*

Sane comprehensive survey... absolutely worth the price.

—*Miami Herald*

Put away the aspirin, because there's a new book... that should make your toy-buying decisions smart and easy.

—*Houston Post*

Definite parental appeal.

—*Booklist*

The authors of the Oppenheim Toy Portfolio have yet again answered the call of parents who are tired of guessing which are the best toys and products for children—they've published a book.

—*New York Family*

The Oppenheim Toy Portfolio tells parents which are the best and dumbest toys.

—*Business Week*

OPPENHEIM TOY PORTFOLIO

2006 Edition

The Best Toys, Books, Videos,
Music & Software For Kids

Joanne Oppenheim
and **Stephanie Oppenheim**

Illustrations by **Joan Auclair**

With thanks to our family and the many other families who helped us test for the best.

—Joanne & Stephanie

Designed by Joan Auclair

ISBN: 0-9721050-3-4

Contents

Introduction

Our Thirteenth Edition

Once again we have spent the year testing the hundreds of new toys, books, videos, and audios that you will be considering for the children in your life. Whether you are a new parent or grandparent, or an uncle, aunt, or family friend, you will find reviews in these pages that can help you bring home memorable and engaging products that will entertain and fit your child's developing needs. That is what we do for you.

Why a guide to children's media? Anyone who has walked the aisles of a giant toy supermarket or tried to sift through the mountains of books, DVDs, and music designed for children appreciates how hard it is to know what to buy. Our goal is to take the guesswork out of choosing products that are not a waste of your money or your child's time.

Over the last two decades of reviewing products targeted to kids, we've noted that the expectations of what a toy does have changed radically, although not always to the benefit of children and their play lives.

Quick Rating at a Glance. In addition to awarding products with a Platinum, Gold, or Blue Chip rating, we have also marked products with "play balls" right after the price to give you a quicker read on what worked and what didn't. You'll find our lists of this year's award-winning and top-rated products in the opening pages of this book. In addition to our PLATINUM AWARD Winners list, you'll find lists of outstanding products for group play, parent-child interactions, and office quiet time; top-rated science, educational, special needs, and gender-free products; our top picks for Under $10, $15, and $20; as well as Break-the-Bank (grandparent!) gifts.

You'll find full descriptions of these as well as other excellent new products, along with shopping information, in each of the age-appropriate chapters of the book. As always, we've included our BLUE CHIP classics, since we believe it would be a shame for kids to miss such products just because they weren't invented yesterday.

Children's products have a short shelf life. In fact, over 60 percent of this year's book is entirely new content—a response to the thousands of new choices introduced this year (6,000 new toys alone).

As always, we tested plenty of products that just didn't work or live up to our expectations. Yet as the process moved along, we were relieved and ultimately delighted with the range of wonderful choices available to consumers this year.

What Are the Trends for 2006?

Notable Trends

Generational Markers. Want to feel old? The Rubik's Cube is 25 years old. Monopoly is 70, Operation is 40, as is Trouble Pop O Matic (a favorite here); Mystery Date is 40 and Pictionary is 20. So, what's old is new again, except, of course, those of us who played with these toys as kids!

Yo-yos for Idiots. Obviously not what the company calls their new Power Brain YoYo from Hasbro—but if you were ever challenged, as were we, to get the yo-yo to return to your sweaty palm, much less do a trick, look no further. But beware—these yo-yos are so smart they whip back up quickly enough to chip a tooth.

Tiddlywinks. Another wink to the olden days, we saw at least a half a dozen variations on tiddlywinks. Now you can launch everything from frogs to meatballs. CareBears are also back (they glow in the dark) and Trollz are also trying hard to be even tackier than before.

American Idol Wannabes. The hit show has spawned its own dolls (even Barbie, herself an American icon, wants in on the pop culture phenomenon). Karaoke machines, floor and head microphones (pink of course), and even a vanity set with built in pop songs are among the entries designed to appeal to the American Idol in training for the year 2020!

Dogs that Bite and other creatures! Beware some of those furry, sweet-looking dogs called Smoochy Pups (stick your finger in his mouth and they clamp down). There's also the new high-tech Roboraptor that hisses and goes into stalk mode and generally spooked us out. The same company's Chimp Head looks like a prop from Escape from the Planet of the Apes movie. Amazing.

Career Planning? One of the more curious doll lines of the year—dolls that pop out of plastic cupcakes. Somehow this reminded us of a bad movie reference to the girl jumping out of the cake at a stag party.

Plug and Play for the Preschool Set. Before your child enters the land of video games (from which many never return), companies are hoping that you'll buy one of their gaming systems for your preschooler. Our testers gave mixed reviews to the lastest offerings.

Potty Dolls and Potty Books. Last year we were amazed by the number of potty dolls we received for review. This year, books have caught up with what we can only gather is a national preoccupation. Titles such as *Potty Poo-Poo Wee-Wee!*, *Time to Pee*, and *Pee-Ew!* (a book about farting), are just some of the books we passed on for preschoolers. Perhaps this recent run of books got their impetus from the best-selling *Walter, the Farting Dog*—the ultimate bathroom reading.

Pseudo Book Connection. Many toy manufacturers are packaging storybooks with construction toys and pretend settings. While the concept is one we applaud, the execution is often tacky.

Talking Capes. Action figures are bigger than ever—they are as big as your child—in fact, they are your child. With a talking Superman or Batman cape and a simple push of a button, you'll get a pre-recorded line delivered on cue. No input from your child required.

Castles. Last year we reported about great castle settings for preschoolers and early school-age kids. Oddly enough, this theme has now trickled down to infant and toddler toys.

Fairies. You'd almost think fairies were real. (Can you tell we don't get out much?) There are so many fairy toys this year. Fairy settings, fairy costumes, fairy dolls, fairy books—you get the idea. Most fairy nice.

The Zen of Knitting. One of the strongest trends in crafts remains knitting and crocheting. Can you imagine that granny squares are cool? In fact, some of the kits are a really good deal for adults as well (bamboo needles and quality chunky yarn are included in many).

Get Up! In perhaps one of the best trends of the year, games are encouraging kids to get up and move. Interestingly, many of these come from the plug-in TV games that have in past been responsible for a new generation of couch potoatoes.

What was that? At first we thought it was a symptom of our age, but then we also heard from our testers that many toys were notably too soft in sound level. After years of complaining about too much noise, we're not sure we should even mention this one. We also loved that many of our toddler testers loved playing with the volume controls!

A retro-ized toyland. Bingo, knitting, wooden push toys . . . our award list has a particularly strong throwback to a kinder and gentler time.

On the Upside

Wood Toys. We saw a resurgence in wooden toys this year. Push toys, cars, wonderful marble runs, castles, dollhouses. They are beautifully crafted and likely to have a long play life.

Fewer Stupid "Smart" Toys. Toys that claim to teach babies school skills before they can talk are thankfully on the decline. There are still notable exceptions . . . for example, a toy labeled for six-month-olds, who are not yet walking, to find the shape or color object and fit it in place.

Pretend Power. There's a miniature play setting for every interest: castles, a pirate ship, a zoo, an amazing crane, and a treehouse are just some of the great props for pretend that made our top list.

Game Time. Classic games, as well as a new crop of innovative games, are among the best choices in toyland. Most kids will jump at a chance to play any truly "interactive" game with their folks. Games are also a no-tears way of developing math, language, geography, and reading skills, and gamesmanship, too. They give families an opportunity to share some important values (being a good sport, for example) and also time to talk while the game's being played.

Volume Controls Are In! Perhaps to bolster parental sanity, toy makers have added volume controls to their electronic wonders (and even the revolutionary option of playing with the sound off). We usually find that less noise means more play value in the long run.

Who's the Boss? Thank goodness there seem to be fewer intrusive toys that dictate how kids are to play. Indeed, play is one of the areas where kids can and should be empowered to use their own creative powers.

On the Downside

Extreme Makeover. Reality makeover shows are all the rage and now there's a doll that takes the concept to the limit. The new My Scene Swappin' Styles from Mattel allows girls unhappy with the doll's look to pop off the head and replace it with two other alternatives. We hope the networks don't get any ideas.

Rococo Plastic. We have never seen so many truly ugly toys that we know will exist in some landfill for centuries. Take, for example, the My Little Pony Butterfly Island. It's a dream world of plastic ponies clearly inspired by Liberace's decorator. While there's nothing technically wrong with many of the toys in this category, they are just too ugly to have around.

Puzzles for Babies? We were sent several puzzles with oversized pieces marked for 12- and 18-month-olds. It doesn't matter how big the pieces are, babies do not have the visual discrimination to see part/whole images or to understand the logic of putting them together. Nor do they have the dexterity to turn and fit pieces of a jigsaw puzzle together. Putting babies' images on the puzzle pieces does not make them appropriate for babies! It's like reading *War and Peace* to your preschooler. We wonder if any of these puzzle makers have ever played with a 12–18-month-old baby?

Your child's not stupid. Age labels are off kilter . . . not just for babies and toddlers, but for older kids as well. We had bead kits and construction sets that are misleadingly labeled at much younger ages than would be possible. While we are all for parental assistance, we think a lot of frustration could be saved if toys were more honestly labeled to fit.

PhD required. While some games had ambiguous directions, others had direction overkill. One card game designed for 8-year-olds was tested by a family with numerous post-graduate degrees—even with all that brain power, no one could keep track of all the permutations.

Misleading Boxes. Our testers were particularly up in arms about boxes that did not warn that additional purchases were required, or boxes where it looked like you were getting more than you actually were.

No More Steering. In what we assume is a cost-saving move, most ride-on toys for the youngest riders no longer have real steering—forcing kids to lift the whole toy up when they want to change direction.

Where's the story? Hands down, the most disappointing year we've had in reviewing children's books. We usually have a stack of entertaining picture books with engaging stories and compelling artwork. This year's stories were flat and so much of the artwork presented a disturbingly ugly view of the world, both real and make-believe. Most upsetting was the absence of humor, seemingly replaced with a negative view of life. While this may reflect a grownup sensibility at the moment, children need an optimistic view.

Hurry Up, Baby! The marketing message to new parents is clear. "Smart toys" will help your baby learn faster and achieve more. They don't mention that developmentally, babies learn best through real-life experiences and that too many lights and sounds can stimulate babies to distraction. Babies and toddlers are not ready for symbolic learning. The fact that a toddler can recite the alphabet is nothing more than a great parlor trick—ask the same toddler what "l-m-n-o-p" means and see what happens. There is no one magic toy that will guarantee an Ivy League acceptance (or even a spot in your city's competitive preschools)!

The Ultimate Downside. All of this rushing gives kids the unfortunate message that learning is hard and that maybe they're not very good learners. The most important thing parents can do is provide an environment that helps develop their children's confidence and a positive sense of themselves as learners. Many of the academic skills will be learned with much less difficulty later on, when children are more developmentally ready.

Trust your instincts and relax; the misguided "sooner is better" mentality is not a view shared by the majority of child development experts. Your toddler does not need to know how to spell *cat* or five words that rhyme with *star*. For children at every stage of development, toys that match their emerging abilities can best foster learning.

Talk, read, play with, and enjoy your child. Children learn language when people talk and listen to them. Literacy grows from the pleasures discovered in sharing books with meaningful stories and memorable illustrations. It is not served by rushing babies and toddlers with letter and sound drills. During early childhood the everyday discoveries of life have more educational value than any quiz machine you can bring home. Interactive people are far more important to learning than interactive machines!

Just Toys—What Difference Do They Make?

So what's the harm? After all, this is the 21st century. This is the age of technology, and even the Consumer Product Safety Commission is considering adjusting its age guidelines.

But pushing kids to do things that are developmentally inappropriate delivers a powerfully negative message that colors how kids think about themselves as competent, able doers. Parents, bombarded with the "smart toy, smart child" message, may also wonder if there's something wrong with their toddler who's incapable of rhyming in three languages or spelling *unicorn* by age three!

We used to "invest" in our toys. A favorite doll would be your companion in good times and bad (real and pretend), and our toys grew with us. Preprogrammed toys do not have the same lasting play value, however. For the most part, they are the Toyland equivalent of a one-trick pony.

Pretend No More. Pretend play is not merely something

cute that children do while they are waiting to grow up. It's through pretending that children begin to think symbolically, letting one thing stand for another. The ability to make their own symbols, by turning a mud pie with sticks into a birthday cake with candles, provides the underpinnings for more abstract symbolic systems.

Changing Expectations. Play is also one of those wonderful states where kids can step into roles of control—even if it is pretend. So playhouses with sound effects that tell kids it's raining—"shut the window"—or small trucks with drivers who run the show with voice commands, steal words from the mouths of babes. As more and more tech toys invade Toyland, the expectations of what a toy does seem to be changing in the minds of children as well as adults. As toys become more literal, children also become more passive observers; the true value of play is turned upside down, with children reduced to pushing buttons and reacting to what the toy does instead of being active players. Kids end up moving around the play schemes dreamed up by adults—and being robbed of the power of play.

We're all for technology, but not when it is used to strip the value and fun of play from children.

Expanded Coverage

We have included reviews of the best products we tested this year as well as highlighting some notable losers. Unfortunately, there isn't space for all the products we review—so be sure to visit our website, www.toyportfolio.com, where our database of reviews is available. We'd like to thank all the families that contributed to this book. As always, we welcome you, our readers, to give us your feedback on the selections. For new readers, you'll find our review process and criteria for our award program below.

Happy playing!

Joanne   Stephanie

How We Select the Best

We shop for children year 'round—only we get to do what most parents wish they could do before they buy. We open the toys, run the DVDs, read the books, and play the music. We get to compare all the toys that may look remarkably similar but often turn out to be quite different. For example, we put the toy trains together and find out which ones don't stay on the tracks.

How We're Different

We don't sell products. We don't take fees for looking at products. The **Oppenheim Toy Portfolio** was introduced in 1989 as the only independent consumer review of children's media. Unlike most other groups that rate products, we do not charge entry fees or accept ads from manufacturers. When you see our award seals on products, you can be assured that they are "award-winning" because they were selected by a noted expert in child development, children's literature, or education, and then rated by the most objective panel of judges—kids.

The Real Experts Speak: Kids and Their Families

To get a meaningful sampling, we deal with families from all walks of life. We have testers in the city and in the country, in diapers and in blue jeans, in school clothes and in tutus. They have parents who are teachers, secretaries, lawyers, doctors, writers, engineers, doormen, software programmers, editors, psychologists, librarians, engineers, business people, architects, family therapists, musicians, artists, nurses, and early childhood educators. In some instances we have tested products in preschool and after-school settings where we can get feedback from groups of children. Since all new products tend to have novelty appeal, we ask our testers to live with a product for a while before assessing it. Among other things, we always ask, Would you recommend it to others?

Criteria We Use for Choosing Quality Products

- What is this product designed to do and how well does it do it?

- What can the child do with the product? Does it invite active doing and thinking or simply passive watching?

- Is it safe and well designed, and can it withstand the unexpected?

- Does it "fit" the developmental needs, interests, and typical skills of the children for whom it was designed?

- What message does it convey? Toys as well as books and videos can say a great deal about values that parents are trying to convey. For example, does the product reflect old sexual stereotypes that limit children's views of themselves and others?

- What will a child learn from this product? Is it a "smart" product that will engage the child's mind or simply a novelty with limited play value?

- Is it entertaining? No product makes our list if kids find it boring, no matter how "good" or "educational" it claims to be.

- Is the age label correct? Is the product so easy that it will be boring or so challenging that it will be frustrating?

Rating System

Outstanding products, selected by our testers, are awarded one of four honors:

 Oppenheim Toy Portfolio Platinum Award— These represent the most innovative, engaging new products of the year. See the 2006 Platinum Award List.

 Oppenheim Toy Portfolio Gold Seal Award— Given to outstanding new products that enhance the lives of children. Products listed with four play balls have received a Gold Seal Award.

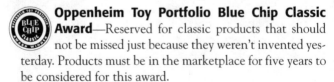 **Oppenheim Toy Portfolio Blue Chip Classic Award**—Reserved for classic products that should not be missed just because they weren't invented yesterday. Products must be in the marketplace for five years to be considered for this award.

Oppenheim Toy Portfolio SNAP Award—Our Special Needs Adaptable Product Award is given to products that can be used by or easily adapted for children with special needs. All products reviewed in that chapter are recommended; the most outstanding are SNAP Award winners.

Using This Book

Each section begins with a play profile that tells you what to expect during each developmental stage and what "basic gear" will enhance learning and play. We also give you suggestions for best gifts for your budget and, perhaps most importantly, a stage-by-stage list of toys to avoid.

Because we know how busy people are these days, our reviews are purposely short and provide information on how to get your hands on the product.

A word about prices: Our award-winning products are not all high-ticket items. We have selected the very best products in toy supermarkets, as well as those that you will find in specialty stores, museum shops, and quality catalogs. We have listed the suggested retail prices, but they will vary tremendously depending on where you shop.

Telephone numbers: Where available, we have given a customer service number in case you have difficulty locating the product in your area. For some educational products, you'll find a catalog number for ordering.

Child's Play—More Than Fun!

For children, playing is more than a fun way to fill the day. It's through play that children learn and develop all sorts of important physical, intellectual, and social skills. Like musicians, children use well-chosen toys, books, and music to orchestrate their play. As they grow and develop, so does their need for more complex playthings that challenge and enhance their learning. Toys and stories with the right developmental fit help create a marvelous harmony for learning and fun. The **Oppenheim Toy Portfolio** is a resource book you can use to make that kind of mix.

OPPENHEIM TOY PORTFOLIO
PLATINUM TOY AWARDS 2006

INFANTS

Gymini Total Playground Kick & Play
(Tiny Love), *pp. 9, 258*

Bucket Buddies (Infantino), *p. 16*

**Lamaze Lights & Sounds Barnyard Crawl
Toy*/Lamaze Whirl & Twirl Jungle***
(RC2/Learning Curve), *pp. 21, 23, 29, 30, 259*

Press N Go Inchworm (International Playthings), *p. 24*

Tutti Frutti Dog (Gund), *p. 27*

TODDLERS

Pushing Car and Doll Pram (Haba), *p. 36*

Rocking Wobble Whale (Mamas & Papas), *p. 38*

Learn-Around Playground (LeapFrog), *pp. 45, 261*

Super Spiral Play Tower (International Playthings),
pp. 46, 264

Lego Duplo Thomas Load and Carry Train Set
(Lego Systems), *p. 47*

Rick the Frog & Friends (Rich Frog), *p. 53*

Latitude Enfant Grannimals Collection (Pint Size
Productions), *p. 53*

Small World Living Wooden Kitchen Appliances
(Small World Toys), *p. 59*

PRESCHOOLERS

Dolls, Bears, & Dollhouse

Calico Critters Townhome (International Playthings),
p. 82

Jules*/Lili* (Corolle), *pp. 76, 122*

Great Big Creamy Bear* (Mary Meyer), *p. 79*

*indicates a tie in the category

PRESCHOOLERS *(cont.)*

Smushy Bear* (North American Bear Co.), *p. 79*

Cuddly Pals Big Pokey* (Gund), *p. 79*

Construction

Legoville Fire Station (Lego Systems), *p. 92*

Magneatos (Guidecraft), *pp. 92, 269*

Games & Art

Candy Land DVD (Milton Bradley), *pp. 267, 290*

Super Rolling Art Center (Alex), *p. 110*

Vehicles

Automoblox (Automoblox), *p. 85*

My First RC Buggies (Kid Galaxy), *pp. 85, 273*

Shake 'N Go Speedway (Fisher-Price), *p. 87*

Read With Me DVD (Fisher-Price/Scholastic), *p. 96*

Outdoor

Endless Adventures Tikes Town Playhouse* (Little Tikes), *p. 107*

Naturally Playful Welcome Home Playhouse* (Step 2), *p. 106*

Plasmacar (PlaSmart), *p. 105*

EARLY SCHOOL YEARS

Construction

Lego Pirate Ship (Lego Systems), *p. 120*

Flex K'nex (K'nex), *p. 128*

Knights' Empire Castle*/Grande Mansion* (Playmobil), *p. 119*

Magbots Scorpion (Mindscope), *p. 129*

Quadrilla (HaPe), *p. 130*

Star Wars ARC-170 Starfighter*/Wild Hunters* (Lego Systems), *p. 130*

Crafts

Ceramic Swirl Art (Alex), *p. 147*

EZ 2 Quikrochet Kit (The Bead Shop), *p. 149*

Funky and **Inspire Bead Chests** (Bead Bazaar), *p. 148*

*indicates a tie in the category

*indicates a tie in the category

OPPENHEIM TOY PORTFOLIO PLATINUM BOOK AWARDS 2006

INFANTS AND TODDLERS

Fluffy Chick and Friends (Priddy Books), *p. 164*
Playtime Peekaboo! (Sirett, et al., DK), *p. 165*
Quack! (Root/Meade, Candlewick), *p. 168*
Cornelius P. Mud, Are You Ready For Bed? (Saltzberg, Candlewick), *p.*
Food for Thought (Freymann, Scholastic), *p. 170*
If You're Happy and You Know It! (Cabrera, Holiday House), *p. 172*

PRESCHOOLERS

Carl's Sleepy Afternoon (Day, Farrar Straus), *p. 173*
Here Comes Grandma (Lord/Paschkis, Holt), *p. 176*
If You Give Pig A Party (Numeroff/Bond, HarperCollins), *p. 175*
Leonardo the Terrible Monster (Willems, Hyperion), *p. 175*
Sleep Tight, Little Bear (Waddell/Firth, Candlewick), *p. 178*
Tall (Alborough, Candlewick), *p. 180*
We've All Got Bellybuttons! (Martin/Cecil, Candlewick), *p. 181*
Winter's Tale (Sabuda, Simon & Schuster), *p. 182*

EARLY SCHOOL YEARS

Fiction
Diary of a Spider (Cronin/Bliss, HarperCollins), *p. 183*
The Dog Who Cried Wolf (Kasza, Putnam), *p. 183*
Froggy's Sleepover (London/Remkiewicz, Viking), *p. 202*
Pirate Girl (Funke/Meyer, Scholastic), *p. 184*
The Witch's Walking Stick (Meddaugh, Houghton Mifflin), *p. 175*
The Wolf's Story (Forward/Cohen, Candlewick), *p. 187*

OPPENHEIM TOY PORTFOLIO PLATINUM BOOK AWARDS 2006

EARLY SCHOOL YEARS *(cont.)*

Nonfiction

Encyclopedia Prehistorica Dinosaurs
(Sabuda/Reinhart, Candlewick), *p. 191*

Joe Louis: America's Fighter (Adler/Widener,
Harcourt), *p. 192*

The Usborne Complete Book of Art Ideas (Watt et
al., Usborne), *p. 193*

First Picture Dictionary (Scholastic), *p. 210*

Chapter books

Eldest (Paolini, Knopf), *p. 198*

Harry Potter and the Half-Blood Prince (Rowling,
Scholastic), *p. 255*

Inkspell (Funke, Scholastic), *p. 199*

The Sisters Grimm (Buckley, Amulet), *p. 200*

Holiday books

Santa Claus: The World's Number One Toy Expert
(Frazee, Harcourt), *p. 208*

Three French Hens (Palatini/Egielski, Hyperion), *p. 210*

OPPENHEIM TOY PORTFOLIO PLATINUM AUDIO AWARDS 2006

Disney Wishes! (Disney), *p. 247*

Hey, Picasso (Rounder), *p. 248*

Scat Like That: A Musical Word Odyssey
(Rounder), *p. 249*

Harry Potter and the Half-Blood Prince
(Listening Library), *p. 255*

OPPENHEIM TOY PORTFOLIO PLATINUM DVD AWARDS 2006

Happy Healthy Monsters (Sony), p. 218
Angelina Ballerina The Big Performance (HIT Entertainment), p. 220
Nova: Welcome to Mars (WGBH), p. 241
Peep and the Big Wide World (WGBH), p. 233
Pollyanna (WGBH/Masterpiece Theatre), p. 227
The Incredibles (Disney), p. 229
March of the Penguins (National Geographic), p. 240
Rainy Day Art (Jumby Bay), p. 234
Samantha: An American Girl Holiday (Warner Bros.), p. 230
Charlie and the Chocolate Factory (Warner Bros.), p. 228

OPPENHEIM TOY PORTFOLIO SPECIAL NEEDS ADAPTABLE PRODUCT AWARDS 2006

Gymini Total Playground Kick & Play (Tiny Love), p. 258
Lamaze Whirl & Twirl Jungle (RC2/Learning Curve), p. 259
Learn-Around Playground (LeapFrog), p. 261
Neurosmith Music Blocks (Small World Toys), p. 260
Candy Land DVD Game (Milton Bradley), pp. 267, 290
WonderFoam Dominoes (Chenille Kraft), p. 267
Bendos My First RC Buggies (Kid Galaxy), p. 273
Check-up Time Elmo (Fisher-Price), p. 274

TOP-RATED GROUP TOYS 2006

Kids are by nature social beings and enjoy few things more than being with other kids. Still, learning to share and play together can be rough going. We kept an eye out this year for toys that work especially well with groups of kids. For kids who are still at the "it's mine" stage, the key is to find toys with enough pieces to go around. We also looked for products that lend themselves to cooperative play—board games or activity kits that two or more children can enjoy together—or simply play with side by side. We often talk these days about interactive toys, but here are some wonderful products for interactive kids.

Candy Land DVD Game (Hasbro), *pp. 267, 290*
Colossal Barrel of Crafts (Chenille Krafts), *p. 109*
Egg and Spoon Race (International Playthings), *p. 92*
The Family Fun Game (Cranium), *p. 134*
Finger Painting Party (Alex), *pp. 109, 279*
Lego Quatro (Lego Systems), *p. 47, 261*
My Playhouse (Alex), *p. 107*
Naturally Playful Clubhouse Climber (Step 2), *p. 41*
Wooden Trains/Unit Wooden Blocks
  (various makers), *pp. 47, 89*

GREAT LEARNING TOYS FOR THE 3 RS 2006

Whether your kids are getting top grades or the other kind, there are playful ways you can help. Here are some of our highlighted favorites that give school skills a boost without your having to break out the flashcards.

Reading, Storytelling, Listening, & Language Skills
4 Way Spelldown (Cadaco), *p. 136*
Maya & Miguel World Scramble (Briarpatch), *p. 136*
Leapster L-Max (LeapFrog), *p. 159*
Audio Books, *p. 253*

Prewriting/Fine-Motor Skills
Lacing Games (various makers), *pp. 99, 124, 263*
Leap Pad Plus Writing System (LeapFrog), *pp. 141, 268*

Math, Logic, & Visual Perception
Da Vinci's Challenge (Briarpatch), *p. 163*
I Never Forget A Face Memory Game (eeBoo), *p. 94*
Make 'N' Break (Ravensburger), *p. 132*
Castle Keep (Gamewright), *p. 132*
Toot and Otto Game (Thinkfun), *p. 136*
Quadrilla (HaPe), *p. 130*
Zig Zag (Educational Insights), *p. 136*

Staying Power & Problem Solving
Bead Kits (various makers), *pp. 109, 148–150, 160*
Construction Toys (various makers), *pp. 47–49, 88–92, 127–131, 268–269*
Magnetic Building sets (various makers), *pp. 92, 130, 269*
Puzzles (various makers), *pp. 44, 97, 142, 262*

TOP-RATED OFFICE TOYS **2006**

Whether your office is in a complex or in a corner of your home, when kids come to visit, having a few quiet toys can make the time more enjoyable for everyone. Besides a pack of crayons and paper, here are some top choices:

TODDLERS AND PRESCHOOLERS

Crayola Color Wonder Paper & Markers (Binney & Smith), *pp. 61, 109, 278*

Fairy Collection Woodkins (Pamela Drake), *pp. 114, 275*

Lego Quatro Bucket (Lego Systems), *pp. 47, 261*

Kid K'nex Crimpy Critters (K'nex), *p. 91*

Play Scene: A Day at the Zoo (Mudpuppy), *p. 113*

EARLY SCHOOL YEARS

Bead Kits (various makers), *pp. 148, 149*

Pixter Multi-Media (Fisher-Price), *p. 161*

Fashion Angels Fashion Design Sketch Book (The Bead Shop), *p. 159*

Leapster L-Max (LeapFrog), *p. 159*

Gameboy DS (Nintendo), *p. 294*

Lacing Puppets (Lauri), *p. 124*

While it's important for kids to know how to play independently, games and cooperative projects provide the raw materials for interactions that can be rewarding for adult and child. Without taking over, adults can help kids get started and be there as "consultants," giving kids strategies for working in an orderly fashion. Making time to do such things together gives you a chance to play and experiment together—a chance to solve problems, think creatively, and even have fun learning together.

Here are some of our favorites:

PRESCHOOLERS

Puppets & Puppet Stage (various makers), *pp. 80–81*
Puzzles (various makers), *pp. 44, 97, 142, 262*
WonderFoam Dominoes (Chenille Kraft), *p. 267*
Wooden Trains (various makers), *p. 47*

EARLY SCHOOL YEARS

Castle (Playmobil), *pp. 119–120*
Construction sets (various makers), *pp. 47–49, 88–92, 127–131, 268–269*
Hanging Bird House & Feeder Kits
(TWC of America), *p. 158*
Sir Steps-A-Lot (imadethat), *p. 109*
Whoonu (Cranium), *p. 137*

Many of the toys, books, and videos you bring home may have a built-in Gender Agenda™—products that reinforce stereotypes and shape your child's self-image. It often begins innocently in the nursery with pastel color coding, but quickly moves on to a glut of products with themes of hair-play for girls and gunplay for boys. The gender issue is not just one that is important to girls. The overly aggressive and violent-themed toys and video games directed at boys are even more alarming to us than the dating games or lavender blocks that come with blueprints for a shopping mall.

Can you avoid all gender-specific toys? Probably not. These are often the products kids want the most, not only because they are heavily promoted on TV, but also because children tend to sort the world out in the simple and absolute terms of right or wrong, hard or easy, boy or girl. There are, however, positive choices you can make—where a gender-free product will work for both boys and girls... and products that break gender stereotypes.

Whoonu (Cranium), *p. 137*

Deluxe Tumble Treehouse (Maxim Enterprises), *p. 84*

Dudley Musical Pull-Along Duck (Mamas & Papas), *pp. 30, 39*

Lamaze Whirl & Twirl Jungle (RC2/Learning Curve), *pp. 21, 29, 30, 259*

Retro Rocket (Radio Flyer), *p. 37*

Our World (Mudpuppy Press), *p. 98*

Trikke 5 (Trikke Tech), *p. 156*

Wooden Kitchen Appliances (Small World Toys), *p. 59*

MAKE A GIFT LIST 2006

Teaching kids to give, not just get, can be fun with any one of these craft kits. These are just a few of our favorite kits that make a finished product that kids can give with pride to family, friends, or teachers.

Beeswax Candles (Creativity for Kids), *p. 147*
Friendship Wheel (Alex), *p. 151*
I Knit This Poncho! (The Bead Shop), *p. 151*
Inspire Bead Chest (Bead Bazaar), *p. 148*
My Star Box Kit (Balitono), *p. 146*
Potholders & Other Loopy Projects (Klutz), *p. 152*
Wake Up! Alarm Clock (Creativity for Kids), *p. 145*

One of the best ways to excite kids about science is to make it a hands-on experience. Here are our favorite picks of this year's top science toys. Many require some adult involvement—providing a chance to make discoveries together. Be sure to check our science books, videos, and software recommendations.

TOP-RATED PRODUCTS UNDER $10 ⭐ *2006*

20Q (Radica), *p. 159*

Bendos (Kid Galaxy), *pp. 89, 275*

Circle Rattle (Sassy), *p. 11*

Crayola Color Wonder Paper & Markers (Binney & Smith), *pp. 61, 109, 278*

Gertie Balls (Small World Toys), *pp. 102, 280*

Power Brain YoYo (Hasbro), *p. 161*

Puzzles (Lauri/Ravensburger), *pp. 44, 97, 142, 262*

Rugged Riggz Trucks (Little Tikes), *p. 85*

Toot and Otto Game (ThinkFun), *p. 136*

Wig Out (Gamewright), *p. 161*

Wish Weaver (The Bead Shop), *p. 149*

TOP-RATED PRODUCTS UNDER $15 ⭐ *2006*

Backyard Flyer (Kid Galaxy), *p. 153*

Bialo (HaPe), *p. 133*

Ceramic Allowance Bank (Creativity for Kids), *pp. 145, 278*

Dishes (various makers), *pp. 58, 75*

Lamaze Stack 'n Nest Birds (RC2/Learning Curve), *pp. 17, 261*

Lego Quatro Bucket (Lego Systems), *pp. 47, 261*

Me in the Mirror (Sassy), *p. 11*

Storefront Bingo (eeBoo), *p. 133*

Zigity (Cranium), *p. 137*

TOP-RATED PRODUCTS UNDER $25 ⭐2006⭐

Alfredo's Food Fight (Fundex), *p. 132*
Bumparena (Cranium), *p. 131*
Duck Duck Goose (Milton Bradley), *p. 93*
Spool Knit Jewelry (Klutz), *p. 201*
Lamaze Whirl & Twirl Jungle (RC2/Learning Curve),
  pp. 21, 29, 30, 259
Musical Stack & Play (Tiny Love), *pp. 30, 45, 261*

TOP-RATED BIG TICKET LIST ⭐2006⭐

American Girl Elizabeth (American Girl), *p. 122*
Pixter Multi-Media (Fisher-Price), *p.161*
Great Big Creamy Bear (Mary Meyer), *p. 79*
Gymini Total Playground Kick & Play (Tiny Love)
  pp. 9, 258
Leapster L-Max (LeapFrog), *p. 159*
Learn-Around Playground (LeapFrog), *pp. 45, 261*
Lila (Corolle), *p. 76*
Monster Art Center (Alex), *p. 146*
Pushing Car (Haba), *p.36*
Retro Rocket (Radio Flyer), *p. 37*
Robosapien V2 (WowWee), *p. 126*
Rocking Horses (Mamas & Papas), *p. 38*
Super Art Table (Alex), *p. 112*
Wooden Blocks/Trains (various makers), *pp. 47, 89*

I • Toys

1 • Infants
Birth to One Year

The Horizontal Infant

What to Expect Developmentally

Your Role in Play. To your newborn, no toy in the world is more interesting than you! Babies are more interested in people than things. Your smiling face, your gentle touch, the sound of your voice, even your familiar scent make you the most perfect plaything. Don't worry about spoiling your newborn with attention. Responding to your baby's needs now will make him less needy later. Playing with your baby is not just fun—it's one of the most important ways babies learn about themselves and the world of people and things!

Learning Through the Senses. Right from the start, babies begin learning by looking, listening, touching, smelling, and tasting. It's through their senses that they learn about the world. In this first remarkable year, babies progress from gazing to grasping, from touching to tossing, from watching to doing. By selecting a rich variety of playthings, parents can match their baby's sensory learning style.

Reaching Out. Initially, you will be the one to activate the mobile, shake the rattle, squeeze the squeaker. But before long, baby will be reaching out and taking hold of things and engaging you in a game of peekaboo.

Toys and Development. As babies develop, so does their need for playthings that fit their growing abilities. Like clothes, good toys need to fit. Some of the toys for newborns will have short-term use and then get packed away or passed along to a new cousin or friend. Others will be used in new ways as your child grows. During this first year, babies need toys to gaze at, listen to, grasp, chomp on, shake, pass from one hand to another, bang together, toss, chase, and hug.

 BASIC GEAR CHECKLIST
FOR THE HORIZONTAL INFANT

✓Mobile   ✓Crib mirror
✓Musical toys   ✓Activity mat
✓Soft fabric toys with differing sounds and textures
✓Fabric dolls or animals with easy-to-grab limbs

🚫 **Toys to Avoid**
These toys pose choking and/or suffocation hazards:
✓Antique rattles
✓Foam toys
✓Toys with elastic
✓Toys with buttons, bells, or ribbons
✓Old wooden toys that may contain lead paint
✓Furry plush dolls that shed
✓Any toys with small parts

Crib Toys: Musical Toys, Mobiles, and Mirrors

Mobiles

A musical mobile attached to crib rail or changing table provides baby with fascinating sights and sounds. During the first 3 months, infants can focus only on objects that are relatively close. Toys should be between 8" and 14" from their eyes. Mobiles with bright colors and high contrast are easier for baby to see than pastels. Before you buy any mobile, look at it from the baby's perspective. What can you see? Many attractive mobiles are purely for decoration and do not have images that face the baby in the crib. **Editors' Note:** Unfortunately most mobiles we reviewed this year were both pastel and had images not directed at baby!

Here are our favorites (all gender-free):

■ Changing Table Flutter Bug Musical Mobile ✦2006✦

(Infantino $23 ✪✪✪) Cleverly designed, this "bug" has four patterned wings with colorful ribbons that flutter as they turn to the music. It's a windup music box with old-fashioned sound, rather than the usual electronic type. This attaches to the changing table for three minutes' worth of diversion. (800) 840-4916.

■ Flutterbye Dreams ✦2006✦

(Fisher-Price $24.95 ✪✪) The concept of this toy is well intentioned: the *tweet-tweet* of birdies—think the opening of a Bugs Bunny nature scene and you get the picture. Our problem is that the *tweet-tweet* is very high pitched, making us wince instead of relax. So we'd pass on this one. The **Ocean Wonders** (✪✪) mobile has three fish that spin around (not particularly eye-catching), but we didn't like the gel-like "fishbowl" intended for baby to push on. There's a disconnect with the packaging since no mobile should be left in a crib when a baby is sitting up. (800) 432-5437.

■ Lamaze Shine On Me Musical Mobile

(RC2/Learning Curve $50 ✪✪✪✪✪) A cheerful mobile with a bright smiley sun face tilted down for baby to see. A bird, a butterfly, and some friendly bugs spin as the mobile rotates. Plays jazz, classical, and Latin music that can be activated with a remote control. PLATINUM AWARD '04. (800) 704-8697.

■ Symphony in Motion Deluxe

(Tiny Love $49.95 ✪✪✪✪✪) How do you make a good thing better? Add a remote control and new animals to this clever musical mobile with innovative motion. Small shapes slide on the arms of the mobile, making clicking sounds as the mobile turns. The sound quality is better than most and it plays several classical selections.

PLATINUM AWARD '02. New for **2006**, the **Symphony-in-Motion Nature Mobile** ($49.95) with 15 minutes of nature sounds and music. Done in a nature motif (we prefer the look of the original). Was not ready for testing. (800) 843-6292.

■ **Wimmer-Ferguson Infant Stim-Mobile** BLUE CHIP

(Manhattan Toy $20 ❍❍❍❍❍) Newborns will be fascinated with the black-and-white, high-contrast patterns of the ten vinyl 3" discs and squares that dance and dangle on this nonmusical mobile. Not as cute looking as other mobiles, but babies do react to the visual stimulation of this crib toy. (800) 541-1345.

☞ **SAFETY TIP: Mobiles should be removed by the time baby is 5 months old, or whenever baby can reach out and touch them, to avoid the danger of strangulations or choking on small parts.**

SMART BABY TRICK: Monkey See, Monkey Do. Here's the first really neat trick your baby will be able to do. Almost from the start your baby will be able to imitate your expressions. Try sticking your tongue out and see what happens! Who says you need words to "talk"?

SMART PARENT TRICK: Babies stop looking at things that are always there, just as you stop looking at a vase that's always in the same place. Changing things to gaze at will interest babies more. Also, it's hard to focus on too many objects at once. So less may be more.

Musicals

Few toys are as soothing to newborns as a music box with its quiet sounds. Today, most musical toys for infants don't come as boxes but as plush toys. We prefer some of the newer pull-down musical toys to dolls with hard metal windup keys that older babies may chew on or get poked with by accident.

■ Bethany Butterfly Musical Activity Toy

(Mamas & Papas $19.99 ●●●●½) Hang this brightly colored velour and patterned butterfly in the crib or on a stroller for gazing. Plays "Somewhere Over the Rainbow." Also sweet, **Munch Giraffe** ($21.99 ●●●●): a gentle pull on her tail and she plays "Hush Little Baby"—very soothing. (310) 631-2222.

■ Cuddly Pals Pokey & Spunky
2006 PLATINUM AWARDS

(Gund $20 each, ●●●●●) Wind up either Pokey (a bear) or Spunky (a pup), and they will play you a lullaby as they move their heads slowly. The little honey-colored bear plays "Beautiful Dreamer" while honey-toned-with-white-patches Spunky plays Brahms' "Lullaby." Both have stitched features and a big plastic key. These are also available in pastel tones. Birth & up. Still top rated, **Peter Rabbit Musical** ($25) Peter Rabbit moves his head very slowly as he plays Brahms' "Lullaby." (800) 448-4863.

■ Flutterbye Dreams Lullabye Birdies Soother **2006**

(Fisher-Price $29.99 ●●●●) A musical crib toy that has four moving plastic chirping birds that baby can watch as she listens to four different tunes. We found the chirping less high-pitched than on the mobile from the same line (see p. 3). The toy also provides a light show on the ceiling. Similar to their old ocean-themed toy, but without the bubbles. We found the bubbles a bit more soothing than the birds—listen before you buy. We would skip the new **Ocean Wonders Musical Activity Mirror** ($15 ●●); the sound was not pleasing and it is designed to be hung over the baby's head with toys to pull on—looked worrisome to us. (800) 432-5437.

■ Sleepyhead Bunny

(North American Bear Co. $29 ●●●●●) Pull the long blue-and-white sleeping cap on this floppy pastel bunny, and it plays "Beautiful Dreamer" with an old-fashioned musical sound.

Also comes in pink. PLATINUM AWARD '05. (800) 682-3427.

■ Whoozit Pull Musical

(Manhattan Toy $19.95 **oooo**) Fans of the zany Whoozit line will consider this pull-down musical a must-have for the crib. A little Whoozit face pulls down from a collection of brightly colored stars, and plays "Twinkle, Twinkle, Little Star" with a lovely sound quality. (800) 541-1345.

Crib Mirrors

Even before your baby can reach out and touch, a crib mirror provides her with ever-changing images. It will be a while before baby knows whose face and hands she sees. In time, she'll be babbling to that face and studying the reflection of her hands.

■ Earlyears Crib Mirror ⚑ *2006*

(International Playthings $16.99 **oooo**) Best choice for newborns, this 14½" x 11" black-and-white, high-contrast graphic will attract baby's attention. Reverse it and you have an infant-safe, distortion-free mirror with colorful trim. (800) 445-8347.

■ Me in the Mirror

(Sassy $14.95 **oooo**) This large (9½") mirror has interesting toys attached for gazing, and even a place for adding your own photo. Great for tummy time on the floor, or you can attach it to the side of the crib. (800) 323-6336.

🖝 **SAFETY TIP: Many catalogs and picture books show baby cribs overflowing with quilts, pillows, and toys. These are pretty to look at, but totally unsafe!**

BABY TRACKING GAMES
Following a moving object is no small feat for the new baby. Use a boldly patterned soft toy with quiet rattle or squeaky sound to get baby's attention. Give

it a shake and move it slowly from side to side in baby's line of vision. In time baby will reach out to touch, but for now, looking and listening is the name of the game. Remember, newborns can't focus on objects more than 8–14 inches from their eyes.

Everything That Goes Up: Here's a little baby science lesson. Hold your hand up in the air in baby's sight line, saying:
"Everything that goes up comes down, down, down!"
(Gradually spiral your hand down, down, down 'til you gently tickle baby under the chin or on the tummy.) Before long baby will anticipate the tickles, and giggle before your fingers touch!

Equipment for Playtime

Babies are such social beings that they are often happiest when they are in the midst of the action. Many of the following products have serious safety issues that you should be aware of before you buy:

SAFETY TIP: Swings, baby seats, playpens, and saucers are often recalled because they can tip or collapse with frightening consequences. Be sure to check the Consumer Product Safety Commission website if you have inherited a product or find one at a yard sale.

SAFETY TIP: Never place any type of baby carrier on a table, bed, or counter. Even though the baby has never done it before, there's no way of predicting when he will make a move that can tip the carrier.

☞ **SAFETY TIP:** Many parents find the back-and-forth action of a swing a soothing diversion for a restless infant. We find it difficult to recommend any infant swings, however, because they can entrap limbs and necks, or even collapse. If you choose to use one, we urge you not to leave the room. Use it only with constant supervision.

☞ **SAFETY TIP:** While stationary entertainment units are safer than the walkers most of us had as kids, you should know that they do not build muscles for walking, and time in these seats should be limited and supervised. Babies do need to crawl before they walk!

SMART PARENT TRICKS

You Don't Say! Some new parents feel awkward about speaking to a baby who can't talk yet. What can you talk about? Anything. Talk about what you are doing, even if you are changing a diaper. Imitate baby's coos, gurgles, and squeals. In the beginning you'll do most of the talking . . . but before long baby will be answering. Pause, so baby can take turns! Before long you'll be having real "chats." Research indicates that babies who are frequently talked to have almost 300 more words by age 2 than tots who are rarely spoken to.

Puff 'n' Pop. Puff your cheeks. Then use your hands to pop them to make a funny noise. Soon, baby will reach out to pop your cheeks for you.

Playmats/Activity Gyms

WHAT TO AVOID: As a general rule, avoid playmats and blankets that have lots of doodads, which pose a choking hazard. Also avoid mats with activities all over and no really comfortable place for baby to lie down on. In addition, we do not recommend plastic activity gyms that now come with a cacophony of frenetic lights and sounds. These gyms have too much heavy plastic over your child's head (it takes only a baby's kick or a big sibling to knock into one of these things to send them over). Most offer the convertibility factor for older babies, but instead, we'd recommend buying a toy for a sitting-up baby when he's ready. See Vertical Infants, Toys for Making Things Happen, p. 19.

Best in Category

■ Gymini Total Playground Kick & Play
2006 PLATINUM AWARD

(Tiny Love $69 ooooo) This company continues to be the leader in activity mats for young babies. We'd put this mat on the "must have" list for the baby shower. The new feature this year is a kick-and-play area that babies can activate with their feet or bat at from their tummies as they get older. The key difference between this mat and so many others we tested is that the lights and music are soothing and not over-the-top loud or jarring. Comes with a mirror that babies will enjoy. Like the original, this has two arches and dangly toys for gazing at and batting. We also recommend the less expensive version without the lights and music. PLATINUM AWARD '03. (800) 843-6292.

■ Taf Toys Smart Mat 2006

(Edushape $59.95 oooo½) Our family with triplets raved about this amazing oversized playmat (39" x 59"). "There's enough room for all our girls." Another family wrote: "it was perfect for our den that has bare floors. It's very cushy and I find it attractive to have out in the room." It has bright graphics and interesting textures and sounds. Comes with several attached toys as well as three separate toys that have interesting textures to explore.

This is an unusually attractive and versatile mat that will get miles of use until baby takes off as a crawler. (800) 404-4744.

■ Locking Links 3-in-1 Gym *2006*

(Little Tikes $50 **oo**) This may look like a lot of other baby mats, but you will be surprised by the over-the-top sounds when you activate this one. Each song is introduced with the grating sound of chirping birds—sure to startle little ones. The quality of the music leaves a lot to be desired and, finally, the dangly toys (designed to be handled by baby eventually) have a tiny screw on the links. This is the same problem we had with their new rattle/teethers. (800) 321-0183.

■ Lamaze 2-in-1 Gym

(RC2/Learning Curve $60 **oooo**) A reversible playmat with high-contrast red, black, and white on one side, and bright colors on flip side. Closes up easily with a Velcro closure. Comes with three hanging toys for early gazing. (800) 704-8697.

■ Whoozit Gym to Go

(Manhattan Toy $50 **ooo**) Handsome playmat with signature Whoozit design but smaller than both the Gymini and Lamaze versions, folds up with a small handle that our tester found not as easy to carry as the Gymini, which she preferred. (800) 541-1345.

☞ **SAFETY TIP: With any gym you use, total supervision is required. Gyms are also not for babies who are beginning to pull themselves up. We prefer fabric playmats to most plastic gyms, which can be accidentally kicked over. Yes, we are repeating ourselves . . . but it's worth repeating.**

First Lap and Floor Toys: Rattles, Sound Toys, and More

Infant toys can help adults engage and interact with newborns. A bright rattle that baby tracks visually, a quiet music box that soothes, or an interesting doll to gaze or swipe at, are ideal for getting-acquainted games. These toys can be used on the changing table or for lap games during playful moments after a feeding, before a bath, or whenever. ***Editors' Note:*** Since babies are no longer put to sleep on their tummies, giving them supervised tummy time is very important for developing neck and upper body strength. Some of these toys can be put in front of them.

■ Lamaze First Mirror BLUE CHIP

(RC2/Learning Curve $19.99 ●●●●●) A fabric-covered wedge with a mirror is covered in eye-grabbing bold black-and-white patterns with red piping. The distortion-free mirror is now padded and, like the original, can be removed and hung in the crib. PLATINUM AWARD '98. (800) 704-8697. You can also use the **Me in the Mirror** from Sassy (see p. 6) on the floor.

Smart Baby Trick. Since babies are no longer put to sleep on their tummies, many of our testing families are telling us that their babies are not learning to crawl in the traditional way. To build those little muscles, it's a good idea to build some brief tummy time into their playtime. Most toys designed for this sound better than they are. Many are just too gimmicky. Nothing replaces your getting down there and playing. Putting interesting toys in their reach will encourage babies to use the arm, leg, and neck muscles they'll need to get about as crawlers.

Rattles

Many rattles are too noisy, hard, and heavy for newborns. While most will be used by adults to get baby's attention, the best choice for newborns is a rattle with a soft sound that won't startle and a soft finish that won't hurt. During the first months, an infant's arm and hand movements are not yet refined. Here are some of the best rattles for early playtimes:

■ Circle Rattle 2006

(Sassy $3.99 ●●●●½) Good for early tracking games, this colorful ring has a spotted ball, interesting textures, and smaller rings that clack. So there's a lot to look at, feel, and, last but not least, chew on. This is a classic shape reintroduced in new colors. Also new for 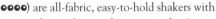, **Swing on a Ring Monkey Rattle** ($3.99 **oooo**): purple, red, and green monkeys with fabric arms, legs, and tails are attached to a ring. (800) 323-6336.

■ Razzy Rattles *2006*

(Mary Meyer $4.50 **oooo**) Choose a very quiet floppy little red pig, green turtle, blue elephant, or yellow lion in washable terry with gingham trim and stitched features. Also, **See Me? Rattles** ($4.50

oooo) are all-fabric, easy-to-hold shakers with happy faces and a quiet jingle. A nice toy for older sibs to use with baby. A "mirror" on the back of the rattle face is distorted, but not to worry, baby is going to be attracted to the patterns and stitched face and big brother's antics. (800) 451-4387.

■ Itty Bitty Bugs Rattles

(Gund $5 **ooooo**) If you have a preemie, these lightweight rattles will be a better choice as your baby's hand strength grows. They are covered with brightly colored terry and have a hole in the middle, making them easier for little hands to grasp. PLATINUM AWARD '05. Also, **Mini Pro Grabbies** (Gund $5 **oooo**) are even lighter, done in velour, and have a sports theme. (800) 4863.

■ Let's Play Puppets *2006*

(Gund $12.99 **oooo**½) Choose a blue elephant, **Tootie,** lavender hippo, **Tibs,** or mint green frog, **Pippy,** for early tracking games and heart-to-heart talks. These soft hand puppets come with a baby puppet so parent and child can sing and talk together. These are fun to share with an older sibling as you play with baby together. Also a good take-along toy for distractions on small trips. (800) 448-4863.

■ Harold Hound Teether Rattle

(Mamas & Papas $7.99 **ooooo**) A colorful patchwork velour dog rattle with floppy ears, striped handle, little noise, but big eye appeal. PLATINUM AWARD '05. Still top rated, last year's **Molly Moo Teether Rattle** ($8.99 **oooo**½). (310) 631-2222.

BABY MUSIC GAMES

Sing, Sing a Song! Okay, it doesn't matter if you sing off key or you don't know all the words. To your baby, you deserve a Grammy! Singing can soothe a crying baby or refresh and surprise a fussy baby. Go ahead! Add his name to the songs you sing and you'll really have a fan! Don't be afraid to do a little dancing—it's a great way to release your tension as well as baby's.

The Vertical Infant

What to Expect Developmentally

Once babies can sit up, they have a new view of and fascination with the world of things. Now they don't just grasp at toys, they can use their hands and mouths to explore and feel objects. At around 9 months, babies gain fuller control of their separate fingers and begin to use their index fingers to point and poke at openings. Now they can activate toys with spinners. It's also at this stage that they can handle two objects at the same time.

Watch how your baby explores any toy, examining every angle. She looks at it, fingers it, tastes it. Using two hands, she bangs two blocks together, or spends many moments passing a toy from one hand to another. This is serious work, a way of discovering how things function and what she can do to make things happen.

During this exciting time your baby will begin to crawl and even pull himself up on his two little feet. Some babies may even take their first steps. In a matter of just a few months, your baby grows from needing others to play a game of patty-cake, to putting out his hands and leading others to play patty-cake with him.

Many of the toys from the horizontal stage will still be used. By now, however, the mobile should be removed from the crib, and other interesting playthings should be added gradually. As new toys are introduced, put some of the older things away. Recycle toys that have lost their novelty by putting them out of sight for a while, then reintroduce them or give them away. A clutter of playthings can become more of a distraction than an attraction.

> ## ⚙ BASIC GEAR CHECKLIST
> ##   FOR THE VERTICAL INFANT
>
> ✓Rattles and teething toys
> ✓Manipulatives with differing shapes, sounds, textures
> ✓Plastic containers for filling and dumping games
> ✓Cloth or sturdy cardboard books
> ✓Washable dolls and animals   ✓Musical toys
> ✓Soft fabric-covered ball   ✓Cloth blocks
> ✓Rolling toys or vehicles   ✓Bath toys
>
> ## 🚫 Toys to Avoid
>   These toys pose choking and/or suffocation hazards:
> ✓Antique rattles
> ✓Foam toys
> ✓Toys with elastic
> ✓Toys with buttons, bells, and ribbons
> ✓Old wooden toys that may contain lead paint
> ✓Furry plush dolls that shed
> ✓Any toys with small parts
>
> These toys are developmentally inappropriate:
> ✓Shape sorters and ring-and-post toys—these call for
>   skills beyond those of an infant

Rattles and Teethers

Now is the time for manipulatives that encourage two-handed exploration while providing interesting textures and sounds, and safe, chewable surfaces for teething. You can't teach eye-hand coordination, but you can motivate exploration by providing toys that develop baby's ability to use hands and fingers in new and more complex ways.

■ Baby Smiley Face Rattle BLUE CHIP

(Sassy $5.99 ●●●●●) Older babies will enjoy exploring this friendly rattle with a smiling face, jiggly eyes, squeaky nose, and chewy, polka-dotted, handle-shaped ears. It reverses to a distortion-free mirror. Also easy to grasp, interesting to exam-

ine, and ideal for teething, the **Hourglass Rattle** ($4.99 oooo)
newly refreshed with bright colors. (800) 323-6336.

■ Cuddly Teether Blanket 2006

(Infantino $9 oooo½) Choose a terry cloth
blanket (the size of a washcloth) with satin
binding and teethers in each corner, topped
off with a velour and satin head of a frog
or pup. A soft, safe, and interesting sensory toy. (800) 840-4916.

■ Earlyears Click & Play Triangles 2006

(International Playthings $6.99 oooo) Ideal for two-handed play,
these three-hinged triangles click as they are
opened and closed. A central triangle has a small
mirror and the textured triangles are fine for
teething. Also new for **2006**, **Busy
Bead Rattle** ($9.99 oooo); this hour-
glass-shaped toy has beads that drop
from one cone to another. The cones
turn with a quiet click and the colorful
central ring has beads that turn. (800) 445-8347.

■ Tolo Abacus Rattle BLUE CHIP

(Small World Toys $5.95 ooooo) There are lots of moving parts to
explore as they clack and move on this colorful plastic rattle for two-
handed play. Also, still top rated, the **Tolo Roller Ball** with a small ball
inside a larger ball and easy grip openings. Both beautifully crafted in
sturdy, primary-colored plastic with interesting action for baby to
manipulate. (800) 421-4153.

■ Whoozit Touch & Teethe

(Manhattan Toy $12 oooo½) An easy-to-
hold, visually exciting rattle. The
Whoozit face with a squeaky nose is on
one side, and a mirror is on the other. A
ring with hearts, stars, and other textured
shapes surrounds the face and is ideal for
two-handed exploration and teething. Also
interesting, **Winkle** ($12 oooo); put this in the
fridge to chill the plastic loops for teething. This toy has a quiet rattle
sound and many loops for easy holding and two-handed play. (800)
541-1345.

SMART PARENT TRICKS: Who's That? Your baby in arms will be amazed to catch sight of herself and you in a mirror. Watch her surprise as she sees you twice—the real you and your reflection. Talk about what she sees and let her touch your face and your reflection. In time, you can play little games of "Where is my nose? Where is baby's nose?" Move baby in and out of the sight line of the mirror, playing yet another variation of peekaboo!

Floor Toys

Many of the toys here are truly "interactive," but not electronic. They depend on an adult interacting with the baby to make something happen. Some testers complained that their babies did not know what do to with the stacking toy. True. Stacking, knocking down, and playing peek a boo are all the tricks you'll teach your baby. There is no button to push—you are the button! They also complained that the toy did not hold the baby's interest. Also true. You are the only plaything that will hold your baby's interest for long stretches of time. These toys are really just props for introducing games and being sociable. Especially for this stage of the game, interacting with your baby on the floor is more important than what toy you brought home. It is the dialogue you share with your baby that's the key.

■ Bucket Buddies *2006* PLATINUM AWARD

(Infantino $20 ●●●●●) Three fabric buckets with happy stitched faces and crinkle ears can nest or stack. There are squeakers, rattles, and jingle sounds along with three crinkly soft play pieces to put in and take out of the buckets. Beautifully crafted in colorful patterned fabrics, a good toy for parent–child games of "knock it down" or "hide and find." (800) 840-4916.

■ Lamaze Stack 'n Nest Birds 2006

(RC2/Learning Curve $14.99 oooo½) There are
four birds that can be stacked in a tower or nest-
ed one over the other. Three are done in fabric
with zippy patterns, touchy-feely textures, and
interesting sounds that rattle, crinkle, and
squeak. The littlest bird is a funny-faced
squeeze toy that can hide under all the others.
Size order is built into the fun for peek-a-boo
games of "Where's the birdie?" 9 mos. & up. (800) 704-8697.

First Blocks

We like the **Discover & Play Color Blocks** (Baby Einstein
$12.99 oooo½), which have interesting textures on each side.
One block makes a quacking sound that your baby will enjoy
hearing long before she'll be able to make it happen. These are
fun for stacking and knocking down. (800) 793-1454. We also
still recommend **Earlyears Soft Busy Blocks** (International
Playthings $15 oooo½) which have softer sides and corded
piping, making them easier for baby to grasp. Colorful graphics and patterns and quiet sounds make these good floor toys
for beginners. Also, **Earlyears Sweet Baby Blocks** ($10
oooo). Six soft, squeezable vinyl blocks, easy to grasp, with a
colorful single image on each face of the cubes. Fun for stacking, knocking down, and tossing. (800) 445-8347.

■ Peek Rattle and Teethe 2006

(Infantino $13 oooo½) Four easy-to-grasp hollow
fabric blocks, each has a teether attached and
interesting textures and patterns to explore. Best of
all, one side of each block has a soft see-through
vinyl "window" so baby can see and hear the
bright plastic rings that are locked inside. Stack
them, roll them, toss or taste them, these are a
good choice for sitting-up babies. (800) 840-4916.

TWO-WAY BABY GAME Booom!
Before baby starts stacking
blocks, he'll like knocking
them down. Use fabric

blocks or a stack of big plastic ones. How high can you stack them before your little playmate makes them go BOOOOOOOOM? Baby loves the powerful feeling of making this happen, especially if you laugh it up.

Filling and Spilling Games

With their newly acquired skills of grasping and letting go comes the favorite game of filling and dumping multiple objects in and out of containers.

■ **Baby's First Blocks** and **Snap-Lock Beads** BLUE CHIP

(Fisher-Price $8 & $3.99 ❍❍❍❍❍) Babies will enjoy these toys long before they can do what the boxes promise. **Baby's First Blocks** is technically a shape-sorter, but the 12 blocks will be used to fill, spill, and throw long before baby can fit them into the four-place shape-sorter lid of the container. Put the lid away for now. The same is true of the lemon-sized **Snap-Lock** plastic beads that will be enjoyed for chomping on, picking up, tossing, and little games of fill and dump. Putting them together comes much later. Great for developing fine motor skills and the ability to litter the floor. (800) 432-5437.

■ **Lamaze Multi-Sensory Soft Sorter**

(RC2/Learning Curve $19.99 ❍❍❍❍) Babies don't need to know their shapes to use this big colorful fabric cube with a lift-up lid and different geometric openings on each side. The colorful patterns on each side match the four soft rattle shapes that fit into the cube. However, the openings are big enough to allow baby to put any shape into any opening. New for **2006**, the toy has an apple scent (we didn't find it overwhelming but it's a personal preference). (800) 704-8697.

How Many Socks? Game The Lamaze Soft Sorter is a perfect prop to fill with all those unmatched socks you keep saving. Leave the wide door open and let some stick out of the other openings on the cube.

This is almost as much fun to empty as a box of tissues, and much safer, since tissues fall apart when they are tasted. Strengthens hands and fingers while exploring textures, colors, and patterns.

■ Put and Peek Birdhouse

(Manhattan Toy $19.95 **oooo**) This cheerful fabric birdhouse is a parent-intensive toy with lots of possibilities for hamming it up. You can fly the four birds into the house (the roof opens wide, as does one side). Our nine-month-old tester favored holding (and tasting) the red bird as he watched his father fly the other ones about. 6 mos. & up. (800) 541-1345. Preferable to Infantino's **Puppies Playhouse** (**ooo**) (same idea, but the animals aren't as nice and the house is smaller and not see-through). **Editors' Note:** Manhattan Toy also introduced two new fill 'n' dump toys this year (one circus-themed, the other Whoozits). We found for once that both toys were a little bit too quiet and that the opening for the toys at the top should have been wider.

Toys for Making Things Happen

Some of the best infant toys introduce babies to their first lessons in cause and effect. Such toys respond to baby with sounds or motion that give even the youngest players a sense of "can do" power—of making things happen! **What to Avoid:** toys that do too much. Most are overwhelming to kids and they end up watching rather than doing.

■ Classical Stacker

(Fisher-Price $10 **ooooo**) This former PLATINUM-AWARD winning stacker is back with new colors. The star rings fit on the post in any order (a plus). Post has magical lights that wink and play music when top is pressed. Sound quality is not excellent, but it is a long-term favorite. Says 6 mos. & up, we'd say 9 mos. & up. (800) 432-5437.

■ Developlay Activity Center

(Tiny Love $44.95 **ooooo**) A two-sided activity center loaded with interesting challenges for the senses. A polka-dotted spinner reflects in a mirror; music plays with a press of the happy face; pull a ring to make a "hammer" rise and fall. Flip it over for musical buttons, knobs to turn, a gentle pop-up, and gears that spin. 9 mos. & up. PLATINUM AWARD '04. (800) 843-6292.

■ Discover Sounds Kitchen

(Little Tikes $40 ●●●○) There are multiple fill-and-spill activities built into the doors and chutes of this mini-kitchen. There are some noises but none that our parents found objectionable. In contrast, the new **DiscoverSounds Workshop** (●●) was noisy, with limited playability. 9 mos. & up. (800) 321-0183.

COMPARISON SHOPPER
High Chair Toys

Fascination Station   BLUE CHIP (Sassy $8.99 ●●●●●) Our favorite high chair toy on the market. Little testers can bat at this spinning toy that attaches to a tabletop with a stout suction cup. There is plenty to see, hear, and feel as the balls and clackers with bold graphics and textures turn. 6 mos. & up. PLATINUM AWARD '99. New for *2006*, **Fishy Fascination Station** ($8.99 ●●●●½), with spinners shaped like fish. This too converts to a handheld rattle with textures to explore and chewy ring for teething. (800) 323-6336. Also, new for *2006*, a very interesting **Earlyears Click N Spin Highchair Flower** (International Playthings $15.99 ●●●●½). This colorful flower suctions to the high chair tray. Petals have spinners, a mirror, textures, patterns, and sounds for sitting-up baby to activate. (800) 445-8347.

■ Lamaze Chime Garden *2006*

(RC2/Learning Curve $19.99 ●●●●) We had mixed reviews on this toy. Baby needs some power in those little hands to activate the lights and sounds of the five flowers of this musical toy. An interesting toy but not essential. 6 mos. & up. (800)704-8697.

■ Lamaze Whirl & Twirl Jungle 2006 PLATINUM AWARD

(RC2/Learning Curve $19.99 ●●●●●) One of our all-time favorite toys in this category. Three jolly creatures, a lion, and elephant, and a monkey, spin when placed on the colorful musical platform. A single big button activates the music and motion providing a little lesson in cause and effect. This innovative toy develops motor skills, visual tracking, and a powerful sense of being in charge. Unlike the overly frenetic Fisher-Price's **Jungle Friends Treehouse** (●●), the animals here spin at a reasonable rate. 9 mos. & up. (800) 704-8697.

■ Learning Pots & Pans 2006

(Fisher-Price $17.97 ●●) On the plus side, these pots have encased beads that are fun to move about, but the toy requires the pots to be stacked in one correct order (way too hard for babies and young toddlers). There's a shape sorter in the lid and music in the base. This is one of those toys with the alphabet song and counting that's marked for 6–36 months. In the end, this set tries to do too much and fails. (800) 432-5437.

■ Melody Beads Piano 2006

(Little Tikes $25.99 ●●) What should have been a basic gear kind of toy has missed a beat (sorry). Marked for 6 mos. & up, this musical toy has five musical keys and a bead-on-wire toy above. Sounds great in theory. We found the musical quality to be sub-par and, somehow, having dogs barking music (the second sound option) seem more like music *depreciation* than *appreciation!* The greater problem with the toy is that the lesson in cause and effect is lost since one touch of the button sets off tons of music. The older versions of this toy by all manufacturers used to give kids the option of playing one note at a time. The effect here is way too random. (800) 321-0183.

■ Roll-a-Rounds Drop & Roar Dinosaur 2006

(Fisher-Price $35 ●●●●½) This is a ball run with multiple openings from which balls appear. Played with sounds and lights or in silence, it can be enjoyed by a sitting-down baby. That said, this is a large piece of green plastic and younger babies may have trouble fitting the balls into the holes on the front of the dino, rather than dropping them in—as they can in **Roll-a-Rounds Swirlin' Surprise Gumballs** ($17.99 ○○○○½). This is a much smaller ball drop with a lever that pops the gumballs out. It employs more direct cause and effect, but it does tip over easily. Either is a better choice than the **Jungle Friends Treehouse** (○○), a frenetic ball drop with over-the-top sounds and twirling bases. (800) 432-5437.

■ Wobble Top

(Infantino $15.99 ○○○○) An easy push on the big purple button sets the balls inside the dome wobbling, spinning, and clacking. Five fabric petals around the dome have interesting texture and patterns. (800) 840-4916. Still top rated, **Tolo First Friends Carousel** (Small World Toys $12 ○○○○○)—an easy-to-activate flat-bottomed top with little people that spin inside the see-through dome. PLATINUM AWARD '04. (800) 421-4153.

First Toys for Crawlers

At around 7 months, most babies begin to creep. It takes a few months more before most are up on hands and knees and truly crawling. Rolling toys such as small vehicles and balls can match baby's developing mobility. Toys placed slightly beyond baby's reach can provide the motivation to get moving. But make it fun. Avoid turning this into a teasing time. Your object is to motivate, not frustrate. Games of rolling a ball or car back and forth make for happy social play between baby and older kids as well as adults.

■ Baby Gymnastic Playwall *2006*

(Fisher-Price $54.99 ○○○) You need a good deal of space. There are three "walls": one has "chimes" that move and make electronic sounds; one is a curtained wall to crawl through; and the third has a hanging ball to hit. One tester loved this toy, but we'd recommend **Laugh and Learn Learning Home** (see p. 59), a more versatile play setting, and a much better choice than the new wobbly **Activity Tunnel.** (800) 432-5437.

■ Goofy Giggles Wheelie Wobbler *2006*

(Little Tikes $10 ○○○) We thought this cute wheelie toy would be the perfect push-and-go plaything for babies who are beginning to crawl. Each of our testing parents loved the concept, but, surprisingly, none of the babies was very interested. (800) 321-0183.

■ Lamaze Lights & Sounds Barnyard Crawl Toy
2006 PLATINUM AWARD

(RC2/Learning Curve $24.95 ✪✪✪✪✪) Perfect for rolling back and forth, or set it in motion to motivate your beginning crawler to get moving. You can use this with sounds and lights off, or set the volume low or high. Hourglass shaped, this has beads that rattle inside, colorful cloth knotties to feel, and bright patterns. Interesting to all the senses as well as to emerging locomotion skills. (800) 704-8697.

SMART BABY TRICK: If a young baby drops a toy she is holding, she will not look to see where it goes. Developmentally, at this stage, out of sight is out of mind. If she has a toy in one hand and you show her another, she will drop the first and reach for the offered toy.

■ Movers & Shakers Whale **2006**

(Infantino $14 ✪✪✪✪) A jolly little blue velour whale with satin-knotted spout. Press its head and the music plays, as does the vibration that makes the brightly colored creature scoot across the floor. We don't love the electronic music but beginning crawlers will love chasing after this critter. (800) 840-4916.

■ Poppin' Push Car

(Sassy $6 ✪✪✪✪½) Push this little car forward and the popping beads (safely enclosed in the dome roof) make a pleasing sound. Pull the car back and when you let go the car zooms forward. One of the best toys of the season! Just right for floor time play. (800) 323-6336. Also a great choice, the BLUE CHIP **Ambi Baby's First Car** (Brio $10 ✪✪✪✪✪) A safe and chunky, easy-to-roll car for little hands. **Safety note:** Hot Wheels and Matchbox-styled cars have small parts that pose a choking hazard for kids under 3. (888) 274-6869.

■ Press N Go Inchworm 2006 PLATINUM AWARD

(International Playthings $12 ●●●●●) You can simply push this happy looking Inchworm back and forth or press down on its back and it zooms forward. There are little beads inside the domed wheels. A terrific toy that older siblings will love to demo for their little brother or sister. (800) 445-8347.

COMPARISON SHOPPER
Fabric Balls

Nothing is more basic for this stage than a soft fabric ball that's easy to grasp, toss, and roll. A perfect toy for crawlers to chase and for early back-and-forth roly-poly social games. Our favorites: **Colorfun Ball** BLUE CHIP (Gund $12 ●●●●●) A brightly colored ball done in soft velour. (800) 448-4863. Also of interest, **Whoozit Wiggle Ball** (Manhattan Toy $12 ●●●●) This ball is not solid—it has six satiny arms with bright ribbons that make it even easier for babies to grasp. A black-and-white squeaker attached to the center vibrates when pulled. The **Tiger** and **Ladybug Chime Balls** looked promising but were not ready for testing. (800) 541-1345.

SMART BABY GAMES: Roly-Poly Ball. Your sitting-up and crawling baby will love the back-and-forth fun of rolling a ball. Choose a soft fabric ball with jingle inside or a big beach ball that's slightly soft.

I'll Catch You and You Catch Me! Get down on the floor and take turns playing a crawling catch game. Say, "I'm going to catch you!" and crawl after baby. Or play it in reverse, telling baby to "Try and catch me!" Go slowly enough so baby can catch you. This can be a pretty exciting game!

Tub Time

Bathing a baby can be one of the scariest chores for new parents. (After all, once you take off all those layers, they're so small, and that doesn't even take into account the wobbly neck situation!) For your own comfort as well as baby's, make sure you have everything ready before you begin. The key is to remain calm, comforting, and prepared to get wet! For beginners, a small tub will be more comfortable for both bather and bathee. Little ones don't need much in the way of toys, but once they can sit securely, a few simple bath toys add to the fun.

■ Ambi Family Duck BLUE CHIP

(Brio $13.50 ●●●●●) Three little primary-colored plastic ducks and their parent (we make no gender assumptions). Great fun for the bath. The babies store in big duck's body. Also look for Ambi's **Waterball** ($8.50 ●●●●) with two little ducks inside. (888) 274-6869.

■ Musical Bobbing Sprites

(Sassy $6.99 ●●●●) Attach these three suction-cupped "fish" to the bottom of the tub and they stay put while bobbing about as your little one pushes them. Ideal for sitting-up baby to activate but keep in easy reach. Not really musical, more like squeak, rattle, and snappy sounds. (800) 323-6336.

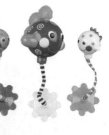

👉 **SAFETY TIP:** The Consumer Product Safety Commission reports 66 deaths since 1983 associated with baby bath "supporting rings," devices that keep baby seated in the bathtub. Never rely on such devices to keep baby safe. Going to answer the door or phone can result in serious injury, or worse, to babies and toddlers.

👉 **SAFETY TIP:** Avoid foam bath toys, which are often labeled in fine print, "Not for children under 3." Babies can choke on bits of foam that break off when babies chew on them.

First Huggables

Babies often receive tons of soft dolls that are too big, too fuzzy, and even unsafe for now. Although they may be decorative and fine for gazing at, fuzzy plush dolls with ribbons, buttons, plastic features that may pull out, or doodads that may be pulled off, are better saved for preschool years.

When shopping for huggables, look for:
✓**Interesting textures**
✓**Easy-to-grasp legs or arms**
✓**Sound effects sewn safely inside**
✓**Washable fabric such as velour or terry cloth**
✓**Stitched-on features; no loose ribbons or bells**
✓**Small enough size for infant to hold with ease**

■ Babipouce

(Corolle $10 & up ooooo) Older babies are fascinated by dolls that look like real babies. The trick is to find dolls that are washable and safe enough for them to handle. Corolle has an assortment of dolls with all-fabric velour rompers in various colors and soft vinyl painted faces. Our favorites this season: **Puppet Blue,** with a tri-knottie hat, or **Puppet Raspberry,** which is easy to grab with an un-stuffed body, or **Miss Grenadine** with a bright red romper. PLATINUM AWARD '05. (800) 668-4846.

■ My Dolly & Sweet Dolly 2006

(Gund $12 each oooo) These cloth dolls come with fabric clothes sewn on, stitched faces, and soft bodies that are easy to grasp. **My Dolly** wears polka dots. **Sweet Dolly** is in stripes and short plush. Both extremely cuddly but only available in Caucasian skin tones and pink clothing. (800) 448-4863.

■ Molly Moo Activity Toy

(Mamas & Papas $29.99 ●●●●●) Pull Molly's tail and she plays "Old MacDonald." With her colorful face and soft body, Molly has interesting textures and patterns at the ends of her front legs, and a dial to spin and a mirror on her back legs—plus a vinyl pocket for a picture you can change. PLATINUM AWARD '04. (310) 631-2222.

■ Tutti Frutti Dog *2006* PLATINUM AWARD

(Gund $22 ●●●●●) So many senses are satisfied with this floppy 11½" velour dog in bright primary colors. His ears crinkle and have corduroy texture. His multicolored terry cloth feet have rattles inside and peek-a-boo mirrors on the bottoms. Squeeze his tummy and he barks! A mostly red, and special pooch for older babies and toddlers. Still top rated, **Tutti Frutti** 5" collection of bright colored animals ($8 each ●●●●●). PLATINUM AWARD '05. (800) 448-4863.

Best Travel Toys for Infants

Having a supply of several small toys can help divert and entertain small travelers, whether you're going out for a day or away for a week. Bring along a familiar comfort toy—a musical toy or doll that's like a touch of home. Pack a variety of toys with different sounds and textures and don't show them all at once; you need to dole them out. Select several very different toys, for example:

✓**Teether**   ✓**Handheld mirror**
✓**Highchair toy**   ✓**Small huggable**
✓**Musical toy**   ✓**Books and pictures to share**
✓**Familiar quilt/playmat to rest on**

■ Baby Whoozit

(Manhattan Toy $10 ●●●●) Updated with a defuzzed nose that lifts for a peek-a-boo surprise, this zany smiley face (5½" diameter) has dangling toys to explore. Also fun for peek-a-boo lap games, the big **Whoozit** ($20 ●●●●) (10½") with lots of dangly toys to tuck in and pull out. (800) 541-1345.

■ New Barn Babies `2006`

(Infantino $13 ●●●●½) This trio includes a black-and-white patterned cow, a bright red bird with crinkle wings, and a pink pig. All have teethers, licks of satin, soft velour, and quiet sounds safely tucked inside. Few toys will hold interest for long at this age, but easy-to-grasp toys with varying patterns, sounds, and textures are good for short-term exploration. Also available as single **Link-Along Friends** ($4.99 each). Birth & up. (800) 840-4916.

■ Car Seat Gallery BLUE CHIP

(Manhattan Toy $12 ●●●●●) Hang the four-way pattern pocket chart on the back of the front seat of the car and use either the included graphic cards or your own photos! (800) 541-1345.

■ Lamaze Traveling Mobile

(RC2/Learning Curve $14.99 ●●●●½) Three happy fabric critters hang from a ring that can be attached to either an infant carrier or stroller. Has a quiet sound and interesting textures for little hands to explore. (800) 704-8697.

Shakers `2006`

All our testers loved the toys that wiggle and shake. Most attach easily to a carseat or stroller. They'll usually buy you a little extra time! Here are our top choices:

■ Bee & Me `2006`

(Infantino $9 ●●●●½) Bee has a happy featured face, satiny ribbons on its crinkly wings, and a bold yellow-and-black striped frame around the mirror. Soft and safe for baby to explore later, but perfect for early gazing. Also nice for take-along gazing, **Tag Along Chimes** ($5.99 ●●●●), two colorful critters that look down at baby with gentle chiming sounds. (800) 840-4916.

■ Most Valuable Baby Pull Toys *2006*

(Gund $10 each **oooo**½) Hook one of these "sports" on the stroller or baby carrier. Give it a tug and it wiggles and shakes its way up. Choose your sport—bear with football, monkey with baseball, frog for soccer, or pup with basketball. Also good for distractions, **MVB rattles** ($9 each) with plush sports at either end and small colorful pieces that move in the easy-to-clutch see-through tube. (800) 448-4863.

■ Tolo Wiggly Jigglies Collection *2006*

(Small World Toys $9.99 each **oooo**) Bring home either the **Ibis Bird** or the **Bug.** Both done in velour and satin with a pull cord that activates a wonderful jiggly sound! (800) 421-4153.

> 👉 **SAFETY TIP:** Links should never be made into a loop, or linked across a crib or playpen. We often see baby strollers draped with long lengths of links. Warning labels say that a chain of links should never be more than 12" long and should be used with adult supervision.

Best New Baby/Shower Gifts

Big Ticket ($40–50)	**Gymini Total Playground Kick & Play** or **Symphony in Motion Deluxe Mobile** (Tiny Love)
Under $40	**Molly Moo Activity Toy** (Mamas & Papas) or **Sleepyhead Bunny** (North American Bear Co.)
Under $25	**Changing Table Flutterbug Musical Mobile** (Infantino) or **Wimmer-Ferguson Infant Stim-Mobile** (Manhattan Toy) or **Cuddly Pals** (Gund)
Under $20	**Bethany Butterfly** (Mamas & Papas) or **Me in the Mirror** (Sassy) or **Lamaze Whirl & Twirl Jungle** (RC2/Learning Curve) or **Roll-A-Rounds Swirlin'**

Surprise (Fisher-Price)

Under $15   **Car Seat Gallery** (Manhattan Toy) or
              Movers & Shakers Whale (Infantino)

Under $10   **Fascination Station** (Sassy)

Under $5   **Snap-Lock Beads** (Fisher-Price)

Toddlers-in-Training Toys

Some of the early walking toys found in the following chapter
may be ideal for infants who are seriously working on walking
before their first birthday.

Looking Ahead: Best First-Birthday Gifts for Every Budget

Big Ticket   **Push Cart** (Galt) or **Laugh and Learn
($50 or more) Learning Home** (Fisher-Price)

Under $50   **Discover Sounds Kitchen** (Little Tikes)
               or **Roll-a-Rounds Drop & Roar
               Dinosaur** (Fisher-Price)

Under $25   **Lamaze Nesting Present** (RC2/Learning
               Curve) or **Read to Me Tot Tower**
               (eeBoo) or **Lamaze Whirl & Twirl
               Jungle** (RC2/Learning Curve)

Under $20   **Musical Stack & Play** (Tiny Love) or
               Babipouce (Corolle)

Under $15   **Colorfun Ball** (Gund) or **Roll-a-
               Rounds Swirlin' Surprise Gumballs**
               (Fisher-Price)

Under $10   **Poppin' Push Car** (Sassy)
               or **Dudley Musical
               Pull-Along Duck**
               (Mamas & Papas)

Under $5   Cardboard book (see
               Books section)

2 • Toddlers
Ones and Twos

What to Expect Developmentally

Ones and Twos. There is a tremendous difference between your one-year-old, whose focus is primarily on mastering and enjoying his new-found mobility, and your two-year-old, who is now running, jumping, and making giant leaps with language and imagination. Yet the second and third years are generally known as the toddler years. Many of the toys and games recommended for ones will continue to be used by twos in new and more complex ways. Since some toddlers will be steady on their feet earlier than others or talking and pretending at different times, you'll want to use this chapter in terms of your own child's individual development. This chapter is not arranged chronologically. You'll find toys and games for ones and twos under each of the following main headings: **Active Physical Play, Strictly Outdoors, Sit-Down Play, Pretend Play, Art and Music, Bath Toys, Basic Furniture, Travel Toys,** and **Birthday Gifts.**

Active Exploration. Anyone who spends time with toddlers knows that they are active, on-the-go learners. They don't visit long, because there are so many places and things to explore. Toys that invite active investigation are best for this age group. For toddlers, toys with doors to open, knobs to push, and pieces to fit, fill, and dump provide the raw material for developing

31

fine-motor skills, language, and imagination.

Big-Muscle Play. Toddlers also need playthings that match their newfound mobility and budding sense of independence. Wheeled toys to push, ride on, and even ride in are great favorites. So is equipment they can climb, rock, and slide on. In these two busy years, toddlers grow from wobbly walkers to nimble runners and climbers.

Language and Pretend Power. As language develops, so does the ability to pretend. For beginners, games of make-believe depend more on action than on story lines. Choose props that look like the things they see in the real world.

Toys and Development. As an infant your baby was involved mainly with people. Now your toddler will spend more time investigating things. Some of the toys in this chapter, such as those for beginning walkers, will have short-term use. However, many of the best products are what we call bridge toys, playthings that will be used now and for several years ahead. While no toddler needs all the toys listed here, 1- and 2-year-olds do need a good mix of toys that fit varying play modes—toys for indoors and out, for quiet, solo sit-down times, and social run-and-shout-out-loud times. A variety of playthings (which may include a plain paper shopping bag or some pots and pans) gives kids the learning tools they need to stretch their physical, intellectual, and social development.

Your Role in Play. Playing (and keeping up) with an active toddler requires a sense of humor and realistic expectations. In order to satisfy their growing appetite for independence, select uncomplicated toys that won't frustrate their sense of "can do" power. For example, if your toddler does not want to sit down with you and work on a puzzle now, she may be willing in an hour, or she may be telling you that it's too difficult and should be put away and tried again in a few weeks.

Childproofing:
Setting the Stage for Learning

Childproofing involves more than putting things out of reach. It involves setting the stage for learning by providing appropriate objects that children can safely explore. To avoid a constant monologue of "No! Don't touch!" remove treasures and objects that may be dangerous to handle. Touching is what toddlers do— it's how they learn. Toddlers who lack the freedom to explore get a negative message about learning. Your goal is to encourage their curiosity, not set up roadblocks to the world around them.

Many household items are the most interesting objects to explore. Toddlers need opportunities to discover how things work—knobs to pull, boxes to open, fabrics to feel, and containers to stack. A low cabinet in the kitchen with a stack of paper plates to explore will hold a toddler's interest. Pots and pans with lids to fit on and lift off will keep toddlers occupied while you are working in the kitchen. Toddlers love to take things off shelves. Why not put sturdy cardboard books on a low shelf so they can enjoy them independently?

Enlarging the Circle: Playmates

Your 1-year-old will play mostly with you and the significant people in her life. But 2s are ready to enlarge their social circle. Whether they go to a play group or the park or visit with neighbors, 2s begin to enjoy playing near and ultimately with other children.

A Word on Sharing. Lacking experience, toddlers live by the philosophy that what's mine is mine and what's yours is mine, too. It's not selfishness so much as not really understanding what sharing means. Toddlers consider their toys almost as extensions of themselves—not for sharing. How can you help? If you are having visitors over, keep visits relatively short. An hour is plenty for 2s—always leave them wanting more!

BASIC GEAR CHECKLIST
FOR ONES

✓ Push toys   ✓ Pull toys
✓ Ride-on toy   ✓ Small vehicles
✓ Musical toys   ✓ Huggables
✓ Toy phone   ✓ Lightweight ball

✓Fill-and-dump toys
✓Manipulatives with moving parts

 BASIC GEAR CHECKLIST
FOR TWOS

✓Ride-on/-in toy   ✓Pull and push toy
✓Big lightweight ball   ✓Shovel and pail
✓Climbing/sliding toy   ✓Art supplies
✓Big blocks   ✓Table and chair
✓Huggables   ✓Props for housekeeping
✓Simple puzzles/shape-sorters

🚫 Toys to Avoid

These toys pose choking and/or suffocation hazards:
✓**Foam toys**
✓**Toys with small parts** (including small plastic fake foods)
✓**Dolls and stuffed animals with fuzzy and/or long hair**
✓**Toys labeled 3 & up** (No matter how smart toddlers are! The label almost always indicates that there are small parts in or on the toy.)
✓**Latex balloons** (Note: The Consumer Product Safety Commission reports that latex balloons are the leading cause of suffocation deaths! Since 1973 more than 110 children have died from suffocation involving uninflated balloons or pieces of broken ones. They are not advised for children under age 6.)

These toys are developmentally inappropriate:
✓**Electronic educational drill toys**
✓**Shape-sorters with more than three shapes**
✓**Battery-operated ride-ons**
✓**Most pedal toys**

Active Physical Play

Between 12 and 15 months most babies start toddling. At first they sidestep from one piece of furniture to another. Soon, with arms used for balance, they take their first independent steps. In these first months of the second year they grow from those thrilling wobbly first steps to being sure-footed adventurers. Few toys lend the kind of security you give as you extend your hands to assure him you are there to catch him.

Beginning walkers will get miles of use from a low-to-the-ground, stable, wheeled toy. The products on the market are not all created equal. Here are some basic things to look for:

- Wobbly toddlers may use toys to pull up on, and most are tippable, so save push toys for true walkers.

- Try before you buy. Some ride-ons are scaled for tall kids, others for small kids.

- Toddlers do not need battery-powered ride-ons. Encourage foot power, not push-button action!

- Toddlers are not ready for pedals. Few have the coordination to use pedals before 2½. Four wheels and two feet on the ground are best.

- Toys with loud and constant sound effects may be appealing in the store, but can become annoying in tight spaces.

Walkers, Wagons, & Ride-ons for Steady-on-Their-Feet Toddlers

COMPARISON SHOPPER:
Plastic Push-Around Walkers

None of these are weighted, the way they used to be made, so they are not for tots to pull up on. Testers gave high marks to two versions: **Stride-to-Ride Learning Walker** (Fisher-Price $34.99 oooo) This updated walker converts to a ride-on and has a shape-sorter car front end. Music can be turned off; and steering wheel, key, and gear shift are ready for pretend play. Best for steady-on-their-feet toddlers! (800) 432-5437. Little Tikes' **Wide Tracker Activity Walker** ($19.99 oooo) has

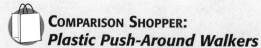

a wider opening in the back so kids are less likely to trip themselves on the wheels! (800) 321-0183.

Top-Rated Wooden Push-Around Walkers

■ Baby Walker BLUE CHIP

(Galt $99 ●●●●●) This classic wooden cart is pricier than any of its plastic counterparts, but it is very stable for early walkers and a perfect first wagon for carting treasures. (800) 899-4258.

■ Classic Walker Wagon

(Radio Flyer $70 ●●●●) This updated version is heavier and slower moving than the original, better suited for new walkers to hold on to. Makes a quiet clicking sound as it moves about. (800) 621-7613. **At press time, the clickers on models sold from 8/03 to 5/05 were recalled. Replacement clickers available from the company.**

■ Pushing Car and Doll Pram
2006 PLATINUM AWARDS

(Haba $159 and $130 ●●●●●) Our test family with three under the age of 4 got right into active pretend play with both of these beautifully styled push-about toys. The **Push Car** ($159 ●●●●●) is low to the ground and balanced enough so that a little sister or a big teddy bear could ride about as a larger child pushed. Furnished with seat cushions and pocket for treasures; made of varnished beech wood with rubber wheels, it maneuvers well, even in tight spaces. Equally well designed, a red and blue **Doll Pram** ($130 ●●●●●) comes with a cushion seat and accommodates several dolls. You can adjust the push bar as children grow, so this will grow into the preschool years. (800) 468-6873.

First Ride-Ons

Unfortunately, most ride-ons no longer have working steering ability, so kids need to move the whole vehicle with their bodies to change direction. Be sure to test-drive with your child before you buy. We found that kids with shorter legs had trouble getting on and off many models.

■ Push Around Buggy

(Step 2 $40 ●●●○) Little toddlers can get into this vehicle without climbing. It is not a toy for them to run with foot power, it is more like a stroller for giving your tot a ride. It has a seat belt, push bar, and a storage compartment up front for treasures. Tested far better than Step 2's other ride-ons such as the **Basket Ride-On** ($21.99 ●●●), a low-to-the-ground red three-wheeler. Testers found its lack of steering a drawback. Step 2's red **Motorcycle** ($21.99 ●●) was not balanced enough for toddlers and the small red **Classy Cruiser** ($34.99 ●●) was too difficult for young riders to get in and out of—and too small for older riders. None have steering. (800) 347-8372.

■ Cozy Coupe II BLUE CHIP

(Little Tikes $44.99 ●●●●●) The classic ride-in toy that a generation of kids has grown up with is still basic gear and will be used into the next age group. One of the only ride-ons with a working steering wheel. They say 1½, we say more like 2 & up. (800) 321-0183.

> **SMART PARENT TRICK:** Ask your toddler what she's bringing as she rides by. Fuel her imagination by "opening" pretend packages she delivers. Modeling pretend games helps tots take the leap into fantasy play.

■ Retro Rocket

(Radio Flyer $69.95 ●●●●●) Our fifteen-month-old testers loved the push-button sound effects, lights, and vibrating motion on this low-to-the-ground ride-on. This vehicle is less wide and lighter than Radio Flyer's **Red Roadster,** and easier for tots to get on and off of. PLATINUM AWARD '05. (800) 621-7613.

Rockers

Low-to-the-ground rockers for toddlers are used for a short time, but match the young toddler's love of motion and repetitive action. These are low enough to the ground so that the older toddler can get on and off with independence, and they're slow enough to be soothing. Often promoted for older infants and young toddlers, these are a better choice for toddlers who are steady on their feet.

■ Angel Fish Rocker 🏆2006

(Step 2 $40 ●●●●½) Reintroduced, this all-plastic fish has been an old favorite for toddlers. The seat is narrow and pretty easy to mount. Can be used indoors or out. But a warning: supervision is needed as rapid rocking can lead to spills. This is bigger than your average rocker and has been known to tip. (800) 347-8372.

■ Rocking Wobble Whale 🏆2006 PLATINUM AWARD

(Mamas & Papas $79.99 ●●●●●) Soft and easy to mount, this blue and green whale has a wooden disc base and plays "If You're Happy and You Know It" when you press its spout. An almost instant hit with our 18-month-old tester. With its quacking moving beak, **Rocking Dudley Duck** ($79.99 ●●●●) seemed almost "alive" to our little tester. Once the surprise passed, the bright yellow bird with crinkle sounds in its wings became a fine un-feathered friend. Some of our testers found the duck quacking fun; others were less amused. (310) 631-2222.

Push and Pull Toys

Push comes before pull. Instead of holding someone's hand, young toddlers often find sheer joy in the independence of walking while holding on to a push toy. You probably started walking with Fisher-Price's BLUE CHIP **Corn Popper** ($8 ●●●●●) or **Melody Push Chime** ($8 ●●●●●). They are still great choices! (800) 432-5437. Pull toys are for older tots who are surefooted and can look over a shoulder without tripping. Ambi's **Max** (Brio $17.50 ●●●●●) is a BLUE CHIP classic pull-along pooch. (888) 274-6869.

■ Dudley Musical Pull-Along Duck

(Mamas & Papas $25 ●●●●●) Dudley is one of the cutest pull toys to come along in years. Yellow with wings that flap as you pull him along and, to make the whole experience even better, if you squeeze his beak, he quacks a tune! Extremely lovable! 1 & up. PLATINUM AWARD '05. Fared better than this year's **Tootle Turtle Pull Along** ($30 ●●●), which comes with a big beaded ball "shell" that our toddlers tried to bounce. The safety cord (a good thing) kept coming undone when pulled (not so good). (310) 631-2222.

■ IQ Preschool Follow-Along Frog

(Small World Toys $15 ●●●●) Here's a really old-fashioned-styled wooden frog that moves up and down as he's pulled. No sound here, just a pleasing motion. 18 mos. & up. (800) 421-4153.

☞ **SAFETY TIP: Avoid pull toys with springs and beads that many toddlers will mouth. Old wooden pull toys from the attic may have dangerous levels of lead paint.**

Balls

Big, lightweight balls for tossing, kicking, and chasing, or for social back-and-forth, roly-poly games are favorite pieces of basic gear. Twos are ready to play bounce and catch. Be sure the ball is lightweight so it won't hurt. Soft fabric balls or slightly deflated beach balls are the best choice for now. Avoid foam- and balloon-filled balls that can be a choking hazard.

■ Little Champs Sports Center *2006*

(Little Tikes $29.95 ●●●●) Toddlers like to imitate older siblings and this little sports set allows them to shoot baskets, hit a baseball, and spin a football. The basketball has a sound chip scoreboard that cheers them on and the baseball clicks as it turns on the post. 9 mos. & up. (800) 321-0183.

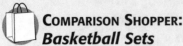

COMPARISON SHOPPER:
Basketball Sets

Baby Play Zone Basketball (Fisher-Price $19.99 **oooo**): small basketball hoop comes with a breakaway net, lights, and music to encourage your toddler to keep going for more baskets! Comes with three small balls. Our tester enjoyed making baskets, but not running after the balls! 9 mos. & up. (800) 432-5437. Testers also liked the similar game play of the LeapFrog's **Learning Hoops Basketball** ($24.95 **ooo**) but not the intrusive alphabet lesson. Making something happen is a big enough deal at this stage! (800) 701-5327.

COMPARISON SHOPPER:
Bowling Sets

Old toddlers and preschoolers like the repetitive action of this game. Two great choices: **Huggy Sport Duck Pins** (Hooray $24.99 **oooo**) Comes with six squat duck pins and a single ball for knocking them down. (866) 278-7785. For a more realistic set, **TotSport Bowling Set** (Little Tikes $14.99 **oooo**): six see-through bowling pins with balls inside make a clattering sound when the lightweight bowling ball knocks them down. 2 & up. (800) 321-0183.

Strictly Outdoors

First Climbers and More

Climbers are great for big-muscle play for toddlers who are steady on their feet. We saw a number of low-to-the-ground climbers with open platforms and some that did not have secure enough sides once tots reached the top. Many looked like an accident waiting to happen. If you are shopping for a young or especially small toddler, stick to the lowest climbers. This is not a product to grow into. You will find climbers scaled for bigger children in the next chapter.

Playhouses

See Preschool chapter.

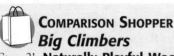

COMPARISON SHOPPER
Big Climbers

Step 2's **Naturally Playful Woodland Climber** ($219.99 ○○○○), done in muted tones, comes with a small ladder up to the 27" high platform with a slide on the other side. 2 & up. Step 2's **Naturally Playful Clubhouse Climber** ($599.99 ○○○○○) is still a great combo gym and playhouse for older toddlers and preschoolers with two towers, a slide, and a connecting bridge. One tower is outfitted with table, chairs, and props. PLATINUM AWARD '01. Little Tikes' **8-in-1 Adjustable Playground** ($315 ○○○○) with tunnels and two slides is packed with places to explore, but without the clubhouse features of Step 2's. Either is ideal for developing coordination, and both are big enough for several kids to share without quarrels! Step 2's towers and bridge were a big hit with our 2- and 3-year-old testers (tall 4s had to bend over to fit). Little Tikes' open-top design extends the age range of their set. Both are hard to assemble. Step 2 (800) 347-8372/Little Tikes (800) 321-0183.

■ Climb and Slide Castle

(Little Tikes $70 ○○○○) Designed for toddlers, this mini-castle-style climber has a low slide and steering wheel on top for dramatic play. It's 43" high. They say one and up; we'd say more like steady-on-their-feet toddlers—who are rarely younger than 18–24 mos. Requires supervision. (800) 321-0183.

■ Triple Play Tunnel *2006*

(Step 2 $39.99 ○○○○) Knowing how toddlers love going in and out of their own spaces, this is great fun—especially for tight spaces. Our toddler tester liked using it for cruising around as well as crawling through (800) 347-8372.

SMART PARENT TRICK: Give 'em a Hand! Toddlers love an appreciative audience—don't we all? When they finish a puzzle, dance a jig, or go down a slide, clap your hands together—give them a hand! Keep in mind that little children see themselves as you see them. During this often negative time, try to accentuate the positive.

Wading Pools and Water Tables

Our testers preferred inexpensive hard-vinyl wading pools to those that had to be blown up or filled with water to hold a shape (most of these had sides that were too high for younger toddlers to climb over by themselves). Prefab wading pools are also easier to lift, dump, and clean. You can find an adequate no-frills pool for under $20.

■ WaterWheel Table 🏆2006

(Step 2 $39.99 ●●●●) We had mixed reviews on this one. For stand-up water play this seems a great choice for the patio or terrace. It doesn't take up a lot of room and allows for spilling, filling, splashing, and getting good and wet! But be forewarned, there seem to be problems with leaks! The plugs on the table are not water tight, so you will have to refill this and not use it indoors. That said, this is also a toy that needs total adult supervision. (800) 347-8372. See Preschool chapter for sand and water table, p. 100.

■ Wagon Set with Bucket 🏆2006

(Small World Toys $15 ●●●●½) A toddler-size red-and-yellow wagon that comes with everything needed for the beach or sandbox—a bucket, sand molds, rake, shovel, sieve, and watering can. 18 mos. & up. (800)421-4153.

> **FREEBIE:** Toddlers love playing with soap and water and covering things with a sudsy lather. Washing kiddie cars, tabletops, and other surfaces is a favorite sport and a good way to cool off on a hot day. A small pail with soapy water and a sponge will provide endless hours of entertainment! As with all water play, supervision is a must.

Sandboxes

While small boxes are good choices when space is a concern, keep in mind that a bigger box will give more than one child enough room to maneuver. We looked for smooth edges and strong sides that will support a child's weight. The motif is really a personal preference. See Sand Tables in Preschool chapter, p. 100.

Our BLUE CHIP favorites: On the small side, **Frog Sandbox** (Step 2 $30) or **Turtle Sandbox** (Little Tikes $35). 1 & up. Bigger choices: **Crabbie Sandbox** (Step 2 $59.99) or **Dinosaur Sandbox** (Little Tikes $59.99). Step 2 (800) 347-8372/Little Tikes (800) 321-0183.

Sandbox Props: A basic bucket from any toy store will do—just be sure to check for smooth edges. To toddlers, sand is another opportunity for spilling and dumping. A simple sand mill or water wheel will have a lot of appeal! Many of the best props for the sandbox are in your kitchen: a plastic colander, empty margarine containers, strainers, squeeze bottles, etc.

Sprinklers 🌟2006

For toddlers ready to get wet, we'd recommend Little Tikes' new **Playful Paws Sprinkler** or **Hook, Line & Sprinkler** ($10 each ●●●●). Both are designed to provide a smaller spray (in one position it's stationary; in the other position it will spin). A better choice than most bigger sprinklers that are often overwhelming. 18 mos. & up. (800) 321-0183.

■ No-Spill Bubble Tumbler BLUE CHIP

(Little Kids $6.95 ooooo) Toddlers love chasing bubbles, even though most are not able to blow their own. When they start, buy one of these no-spill containers that prevent the tears that used to come when the solution would spill! Our testers did not love the new battery-operated **My First Bubble Blower** ($14.95 ooo). "Didn't hold their attention"; "we prefer the original." 18 mos. & up. (800) 545-5437.

The Youngest Gardener

Unfortunately Little Tikes no longer makes their plastic gardening tools that we much prefer to metal sets since toddlers tend to toss and swing tools. Bring home a pretend mower such as Little Tikes' **Mulching Mower** ($19.99 oooo). Our all-time favorite Fisher-Price **Bubble Mower** is now replaced with the **Double Blaster Mower** ($20 ooo)—which works, but not as easily as the original. Little Tikes (800) 321-0183 / Fisher-Price (800) 432-5437.

Sit-Down Play

First Puzzles and Manipulatives

Toddlers enjoy toys that invite investigation but don't demand too much dexterity. Toys with lids to lift, buttons to push, and dials to turn give them satisfying feedback along with playful ways to develop fine-motor skills and eye-hand coordination. Once they understand how to use them, toddlers will enjoy many of the toys in this section independently, and that is very satisfying to the "me do it myself!" toddler.

First Puzzles

Start with whole-piece puzzles. Take the time to introduce a new puzzle or toy. Let your child take the lead, giving time to explore the pieces and experiment with them.

■ Puzzibilities Sounds on the Go

(Small World Toys $15 oooo½) Four big puzzle pieces with easy-to-grasp wooden pegs—each vehicle makes a distinctive sound when

placed in the frame. Also, **Sounds on the Farm**—this one moos, neighs, oinks, and baas. Also top rated, silent, giant peg-handled three-piece **Shapes** or **Numbers** with bold patterns, or **Vehicles** and **Wild Animals** ($9 each **○○○○**). 18 mos. & up. (800) 421-4153.

■ Puzzle Totes

(Lauri $8.99 **○○○○**) Our testers enjoyed playing with this collection of puzzles from Lauri, well known for their textured crepe rubber puz-

zles. Rather than having the traditional tray, these double-thick seven- or eight-piece puzzles have a handle just right for travel and carrying about. Two-toned pieces are able to stand up for dramatic play. Four versions: **Marine Life, Earthmovers, Dinosaurs,** and **Big Shapes.** Older 2s will be able to manipulate these whole-piece puzzles that 3s and 4s will continue to enjoy. (800) 451-0520.

Manipulatives

■ Learn-Around Playground ⭐2006 PLATINUM AWARD

(LeapFrog $59.99 **○○○○○**) This innovative table invites kids to explore and make things happen. A great first birthday gift! Sitting down, tots can play the ball drop and tap the shape tabs and textures. On their feet they can cruise around the sturdy table and test the pop-up and spinning shapes, press the letters that say their names, and activate the keyboard. The ball drop has jazzy percussion sound effects and says the color of each ball as it falls. Has volume control and can be enjoyed with sound off. 9 mos. & up. (800) 701-5327.

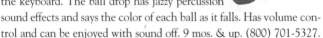

■ Musical Stack & Play

(Tiny Love $19.95 **○○○○○**) This cleverly designed elephant stacking toy has a place for dropping balls in its top. The balls come out at the base with some fanfare (lights/sound) but nothing over the top. Our testers also liked the soft fabric rings for stacking but really spent most of the time playing with the plastic balls. Marked 6 mos. & up, but will be most enjoyed by 1s and up. PLATINUM AWARD '05. (800) 843-6292.

■ Pop-Onz Pop 'n' Twirl Building Table

(Fisher-Price $29.99 ●●●●●) An activity table for the 18-month-and-older crowd that is exactly on target. The pop-ons are big chunky pieces that can be stacked easily on the plastic pegs. Great clear lesson in cause and effect: push the red button, and two parts of the table spin with a little music (volume control—a plus). PLATINUM AWARD '05. New for **2006**, we skipped the **Pop 'n Musical Big Top** (●●), which simply didn't have as much play power as the original. (800) 432-5437. We'd also really skip Playskool's **Spin N' Pop Arcade** (●●) table. It's way too noisy, frenetic, and over the top!

■ Pound-A-Ball

(Small World Toys $15 ●●●●) Most toddlers get to a stage when pounding is just the best! Here's a fun plastic variation with four balls that, once pounded, travel through a small see-through ball run. In the beginning you may need to hold the toy for over-eager pounders! If you prefer a wooden hammer toy, **Ryan's Room Pound Around** ($14.95 ●●●●½) A six-sided pounding board with hammer and colorful pegs that don't come out. Just turn the board and start hammering again and again. Big toddlers love the powerful pounding action. 18 mos. & up. (800) 421-4153.

■ Rollipop Toddler Starter and Advanced Sets

(Edushape $19.95 & $24.95 ●●●●●) These are among our favorite toddler toys. Toddlers love to drop the oversized colorful plastic balls into the starter set (a tower) and track them as they go down. The balls also travel slowly down the advanced set (a bridge), making it an ideal toy for developing visual tracking. 18 mos. & up. PLATINUM AWARD '04. (800) 404-4744.

■ Super Spiral Play Tower
2006 PLATINUM AWARD

(International Playthings $32 ●●●●●) Toddlers love this marvelous toy that they quickly take charge of. Two weighted balls and a little penguin twist down the spiral and slide into different slots. A green froggy slides down a chute and makes a funny sound that ends with a ping of a bell. Repetitive action provides the kind of predictable cause-and-effect results toddlers love. Develops eye-hand skills as well as visual tracking. 18 mos. & up. Their original PLATINUM AWARD-winning **Tomy Ball Party Roll Around Tower** and **Ball Party Bounce** remain top rated (they are very similar to the Edushape toys reviewed above). (800) 445-8347.

First Construction Toys

Few toys have more long-term use and learning value than construction toys. Blocks give children a hands-on understanding of words such as *longer, taller, the same, more, less, bigger, and smaller*. These are basic math concepts built into the play. You can help your toddler connect words to these concepts by using language to describe the pieces or what he is doing. These hands-on experiences have much more educational value than electronic toys that try to teach symbolic numerals. Toddlers need to experience "two-ness" again and again before they make the leap to symbolic representation. Without taking over, get your child started by modeling ways to make an enclosure, or span two blocks with a third. By adding vehicles and small animals and people figures, you provide the ingredients for imaginative play.

■ Lego Quatro 2006

(Lego Systems $9.99 & up ●●●●●) Twos used to graduate to **Lego Duplo** bricks, but now there's a bigger brick (twice the size of Duplo and four times the size of standard Lego). The bricks are made of a softer, easier-to-grasp material. Here, "more is better," so we suggest starting with the **Large Quatro Bucket** ($19.99/75 pieces; $14.99/50 pieces ●●●●●). PLATINUM AWARD '05 1 & up. New, big, and extremely neat for 2006, a big **Mountain Climber** ($24.99 ●●●●½) truck with 20 blocks and a push-button engine sound that tots will love for their dramatic play. (800) 233-8756.

■ Lego Duplo Thomas Load and Carry Train Set 2006 PLATINUM AWARD

(Lego Systems $29.99 ●●●●●) Easy-to-assemble tracks and environment including train, movable light signal, and cargo tower. 61

pieces. Our older toddler testers "loooooved" this set! 2 & up. Still top rated, for Dora fans, **Dora the Explorer,** a 41-piece **Animal Adventure Set** ($29.99 ooooo) with play figures, blocks, and a sound effects box with 8 different sounds—not that kids can't make their own sounds. 2 & up. For other Duplo sets, look at the Preschool chapter, p. 92.

How High? Use blocks to see how high a tower you can build together before it goes kaboom! Take turns adding one more piece—and keep a running count as you go. You can play variations of this game with empty frozen juice cans, wooden thread spools, or other collections.

■ Giant Constructive Blocks BLUE CHIP

(Constructive Playthings $18.99 oooo) These big sturdy blocks (printed like red bricks) are lightweight but satisfyingly hefty for lugging about. Perfect for making tall towers and wide roadways for beginning builders. Strong enough to stand on, these are perennial classics that endure years of creative play. A dozen bricks, 12" x 6" x 4". #CP-626. (800) 832-0572.

■ Mega Blok Lil' Cement Truck and Lil' Dump Truck *2006*

(Mega Bloks $9.99 oooo) These plastic vehicles are just right for 2s and up. They both come with a truckload of Mega Bloks. Just right for pretend construction sites. New for *2006*, **Lil' Train Engine** ($12.99 oooo), a colorful engine that holds a stash of blocks. Still top rated, the larger **Mega Bloks Wagon** ($30 oooo). A tot-sized red wagon loaded with 50 oversized plastic pegged blocks is fun for making big, fast constructions. Pegs on side of wagon can be used for building up and over. (800) 465-6342.

Wooden Blocks

Older twos will begin to enjoy a beginner set of
wooden blocks. We recommend **Ryan's Room
Push-Along Block Cart** PLATINUM
AWARD '03 (Small World Toys $44
ooooo) with 36 pieces, which older tots
will enjoy lugging about. (800) 421-4153. For
larger top-rated sets, see Preschool chapter, p. 88.

Wooden Train Sets

It's a great temptation to buy wooden train sets for older
twos—but be forewarned, most have small figures and other
small parts that make them dangerous for kids under three
who still mouth their toys. See Preschool chapter for reviews
of top-rated sets. To address this issue, Brio has introduced a
new line of trains for toddlers.

First Stacking, Nesting,
and Shape-Sorter Toys

What You Should Know. Classic stacking toys require the
ability to see and arrange objects in size order—a skill that nei-
ther babies nor toddlers have. Such toys are often labeled 6
months & up, but there's nothing wrong if your child can't do
it—the problem is with the label! Happily, there are more for-
giving choices that introduce stacking without the need for size
order. Toddlers will use them to taste, toss, and explore— just
don't expect them to be expert stackers. As you play with your
toddler, use color or size words to describe the pieces.
Such concepts are learned with greater ease
when they are part of everyday experiences.

Two good choices: **Lamaze Spin n
Stack Rings** 2006 (RC2/Learning Curve
$24.99 oooo) has four big plastic rings
decorated with interesting textured
fabric and ribbons that spin when the
music in the post is activated. We thought
the big ring would be too big for little hands, but
our 10-month old tester loved it and soon figured
out how to hit the post to activate music and
make the base spin. (800) 704-8697. Still top

rated, the **Classical Stacker** (Fisher-Price $19.99 ●●●●●) has a post with twinkling lights and sounds as each ring is put on. (800) 432-5437.

Nesting and Stacking Toys

Toddlers like the multiple pieces for pulling apart, banging, and stacking long before they can nest them. Stacking and nesting toys develop eye-hand coordination, size order concepts, and even counting skills. They provide hands-on experience with concepts such as *bigger, smaller, taller, inside, under, top,* and *bottom*—to name but a few. You can make the language connection as you play together.

Here are our top- (and not-so-top-) rated choices:

■ Read to Me Tot Tower

(eeBoo $19 ●●●●●) The latest in a handsome line of sturdy cardboard blocks with storybook-quality illustrations of images to know and name. 1 & up. PLATINUM AWARD '04. (212) 222-0823.

■ Stacking Activity Cubes 2006

(Small World Toys $15 ●●●●) These three cubes can be stacked in any order; the shape fits under the cutout. Each block can be activated by cranking, spinning, or pushing a button. They take some finger power for the motion payoff. Introduce one at a time; once they have them all figured out, introduce the stacking aspect for multi-action surprise! 18 mos. & up. (800) 421-4153.

■ Stacking Cups BLUE CHIP

(Sassy $7.99 ●●●●●) Updated for 2006 in new colors, this is still a great choice. Four boldly patterned cups with interesting textures on the rims. Fun for nesting and stacking and hiding Cheerios under! 1 & up. (800) 323-6336.

■ Stacking Shapes Pegboard 2006

(RC2/Learning Resources $14.95 ●●●●½) A classic toy returns! Little hands will be busy with twenty-five easy-to-grasp, brightly colored chunky pegs that can be sorted by color or shape on the big 10"-square base. Pegs can be stacked and eventually strung like beads. Marked two & up, we'd say this is for slightly older twos and even threes. (800) 222-3909.

■ Zolo Stacrobats *2006*

(Kushies $45.99 **oooo**) Five colorful fabric acrobats and three colorful balls can be balanced (sort of) and arranged in multiple ways on their colorful magnetic fabric balancing three-ring circus-style pad. Magnets inside make for interesting experiments that will be going *ka-boom* on a regular basis. A fun toy for interacting with young toddlers—we think they will have trouble on their own. Play figures store in the magnetic base, so toss the plastic bag they come in. A pricey toy, but attractive. 1 & up. (800) 841-5330.

SAFETY NOTE: Plastic stacking cups should have air holes so they don't form a suction over baby's face. Most toymakers have updated cups, but some old-style products may still be on shelves. Check before you buy!

Shape-Sorters

■ Plan Toys Shape-n-Sort

(Brio $15 **oooo**½) A handsome wooden three-shape sorter. Drop the pieces in place, hit the tray, and pieces drop out. (888) 274-6869.

■ Ryan's Room Get-a-Grip Sorter

(Small World Toys $14.95 **oooo**) A triangular sorter that has a handle and a forgiving opening. Beautifully crafted in wood. A good parent-child toy. (800) 421-4153.

FREEBIE: Many sorters and nesting toys are too hard for young toddlers. You can make your own. Cut holes in the lid of a shoe box for blocks to fall through. Or use a see-through plastic container so tots can see where their pop-beads or blocks have gone.

Pretend Play

As language develops, older toddlers begin their early games of pretend. So much of the real equipment tots see adults using is off-limits to them. Child-sized versions can (sometimes) offer a satisfying alternative and fuel the imagination of little ones, who love to mimic what they see you doing. Never again will sweeping and cleaning be more fun than to a toddler!

Dolls and Huggables

Both boys and girls enjoy playing with dolls and soft animals. For one-year-olds, velour and short-haired plush animals will hold some interest. Twos are ready for both oversized but lightweight huggables to lug about, and small dolls that fit in their fists. Toddlers often get attached to one huggable that becomes an inseparable "lovie." Having a tubbable vinyl doll may also do the trick for a reluctant bather. Since toddlers are still likely to chew on their toys, select uncomplicated dolls without doodads (buttons, long hair). If potty training is on the agenda, see the potty dolls in Preschool, page 78.

> ☞ **SAFETY NOTE:** Do not leave large plush dolls or toys in crib, as they can be stepped on and accidentally give tots a boost over the side. Toddlers should not have pillowlike dolls or toys to sleep with, or dolls with chewable doodads and features that pose a choking hazard.

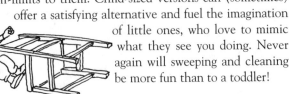

■ Babicorolle 2006

(Corolle $11 & up ●●●●) Corolle has beautiful dolls for every age group. For ones, we recommend soft huggables that feel big but are lightweight. New for 2006, **Babipouce** ($25 ●●●●), an old favorite, is now available with Asian and African-American as well as Caucasian painted vinyl faces and soft bodies. Their clothes are sew-on velour and available in boyish as well as utterly pink choices. Still adorable, **Miss Grenadine** (●●●●●), done in deliciously soft hot pink, red, and orange velour. 1 & up. Twos and up will enjoy Corolle's **Tidoo** collection ($40–$50

●●●●), sweet 12" tubbable/floatable bald-headed dolls with beanbag bodies. Come dressed in knit outfits with Velcro. **Safety note:** Some Tidoo sets have small bottles or fabric balls which we do not recommend for this age group. (800) 668-4846.

■ Rick the Frog & Friends *2006* PLATINUM AWARD

(Rich Frog $12 each ●●●●●) A new line of soft animal dolls with patterned cotton bodies, stitched features, and heads and feet made of terry. These look like storybook characters and are not gender specific. Choose the bunny, elephant, duck, hippo, or frog. Also adorable, **Softies Collection:** a frog, bunny, elephant, and duck ($10 each ●●●●●). These are a little floppier and silky soft to the touch. Just the right-sized handful for toddlers. (802) 865-9225.

■ Latitude Enfant Grannimals Collection *2006* PLATINUM AWARD

(Pint Size Productions $5–$100 each ●●●●●) Done in knitted fabric and stitched features, these are an unusual collection of machine washable soft dolls that are gender neutral. A real departure from the usual plush. Choose Lucien the rabbit, Mona the cow, Sasha the cat, Marie the mouse. The medium (8" $20) and large (16" $30) arrive in a special box that might well turn into a bed. The mini (5" $5) and giant (40" $100) come sans box. (800) 544-9183.

■ Little Mommy Newborn Twin Dolls *2006*

(Fisher-Price $16.99 ●●●●) These bald-headed twin dolls have no moving eyes or small accessories. They're truly toddler friendly. The realistic vinyl features are painted on. Both heavily scented dolls have soft bodies and the rompers they are wearing do not come off. Both come with a chunky molded bottle. Available now in girl/girl; boy/boy, and girl/boy combos. Also available in African American as well as Caucasian dolls. 18 mos. & up. (800) 432-5437.

■ Götz Precious Day Mini Muffin Boy & Girl *2006*

(International Playthings $12 each ●●●●) These little 8" realistic dolls have painted eyes, bald heads, easy-to-hold beanbag bodies, and no small doo-dads. Dressed in striped rompers, they are light enough for older tots to carry and cuter in person than they appear online. 18 mos. & up. (800) 445-8347.

■ Tolo Mother and Baby Elephant *2006*

(Small World Toys $29.99 ●●●●½) Blue velour Mama elephant with floppy plaid ears has magnetic "hands" to hold her elephant child, who looks just like Mama! (800) 220-3669.

■ Baby Beeps *2006*

(North American Bear $15 ●●●●) Colored like pastel sorbets, each of these 15" bears has a big snout with a squeaker inside. Soft, nonshedding plush, they have swinging arms and legs that make them easy to grab, and are big enough to make a good armful for toddlers. Still top rated, **Pastel Pancake Bears with Blankets** ($20 ●●●●) Scrumptious flat bears come with built-in blankies! (800) 682-3427.

■ Big Spunky *2006*

(Gund $59.99 ●●●●½) Older toddlers love big dolls to lug about and flop down on from time to time. The trick is to find something large but light enough for these little ones. Big Spunky fills the order. He's 22" big and available in blue or pink soft plush with patches of white and stitched features for safety's sake. This is what you call a real armful that will get a lot of loving! For smaller but great choices, consider colorful 11" **Tutti Frutti** ($20 ●●●●) elephant, monkey, or cat, or the classic all-time favoite, **Snuffles,** a BLUE CHIP bear ($12 and $20 ●●●●●). (800) 448-4863.

A few words about talking dolls for toddlers

Although soft huggable bears and dolls have long-term play value, interactive dolls that talk, dance, and sing are novelty items that may appeal. Don't be surprised, however, if your toddler is put off by a popular character that comes to life. Toddlers are still sorting out what is real and make-believe—so these "magical" dolls may have more appeal to adults than to the very young.

Doll Accessories

Most toddlers will try to get into doll furniture you buy. Most plastic doll furniture is very tippable. Better to wait until the preschool years for typical baby beds, highchairs, and strollers. Older 2s may enjoy a shopping cart they can push about and use for their dolls. We recommend: **Wooden Doll Cradle Blue Chip** (Community Playthings $90 ●●●●●), a 29" solid maple cradle built to last and big enough for kids to climb in to play baby, or put a family of dolls to sleep in. 2 & up. Item #C140. (800) 777-4244. **Shopping Cart Blue Chip** (Little Tikes $25 ●●●●): this bright yellow cart with baby seat is more gender free than most doll carriers. (800) 321-0183. See the **Doll Pram** from Haba, p. 36.

Vehicles

What to look for: Vehicles with clicky wheels, friction "motors," and passengers to load and unload provide sensory feedback. They are also great props for developing fine-motor skills and pretend play.

What to avoid: A fleet of vehicles with lots of electronic lights, sounds, and voices that will drive you crazy—and, worse, will do nothing to help tots develop language or imagination. Also, avoid small Matchbox or Hot Wheels cars; their small parts can be a choking hazard for kids under 3.

■ Handle Haulers 2006

(Little Tikes $9.99 & up each ●●) Sorry, these trucks might have been award winners, but the age labels saying 12–36 months are totally wrong! For young toddlers, these are not stable enough to keep them from flying into the child's face if he leans on the back or front of the handle for balance. For twos and up, these are uncomplicated props for beginning pretend play. We'd steer clear of the dump truck at any age since it has pinch potential as well. (800) 321-0183.

■ Learning Connections Train 2006

(LeapFrog $24.95 ●●●● ½) This little blue engine and five cars can be pushed without sound, or kids can turn on the sound for music

that either reinforces counting or color concepts. As you add on trains (they connect with magnets), a pleasant voice magically tells you whether you've added an orange car or a car with three ducks. While these concepts are developmentally early for babies, we were delighted that there is no quiz mode here. There is some trial and error in matching positive and negative magnets to connect the trains. The trains can also stack, but only in proper size order, so these can be challenging to younger toddlers. They say 9 months—we'd say more like 15 months. (800) 701-5327.

■ Little Driver

(Small World Toys $32 **oooo** ½) This classic steering wheel with lights and sounds comes with a phone, just right for pretend road trips. 18 mos. & up. (800) 421-4153. Vtech's updated version is much louder than their older model. Try it before you bring it home.

■ Little People Cement Mixer Truck

(Fisher-Price $19.95 **oooo**) Push on the driver's head and the cement mixer tips as the vehicle beeps (not too loudly) with a back-up sound. We also note that the driver is not just female, but she's blond! What next? They say 1 & up. We found this was most enjoyed by 18 mos. & up. (800) 432-5437.

Housekeeping Props

Older toddlers, both boys and girls, adore imitating the real work they see grown-ups doing around the house. Sweeping the floor, vacuuming, cooking, caring for the baby— these are thrilling roles to play. Many of the props for this sort of pretend play will be used for several years. They are what we call "bridge toys," which span the years. These toys are becoming harder and harder to find (a comment on our culture's view of domesticity?). We did receive vacuum cleaners that actually pick things up—but that also meant hair could get caught in the mix, too—so we passed on those. Unfortunately the handle of the **Cleanin' Fun 2 in 1 Vacuum Set** (Little Tikes $19.99 **ooo**), with colorful balls that "pop" when the upright is pushed, is very hard for toddlers to release, and an adult is needed to release the minivac attachment. (800) 321-0183. Fisher-Price took their classic vac out of the line, so your best bet is to sweep up with Schylling's red and yellow **Broom Set** ($7.99 oooo). 2 & up. (800) 541-2929.

☞ **SAFETY TIP: Buckets!** Beware of buckets used in the house for cleaning. Ever-curious toddlers have been known to fall into them and drown. Old buckets from building bricks also pose a problem. Most new play buckets have a safety bar halfway down to prevent tots from putting their heads all the way in.

Phones

Before you buy a play phone with sound, put the receiver to your ear. Many are alarmingly loud. The quietest of the bunch are **Ambi City Phone** (Brio $10 oooo), which has spinning faces, a mirror, a good clicking sound, and lots of buttons to push (888) 274-6869, and **Tolo Mobile Phone** (Small World Toys $12 oooo). (800) 421-4153.

For more bells and whistles: **Talk-to-Me Telephone** (Sassy $17.99 oooo). With an old-fashioned rotary dial on one side and push-button pads on the other, this yellow phone has lots of features for your toddler to explore. The phone counts from 1–9, and says hello and goodbye in English, Spanish, and French. 1 & up. (800) 323-6336.

☞ **SAFETY TIP: An old real phone may seem like lots of fun, but the cord and small parts pose a choking hazard to toddlers.**

It's for You! Game. Older toddlers love talking on the phone. Use the power of pretend to "call" them when lunch is ready or it's time to go out. "Brringggg! Brrringggg! Telephone! It's for you!" Transitions are often easier if you turn them into a game.

Toy Dishes and Pots

Finding a sturdy, gender-free set of plastic dishes isn't easy! Many sets we tested cracked, were too small for little hands, or were very, very pink! Stay away from sets with small parts and sharp cutlery, and of course, save the pottery and china for later.

Dishes and Tea and Cooking Sets:

There are more elaborate sets in the next chapter. For toddlers you want to keep it simple. Model pouring them a pretend cup of something delicious. Don't be afraid to ham it up: "It's too hot!" "This cake is yummy!" For this stage we recommend: **Little Helper's Dining Room & Pots and Pans** (Step 2 $12 oooo) White, magenta, and yellow 22-piece set comes with dishes, pots, and utensils. (800) 347-8372. 2 & up.

Toy Kitchens

Choosing which kitchen center to bring home is really a matter of style preference and space. There are sizes ranging from small single units to elaborate large units that need their own wall, if not room! Few of the sinks hold water, which is too bad. There is also a trend back to pink kitchens—we have noted our gender-free choices because we believe strongly that both boys and girls need to know their way around the kitchen.

■ MagiCook Kitchen

(Little Tikes $90 ooo) This high-tech kitchen will say 100 phrases in three different languages. Unfortunately there is no phrase: "Let's order in." While this may at first seem really neat, this type of directed pretend play robs kids of the pleasure of making their own original creations. 2–5. (800) 321-0183.

■ Lifestyle Dream Kitchen 2006

(Step 2 $149.99 oooo) This combo kitchen with stove, oven, microwave, fridge, and phone (electronic) is 35½" long and is designed for the toddler who needs the dream kitchen (in plastic, of course). This one comes with wainscoting, crown molding, and simulated granite! For an even bigger version, there's the **Lifestyle Deluxe Kitchen** ($219/49" wide oooo)! New for 2006, **Lifestyle Designer Kitchen** ($99 oooo), a smaller scaled kitchen with "stainless" steel fridge and oven, copper-look hood. Has three electronic features: stovetop, light, and phone. (800) 347-8372.

■ Small World Living Wooden Kitchen Appliances
2006 PLATINUM AWARD

(Small World Toys $124 & up each **ooooo**) Wooden sets usually cost a lot more. That's why we were thrilled to find these updated handsome individual pieces (a **sink**, a **stove/oven**, a **refrigerator**) or the **two-in-one sink & stove** ($179). Done in birch-toned wood with bright licks of red. Newest addition, a **BBQ Grill** ($124) with a set of tools. Best of all, the sinks are removable so that you can use "real" water. Most sinks no longer have this feature. These are gender neutral, a plus. They are a bit challenging to put together. (800) 421-4153.

Pretend Settings

■ Laugh and Learn Learning Home **2006**

(Fisher-Price $59.95 **oooo** ½) For the get-about toddler, this "little house" is just the right size for active play and making things happen. It has a door that opens and shuts and is big enough to crawl through, lights that turn off and on, doorbell that rings, ball drop, and shape sorter, among other interesting activities. A great first birthday gift to enjoy throughout this year and probably next. It is a big toy, but if you have the room, it's a good choice for solo or two-tot play! They say 6 months to 3. We'd say one and up would be a better bet. (800) 432-5437.

■ Little People Sweet Sounds Home **2006**

(Fisher-Price $29.99 **oooo**) This fully furnished take-along dollhouse that opens up for lots of pretend play has unfortunately been redesigned with lots of pink trim. In the past, we had applauded the gender-free paint job. Still remains a good choice for older toddlers. 2 & up. New for **2006**, we passed on the **Little People's Castle** (**ooo**) with trumpets that toot and drawbridge that lowers. Our tester kept trying to get the Royals onto their balcony, but they kept falling off! Oops! This fantasy is more appropriate for older kids. We still highly recommend the **Little People Ramps Around Garage** ($29.99 **ooooo**) with a cleverly designed garage that opens up, as well as a car wash, elevator, gas station, two ramps, and repair shop with two cars and drivers. PLATINUM

AWARD '04. We find the classic **Little People Farm** ($29.99 **oo**), with updated built-in electronic sounds, confusing for young children. Put the horse in the hen's "spot," and the horse will cluck! It's what we call a dumb cluck toy! (800) 432-5437.

> **FREEBIE:** Empty, staple-free boxes are among the best toys known to toddlers. Great for sitting in, climbing out of, coloring on, lugging around, crawling through, or loading up.

Art and Music

Art Supplies

Give your toddler opportunities to explore colors and textures. This is not the time for coloring books and drawing within the lines. Scribbling comes before drawing, just as crawling comes before walking! Twos may give names to their drawings and creations after they are done. Finished products are not as important as getting their hands into the doing.

Even one-year-olds get a sense of "can do" power scribbling with big, easy-to-grasp crayons on blank paper. Older tots love the fluid lines they get with fat washable markers, but keep in mind that you'll need to replace covers or the markers will dry out. Twos also enjoy bright tempera paint with thick brushes, or play-dough and finger paints for lively hands-on fun!

You'll need to supervise and establish a place where art materials can be used. You don't really need an easel for now. A low table that children can stand at is fine. In fact, they have less trouble with paint rolling and dripping when they work on a flat surface. If your toddler persists in eating supplies or spreading them on floors or walls, put them away for a while and try again in a month or two.

■ Crayola Kid's First Washable Crayons BLUE CHIP

(Binney & Smith $3 & up **ooooo**) These washable crayons are very big to match toddler's way of grasping with a whole fist. Save the smaller crayons, which snap in tots' hands, for their school days. 1½

& up. (800) 272-9652.

■ Crayola Color Wonder Paper & Markers

(Binney & Smith $8.99 ●●●●●) We thought this prod-
uct should be called color magic! The marker has no
color on the tip and will not "color" on normal paper,
sofas, Grandma's wall (you get the idea!). But when
you color on the special Color Wonder paper . . . voilà!
Magically your design appears. We prefer the open-
ended paper to the coloring books. Drawing at this age should be
more about exploring the materials than worrying about lines or premade art. PLATINUM AWARD '02. We don't recommend **Color
Wonder Finger Paints,** which require more finger pressure than
most kids have at this age. (800) 272-9652.

Play Dough

Playing with premade or homemade dough is marvelous for
twos who love pounding, poking, rolling, crumbling, and
hands-on exploring. At this stage, the finished product is
unimportant. The focus is on smashing a lump flat or pulling
it apart into small pieces or mixing blue and yellow to get
green. Dough should be used with supervision in a placed
established for messy play.

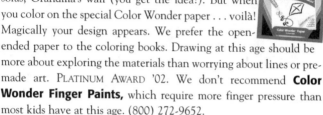

Making Dough Game: Save money
by making your own dough with this homemade play-dough recipe. Kids will
enjoy getting their hands into the bowl and
helping to mix up dough, which can be
stored in a covered container. Mix
together 1 cup of flour, ½ cup salt, a
few drops of vegetable oil, and
enough water to form a ball. Food
coloring or a splash of bright tempera
paint can be added.

■ Play-Doh Case of Colors BLUE CHIP

(Hasbro $7 ●●●●●) Imagine a 10-pack with two-ounce lumps of 10 dif-
ferent colors. Don't let them see all the tubs; open one or two at a time at
most. Add plastic dishes for added pretend! 2 & up. (800) 327-8264.

Paints and Easels

Older toddlers will enjoy painting either at a table where the colors won't run or at a standing easel. Start with three colors at most. Thick brushes and washable tempera paint are good choices available at most toy and art supply stores. Try to have the art supplies ready to go for whenever the creative mood strikes.

See Preschool chapter for easels.

Musical Toys

Once they are steady on their feet, toddlers love to move to music. Play a variety of music for them to dance to or accompany with their "instruments." Aside from the usual music for kids, try some marches, ballet scores, or music from other cultures. Better yet, put on your dancing feet and shake, rattle, and roll along.

■ Bug Tunes Music Set

(Little Tikes $13 ●●●●) Get ready to shake, rattle, and boogie with this 6-piece set of bug-shaped maracas, tamborine, and jingler. Designed for younger players than the Lynn Kleiner set, below—this is more like a set of rattles shaped like instruments. Also fun, **Chimes the Caterpillar** ($13 ●●●●). Two classic musical toys—a xylophone and a keyboard—are combined in one buggy version. Forget the music on the box, the toy is more about exploration than playing a tune. Skip the **Jungle (●●●)** sets with mallets that are more like traditional drumsticks. Our testers tasted all the mallets—so you're better off with the bigger rounder heads. 18 mos. & up. (800) 321-0183.

■ Dance Baby Dance Sit & Stand Danceband

(Fisher-Price $39.99 ●●) Great idea, poorly executed. When toddlers activate sounds by stepping on the play mat or by hitting the keys on the console, too much music plays—so the lessons in cause and effect are lost. Marked 6 mos. & up. (800) 432-5437.

■ Lynn Kleiner Babies Make Music Set

(Remo $40.25 ●●●●½) Many musical instruments for young kids make noise, not music, and many are basically unsafe. Strike up the rhythm band with these instruments that are well crafted with both sound and safety in mind. This set includes a jingle shaker, wrist jingle, small drum, and scarf (all safe enough for toddlers who still mouth their toys). 2 & up. (800) 525-5134.

■ Neurosmith Music Blocks *2006* PLATINUM AWARD

(Small World Toys $45 ●●●●●) Welcome back! Comes with five colored plastic blocks, each side making a different sound. Match the shapes on the blocks or play them in random order—there's no right or wrong way. The "composer" allows you to record and play back your composition. Comes with one jazz cartridge; we'd suggest bringing home the classical cartridge ($15), too. (800) 421-4153.

■ Neurosmith Together Tunes Block *2006*

(Small World Toys $59.99 ●●●●●) Also reintroduced this year, an active musical toy for young toddlers. Just a turn of the oversized fabric block activates a familiar nursery tune along with peek-a-boo surprises built in. Songs include "Wheels on the Bus" and "Old MacDonald." A good choice for cruising toddlers. PLATINUM AWARD '04. (800) 421-4153.

■ Tolo Baby Concerto

(Small World Toys $25 ●●●●½) Toddlers will like lifting the little yellow bear off his sleek red platform or putting him back and watching as he spins to the music. Tots can use the five big key pads to make single notes, or activate one of five melodies by Mozart, Handel, Bach, and Vivaldi. An empowering toy for making things happen. 1 & up. (800) 421-4153.

Follow the Leader Toddler Game. Use a full-length mirror to play a "can-you-do-what-I-do?" game. Use big and little motions from faces to toes. Getting kids to copy what you are doing is more than fun. It helps kids begin to focus on details and translate what they see into actions. Demonstrate a sequence of two motions—pat your head and then your tummy. Can your toddler remember two motions? How about three?

Bath Toys

For young bathers, the tub is just another locale for learning and play. Working up a lather, trying to keep a slippery soap from slipping away, discovering how water spills from a cup, drips from a washcloth, and splashes when you hit it—these are a child's way of finding out how things like soap and water work.

> ☞ **SAFETY TIP: A lot of parents have raised the issue of bath toys that retain water and possibly e.coli bacteria. We saw a lot of toys this season with squirters, tubing, and squeezable parts that produce seemingly appealing water play. But the safety of these toys represents a reasonable concern and we are not recommending them—even though they are really, really cute.**

■ Baby Einstein Bath Puppets *2006*

(Kids II $8.99 each ●●●●½) There's a blue octopus, a two-toothed teal hippo, and a friendly green dragon all done in terry cloth. Use these for playtime in or out of the tub. These are designed with loops to hang and dry after the tub fun is done. (800) 793-1454.

■ Bathtime Kitchen Sink *2006*

(Sassy $15.99 ●●●●½) Now tots can tub with everything including the kitchen sink! This floating "sink" has net basin to hold scooping, squirting, and straining props. Squeeze the squirting spigot for a shower or pour water through the sieve. A clever toy for tubtime. Still top rated, **Sassy's Car Wash** ($15.99 ●●●●) with three little cars that roll down ramps and get "cleaned" with a big yellow shower head nozzle that squirts tub water. They say 9 months, we'd say both are better toddler toys for 18 mos. and up. (800) 323-6336.

> ☞ **SAFETY TIP: Bath toys need to be completely drained and dried between baths to prevent harmful bacteria and/or mold collecting in them. Squeeze toys, although a lot of fun, are particularly susceptible to this problem.**

■ Froggies in the Tub 2006

(Sassy $11 ●●●●½) More like a good piece of equipment than a toy, this happy-faced frog goes over the faucet to protect active toddlers from bumping into metal spout. It comes with a suction-cupped frog with net holder for all those tub toys that make happier tub time for toddlers. (800) 323-6336.

■ Bathketball 2006

(Little Tikes $10 ●●●½) Suction cups hold the hoop securely to the side of the tub. This comes with three squirty balls. The bottom of the net cinches shut for storage. If you are worried about squirty toys in the tub harboring bacteria, pass on this one. We passed on the **Little Tikes Bathtime Band** ($14.99 ●●) This requires 3 AA batteries. Add water to each of the instruments and they play Calypso music. We do not like the idea of battery-operated toys for the tub. Their new **Bathtime Toy Waterfall** (●●) also did not work well. (800) 321-0183.

■ Tolo Animal Water Slide

(Small World Toys $22 ●●●●) Part shape sorter, part pour and spill, this fun bath toy attaches to tub with big suction cups. Pull a lever and shapes slide down chutes and splash into the water. Comes with three shaped pourers to fill and spill. They say 1 & up—we'd say more like 18 months & up. (800) 421-4153.

■ Tub-A-Duck

(International Playthings $12.99 ●●●●) Attach this big yellow duck to the wall of your tub and use the scoops to pour water and make its head bob, wings tip, wheel spin, and beak squirt. Talk about making things happen! 1 & up. (800) 445-8347.

Basic Furniture

Table and Chairs

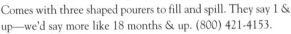

These are basic pieces of gear that will be used for years of snacks, art projects, and tea parties. Best bets are going to have steady legs and a washable surface. After that, it's a matter of budget and style to fit your home. Check the underside of tables and chairs for smooth finishes that won't snag little fingers. Twos also enjoy a rocking chair or armchair scaled to their size. 2 & up.

Some basic safety and design questions you may want to ask:

Can your child get on and off chairs/bench easily?

Is this a set that will work when your child gets a little bigger?

If you're looking at a wooden set, are there exposed screws or nuts (check the underside) that can cut your child?

Is the table surface washable and ready for abuse? (A beautiful painted piece will be destroyed by paint, playdough, crayons, etc.)

Best Travel Toys For Toddlers

We ask almost the impossible from toddlers when we travel by car. Sitting still for long stretches is physically stressful for this age group. Having a plan before you get in the car may help make the transition a little bit easier. The most obvious tip would be to try to plan your car travel to happen at nap time. Of course, that's not always possible. While some kids find the movement of the car soothing and fall asleep easily, others seem to feel the need to co-drive the car—staying alert the entire way!

It's at this age that kids do that straightening-of-the-back trick when being put into their car seats. It will help if you:

- Give your child a heads-up about getting ready to go into the car.

- Leave a special toy in the car that she can look forward to playing with only in the car.

- Bring along favorite tapes to listen to in the car.

- Bring snacks and drinks—especially good if you get caught in traffic!

- Bring along a favorite huggable and/or blanket.

- Bring big washable crayons and pad of paper in a travel sack small enough to fit into a diaper bag or glove compartment.

- Bring an inflatable ball for out-of-the-car breaks and when-you-get-there fun.

- Bring small cardboard books he can handle himself when in his car seat.

- Bring a small set of big plastic blocks or the "favorite toy of the week" for extended stays, one you know she'll be happy to play with while you're unpacking!

Our favorites:

■ S.S. Duckie and Up, Up and Away 🎖2006

(Gund $19.95 ●●●●½) If you're in the back seat with your toddler and you need to go five more exits, these playsets make great choices! These are toys for telling little stories to your tot and hamming it up. There are lots of choices this year! A little ship loaded with two quacking ducks, crinkly starfish, and squeaker fish; or choose a white, red, and blue jet with rattle sounds, male and female pilots, and luggage; or **My Doctor** kit with two medical play figures and stethoscope. Finally, consider the **Lavender Backpack** with **My Little Baby** doll in the carrier and accessories inside the pack. (800) 448-4863.

■ Lamaze Snack Cup Stroller Toy

(RC2/Learning Curve $24.99 ●●●●½) Here's a stroller toy with lots of interesting features. There are a "puppy" snack cup that can detach for washing—ideal for Cheerios on the go—a mini fishbowl with a pull-out fish on tether that won't get away, a squeaky kitten, and a little mouse that pulls forward and wiggles as it vibrates (without music) back to where it started. (800) 704-8697.

■ Magnatudes 🎖2006

(Gund $7.50 ●●●●) Put a few of these soft critters onto the car seat. Attach them by their embedded-magnet hands or feet; your toddler will have fun getting them off and then discovering how their hands and feet attract and repel. Soft, small, and totally ready for imaginative play. These will be enjoyed by preschoolers as well as toddlers who love this small size monkey, bear, or pig that will fit so well in little hands. (800) 448-4863.

■ Puppettos Dog Hand Puppet 🏷2006

(Manhattan Toys $15 **oooo**) A satin-lined doggie hand puppet† to interact with and then pass on as a huggable. Or **Jingle Jungle Giraffe Blankie** ($15 **oooo**), a silky-soft giraffe head with un-stuffed blankie body. A comfy "lovie." (800) 541-1345.

A Present for Me! Game One of the best tips we have for toddlers is to wrap small items for them to unwrap. They don't need to be new—little books, a tape, a box of cereal, or a small toy. Don't show your bag of tricks all at once. Dole them out as you go! Toddlers love surprises, and the unwrapping process is part of the fun and a real time burner.

Best Second-Birthday Gifts For Every Budget

Over $100	**Wooden Blocks** (various makers) or **Playhouse / Large Climber** (Little Tikes / Step 2) or **Toy Kitchen** (Step 2 / Small World Toys) or **Doll Pram** (Haba)
Under $75	**Neurosmith Music Blocks** (Small World Toys) or **Retro Rocket** (Radio Flyer) or **Sandbox** (Little Tikes / Step 2) or **Rocking Wobble Whale** (Mamas & Papas)
Under $50	**Super Spiral Play Tower** (International Playthings) or **Cozy Coupe** (Little Tikes) or **IQ Preschool Push-Along Block Cart** (Small World Toys) or **Tidoo** (Corolle) or **Angel Fish Rocker** (Step 2)

Under $30 **Lego Duplo Thomas Load and Carry Train Set** (Lego Systems) or **Latitude Enfant Grannanimals** (Pint Size Productions) or **Rollipop Advanced Set** (EduShape) or **Giant Cardboard Blocks** (Constructive Playthings)

Under $20 **Quatro** (Lego Systems) or **Toy Dishes** (various makers) or **Puzzibilities Sounds on the Go Puzzle** (Small World Toys) or **Little Mommy Newborn Twin Dolls** (Fisher-Price) or **Bathtime Kitchen Sink** (Sassy)

Under $15 **Rick the Frog & Friends** (Rich Frog) or **Tolo Mobile Phone** (Small World Toys)

Under $10 **Crayola Color Wonder Paper & Markers** (Binney & Smith) or **Mega Bloks Lil' Cement Truck** (Mega Bloks)

Under $5 **Play-Doh** (Hasbro)

A Word about Balloons. Despite the fact that latex balloons are considered unsafe for children under 6, people continue to give them to kids in stores and parks, and at parties. The problem is that kids can suffocate on pieces of latex if they bite and/or inhale a balloon that they break or try to blow up. Yes, they are an old tradition—but a dangerous one. Why take the risk? Stick to Mylar!

3 • Preschool
Three to Four Years

What to Expect Developmentally

Learning Through Pretend. Preschoolers are amazing learning machines! Watch and listen to them at play and you can hear the wheels of their busy minds working full tilt. From sunup to sundown, preschoolers love playing pretend games. Playing all sorts of roles gives kids a chance to become big and powerful people. Providing props for such play gives kids the learning tools to develop language, imagination, and a better understanding of themselves and others.

Social Play. Your once-happy-to-be-only-with-you toddler has blossomed into a much more social being. He enjoys playing with other kids. Sharing is still an issue, but there's a budding understanding of give and take.

Solo Play. Unlike the toddler who moved from one thing to another, preschoolers become able to really focus their attention on building a bridge of blocks, working on a puzzle, or painting pictures.

Toys and Development. Although preschoolers love to play at counting and singing, or even at trying to write the alphabet, informal play is still the best path to learning. Building a tower with blocks, they discover some very basic math concepts. Digging in the sand or floating leaves in puddles, they make early science discoveries.

Big Muscles. Threes and fours also need time and space to run and climb and use their big muscles to develop coordination and a sense of themselves as able doers.

Your Role in Play. A child who has shelves full of stuffed animals or every piece of the hottest licensed character may seem to have tons of toys, but the truth is, no matter how many trucks or dolls a kid has, such collections offer just one kind of play. Take an inventory of your child's toy clutter to see what's really being played with and what needs to be packed away or donated.

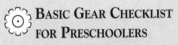

BASIC GEAR CHECKLIST FOR PRESCHOOLERS

✓Set of blocks and props (small vehicles, animals, people)

✓Trike	✓Dolls and/or soft animals
✓Dress-up clothes	✓Housekeeping toys
✓Transportation toys	✓Matching games
✓Picture books	✓Sand and water toys

✓Art materials—crayons, paints, clay
✓Simple puzzles (eight pieces and up)
✓Tape player and music and story tapes

🚫 Toys to Avoid

These toys pose a safety hazard:
✓Electric toys or those that heat up with lightbulbs, which can burn
✓Toys with projectile parts that can injure eyes
✓Toys without volume control, which can damage ears
✓Two-wheelers with training wheels
✓Latex balloons

These toys are developmentally inappropriate:
✓Complex building sets that adults must build while children watch
✓Teaching machines that reduce learning to a series of right or wrong answers
✓Coloring books that limit creativity

Pretend Play

This is the age when pretend play blossoms. Some kids pretend with blocks, trains, and miniatures they move around as they act out little dramas. Others prefer dressing up and playing roles with their whole being. Either way, such games are more than fun. They help children learn to stretch their imaginations, try on powerful new roles, cope with feelings and fears, and develop language and social skills.

Dress-Up Play and Let's-Pretend Props

Old pocketbooks, briefcases, jewelry, hats, or a homemade badge are often all that's needed to transform young players. Below are a few specialty items you may want to buy:

■ Get Real Gear

(Aeromax Toys $49.95 & up ⚫⚫⚫⚫⚫) We were most taken with this company's themed jumpsuits: an orange **Jr. Astronaut** uniform with tons of official looking patches; the **Jr. Air Force Pilot;** and the **Jr. Championship Racer.** Come in sizes for kids 3–12. PLATINUM AWARD '05. They have new gender-specific doctor outfits (not our speed). (877) 776-2291.

■ Let's Pretend Careers 2006

(Small Miracles $29.99 & up ⚫⚫⚫⚫⚫) Handsome enough to wear as real clothes, the newest item in the career line is a **Chef** (with coat, hat, and tools); in the fantasy line, a **Pirate** (outfit comes with a felt hat). Past winners include: **Doctor, Pilot, Equestrian, Firefighter, Construction Worker,** and **Police.** PLATINUM AWARDS '02 & '04. 3–8. (888) 281-1798.

■ Little Pretenders 2006

(Chenille Kraft $24.99 each ⚫⚫⚫⚫) A new line of costumes made of wipe-able vinyl provides the most affordable choice. Each theme comes with accessories (stethoscopes, extinguishers, etc.) and appropriate headgear. Other costumes include **Veterinarian, Hair**

Dresser (the pretend blow dryer makes a great sound), and **Doctor**. 3 & up. (800) 621-1261.

Doctor's Gear

Comparison Shopper
Doctor's & Vet's Kits

Doctors no longer make house calls, and even the traditional black bag from Fisher-Price is gone. Most of the medical kits do not come with cases large enough for easy repacking. The roomiest is **Pretend & Play Doctor Set** (Learning Resources $24.95 ○○○○○). Comes in a large plastic case with 19 pieces including a stethoscope with heartbeat and cough, a beeper, a cellphone, a blood pressure cuff, and other chunky tools. PLATINUM AWARD '04. (888) 800-7893. **Fisher-Price's Medical Kit** (Fisher-Price $10 ○○○○) comes in a smaller plastic case with almost the same basic gear as the original "black bag." (800) 432-5437. For playing Veterinarian, **Small Miracles' Let's Pretend** (Small Miracles $29.99 ○○○○½) has a child-sized jacket, puppy, and stethoscope and other medical tools. (888) 281-1798.

■ Magical Unicorn 2006

(Big Boing Toys $24.99 ○○○○½) White plush with a silver horn and lavender mane fit on child's head without covering eyes. Touch the unicorn and it makes a magical sound—happily, volume control is built in. Comes with furry hooves with their own cloppity magical sound as child runs. Newest addition to last year's award-winning **Roaring Dinosaur, Clippity Clop Horse,** and **Get-up Fairy.** 3–6. (415) 331-7557.

■ Super Star Sing-Along Vanity 2006

(Little Tikes $47 ○○) "Mirror, mirror on the vanity, will I be part of the future American Idol insanity?" We're not big on vanities that come loaded with a karaoke mirror, a wireless microphone (the hairbrush) . . . and an applause button (honest!). Not available for testing. 3 & up. (800) 321-0183.

Housekeeping Tools

Both girls and boys use props for cleaning, cooking, and childcare. Few toys will get more use by both boys and girls than a mini-broom or -mop. This is an inexpensive favorite that you'll find in most toy supermarkets. Kitchen toys are used for playing house and running restaurants. As children's experiences broaden, so does the scope of their games of make-believe. For more kitchens and toy dishes, see Toddlers chapter.

COMPARISON SHOPPER
Dishes 2006

There are three high quality dish sets: **Kitch 'n Carry Sets** (Alex $14.99 & up oooo)—testers loved the brightly colored kitchenware in new see-through zip-up novelty totes. They are gender specific, however, with lots of pink. (800) 666-2539. For gender-free sets, we recommend either: **Earlyplay Sets** (Brio $14.99 & up oooo)—dishes and cutlery in primary colors (888) 274-6869; or **Pretend & Play Dishes** (Learning Resources $12.95 oooo)—service for four includes sturdy plastic cups and saucers, octagonal plates, and cutlery in primary colors. 3 & up. (888) 800-7893.

■ **My First Stove** 2006

(Alex $19.99 oooo) Big kitchens are in the toddler chapter, but this mini kitchen (12" x 11" x 11") fits on a table top; ideal for tight spaces. A painted wooden stovetop with colorful knobs and drawer that opens to store utensils. Companion to **My First Sink.** Don't be fooled by the picture on the box—no pots or dishes in the package! 3 & up. (800) 666-2539.

TOYS

■ Pretend & Play Teaching Telephone BLUE CHIP

(Learning Resources $29.95 ●●●●●) You can program in any phone number and leave a message. When your child calls that number they hear your message. A great way to teach important phone numbers and the concept of 911. Even the concept of taking messages is built into the pretend. 4 & up. PLATINUM AWARD '00. (888) 800-7893.

Dolls and Huggables

Preschoolers love soft animals and dolls as huggable companions for bedtime and playtime. At this age, playing with dolls gives both boys and girls a chance to try out new roles and language.

■ Jules *2006* PLATINUM AWARD

(Corolle $55 ●●●●●) Finding a boy doll is not easy, yet it's a great gift, especially when there's a new baby in the family. Meet Jules, a 17" bald baby doll in blue romper with bottle, bib, and pacifier. Like last year's winner, **Lila,** he cries, laughs, and babbles. Both are a perfect armful for pretend play. 3 & up. PLATINUM AWARD '05. (800) 668-4846.

■ Lili *2006* PLATINUM AWARD

(Corolle $60 ●●●●●) Older preschoolers will love the articulated and fashionable 17" **Lili** dolls. Choose the blond **Rose,** auburn **Melodie,** dark brunette **Belle,** and strawberry blond **Flore.** Each is dressed in a *très jolie* outfit that is totally "now." These will appeal to slightly older girls as well. Think younger American Girl dolls. 4 & up. Also new, **Chouquettes** ($39.95 ●●●●½)— adorable 14" girl dolls come with blond or brunette hair and hairbrush for age-typical play. (800) 668-4846.

■ Madeline BLUE CHIP

(RC2/Learning Curve $19 ●●●●●) Sadly, this line has been cut back dramatically. If you have a Madeline fan, bring home the classic **16" Dressable Madeline** ($19.99 ●●●●) who seems to step right out of the storybook (complete with appendix scar). (800) 704-8697.

■ Topsy Turvy Dolls *2006*

(North American Bear Co. $25 each **oooo**) These very old-fashioned fabric dolls retain their charm. **Cinderella** in rags flips into her ball gown. Also special: **Little Red Riding Hood.** New for *2006*, **Fancy Prancy Princess Topsy Turvy Dusk to Dawn** reverses from purple to a fuchsia gown. Magical! (800) 682-3427.

Multicultural Dolls

Just a few years ago, there were few options that reflected our diversity. Now, there are so many more great choices.

■ Baby Annabell *2006*

(Zapf Creation $39.99 & up **oooo**) For the first time, Annabell cries real tears. After her bottle, she randomly yawns and falls asleep, or starts to cry. Our testers liked the novelty and parents liked the "off" switch option. Crying, babbling **Love Me Chou Chou** ($49.99 **oo**) disappointed our testers, who thought she was "too heavy... it had a seam on her head—looked like she had a brain surgery." Take heart, there is still a **My First Annabell** ($19.95 **ooo**) a 14" baby doll, Caucasian or African American, who does whatever your child imagines. This doll is mislabeled 1 & up, however; the pacifier is too small to be safe for toddlers. (877) 629-9273.

■ Doucette *2006*

(Corolle $24.95 each **ooo**) A multiethnic collection of soft-bodied dolls. We love their polka-dotted outfits and charming faces with painted-on features. These would have been PLATINUM AWARD winners, except for the age label. While these are a perfect choice for 3s & up, small hair accessories and silky hair make them inappropriate for toddlers (the collection is marked 18 mos. & up). Other multicultural collections: **Bebe Do** ($50 **oooo**) come in two skin tones, and **Les Minis Calins** BLUE CHIP ($16 each) come in Asian and African American versions. (800) 668-4846.

■ Groovy Girls and Groovy Boys *2006* BLUE CHIP

(Manhattan Toy $14.95 & up ooooo) All are 13" and soft, with stitched features, yarn hair, and groovy clothes. New for *2006*, a new boy doll, **Kieran,** with strawberry blond curly hair and silver shades; three bathing beauties: African-American **Kassi,** red-headed **Kenna,** and **Kylee** in a sarong. Also new, a royal pair with golden crowns, **Princess Lucinda** & **Prince Lance.** 3 & up. Our Groovy Girl fans also recommend these accessories: **Bombastic Bunk Beds** ($24.99 ooooo) or Mod Place ($50 oooo). Still the superlative gift, consider **Supersize Groovy Girl** ($50 ooooo), a 40" child-sized fabric doll that's like a pretend play pal. (800) 541-1345.

■ Language Littles

(Language Littles $35 oooo) Each of these 16" fabric dolls with yarn hair speaks in English and another language (each says 25 words and phrases). Will they make your child bilingual? Of course not, but they are a place to start. Choose Italian, Greek, French, Chinese, Hebrew, Russian, German, Spanish, or Japanese. 3 & up. (212) 535-8122.

COMPARISON SHOPPER
Drink-and-Wet Dolls

Our testers gave thumbs up to **Bébé Do Emma** or **Paul Fait Pipi** (Corolle $40 each oooo½), anatomically correct girl or boy 14" doll with all-vinyl tubbable body. Comes with potty, bottle, and diaper for pretend play. (800) 668-4846. In the novelty doll category, **Potty Elmo** (Fisher-Price $19 ooooo) is amazing. Give Elmo his sippy cup and you'll hear him drink; if you don't get him to the potty, he says, "Oops, Elmo didn't get to the potty. Accidents happen," and if he makes it, "Elmo can do it and so can you!" One of the best and most polite interactive dolls we've ever tested. PLATINUM AWARD '05. (800) 432-5437. We pass on Zapf Creations' **Baby Born** ($39.99 oo), who got low marks from our testers because they had difficulty getting the pretend poop out (no joke). (877) 629-9273.

Bears of the Year 2006 PLATINUM AWARD

As always, we find selecting one winner totally unbearable! Here are our top picks: a big bear, two medium-sized bears, and a wee little baby bear: **Great Big Creamy Bear** (Mary Meyer $130/36" ⦿⦿⦿⦿⦿) Remember the oversized bear you always dreamed of winning at the fair? This one is much better, because he's totally huggable, soft and delicious! 36" big, this memorable bear will be great to talk to and lean on. Also comes **Kinda Big** ($30/20" ⦿⦿⦿⦿⦿). (800) 451-4387. **Smushy Bear** (North American Bear $40 ⦿⦿⦿⦿⦿) is a floppy tan 25" bear of huggability with a smushy body, floppy head, and velvety nose. (800) 682-3427. **Cuddly Pals Big Pokey** (Gund $20 ⦿⦿⦿⦿⦿) A pudgy 16" soft bear with stitched features and honey-colored fur, all dressed up with an organdy bow. (800) 448-4863.

Best of Show: Dogs of the Year 2006

Doogie Dog Flip Flops (Mary Meyer $15 ⦿⦿⦿⦿) Extremely soft and huggable, this 12" pooch has interesting markings, soft body, velvety nose, and beanbag feet. A smaller 9" version, **Sweet Horace Hound,** is covered in a silky plush with darker brown markings on one eye, tail, and paws. Also special, the dogs from the **Yakety Squeeze Me Critters** collection, see below. (800) 451-4387. Or, in the floppy, understuffed, and very shaggy dog class, our vote goes to **Fluffies** (Manhattan Toy $20 & $40 ⦿⦿⦿⦿) With corduroy noses and weighted paws, these come in two sizes and either pink or white. (800) 541-1345.

Miscellaneous Stuffed Critters

■ **Yakety Squeeze Me Critters** 2006

(Mary Meyer $10 each ⦿⦿⦿⦿½) These are perfect stocking stuffers—soft animals that each make a unique sound when squeezed. Just the right size to fill a child's fist and take along, our favorites are **Yakety Dale Duck, Floyd Frog, Blake Black**

Bear, Paige Poodle, and **Doug the Pug.** (800) 451-4387.

Interactive Dolls 2006

This year's big interactive dolls from Fisher-Price say more than a few words! **Tumble Time Tigger** ($34.99 ●●●●) Sound-activated, just clap your hands to see Tigger tumble, do cartwheels, and even handstands! But be forewarned, his bag of tricks takes 6 AA batteries!

Shout Elmo ($29.99 ●●●●) is designed to get kids up and dancing along. He moves his hands around and moves as he asks kids to sing louder and (thankfully) softer. He takes four AA batteries. Also interesting, **Check-up Time Elmo** ($19.99 ●●●●½), a great prop for getting kids ready for a visit to the doctor. Comes with stethoscope, thermometer, sounds, a song, and a book. Also, techno-savvy tots can have a programmable **Knows Your Name Elmo** or **Winnie the Pooh** ($39.99 each). Not ready for testing, but they promise to know your child's name, favorite food, birthday, and friend's names. (Not sure why, but this seemed a little creepy to one of us.) These are all marked 18 mos. & up, but a better choice for 3 & up. (800) 432-5437.

Notable Doll Accessories

Budget and taste will go into making the choices here. Just like real equipment, there are doll carriers for the silver-spoon set and more practical models for your average doll. Still top rated: American Girl's yellow and blue **Collapsible Stroller** ($34 ●●●●), designed for their 15" Bitty Baby Dolls. Also special, **Bitty Twins Double Stroller** ($48 ●●●●). (800) 845-0005. Community Playthings' BLUE CHIP **Wooden Doll Cradle** ($95 ●●●●●) is made of solid maple and built to last. The large 29" model is big enough so kids can climb in and play baby or put a family of dolls to sleep. 2 & up. #C140. (800) 777-4244.

Puppets and Puppet Stages

Through the mouths of puppets, kids say things that they might not otherwise speak about; so puppets provide a way of venting feelings and developing imagination and language skills. Young puppeteers replay stories, create original tales, and develop skills that link to reading and writing. See Early School Years chapter for more puppets and stages.

■ Animal Puppets

(Gund $16 each **oooo**) Good news! Gund has reintroduced their beautifully made hand puppets. Choose from some of their classic bears such as **Manni,** or other animals, such as **Luke the Lion** or **Bamboo Panda.** (800) 448-4863.

■ Happy Hands Puppets

(Mary Meyer $15 each **oooo**) Just right for a lively telling of "The Three Pigs," bring home these 13" full-body hand puppets. The pig is very cheerful and the wolf is not too scary! Made with a nubby finish, these are pleasing to use and will be enjoyed by the next age group as well. The **Happy Lion** and new **Happy Tiger** and **Dino** are also charming. (800) 451-4387.

■ Puppet Theater

(Alex $79.99 **oooo**½) This has a clock for show time and eye-appealing graphics! This stable floor model is 48" high, with painted trim on one side and a chalk surface for messages. Their tabletop model looks like a fairytale castle and comes with two felt puppets. ($50 **oooo**½). 3 & up. (800) 666-2539. For more stages and puppets, see Early School Years chapter.

FREEBIE: Do it yourself. A large appliance box can be turned into an excellent puppet stage, and so can a cloth-covered card table that kids can hide behind. Another great option is a spring curtain rod and length of fabric that can be used in any doorway.

Pretend Settings:
Doll Houses, Castles, & Garages

Some of the mini-settings listed in the Toddlers chapter will be used in more elaborate ways now. Here are descriptions of recommended settings that are more complex:

Dollhouses

Dollhouses should be kept simple for little hands. Plastic or wood, really comes down to personal preference. Here are our top picks:

Plastic Dollhouses

■ Calico Critters Townhome
2006 PLATINUM AWARD

(International Playthings $84.99 ●●●●●)
Our testers have loved the characters and furnishings from this line for years. Now the new Townhome, in molded plastic, has a woodland look with red tile roof and lights that plug in and turn on with a switch. The animal critter families ($19.99 a set) are like storybook characters. The house opens for play and closes for storing all those little play pieces that kids adore. 4 & up. (800) 445-8347.

■ Twin Time Dollhouse *2006*

(Fisher-Price $69.95●●●½) This big eight-room house has a patio, garage, a mom and dad and twins, plus 10 pieces of furniture and accessories. It opens to a spacious setting that folds up after playtime is done. The color scheme screams plastic, but a good value for the price. 3 & up. (800) 432-5437.

Wooden Dollhouses

There are several great collections. You can't go wrong with any of them.

■ Plan Toys Terrace Dollhouse

(Brio $100 ●●●●●) Complete with a terrace, this is a lovely wooden dollhouse. (888) 274-6869.

■ Ryan's Room Dollhouses

(Small World Toys $100 ●●●●●): **Home Is Where the Heart Is Dollhouse** is a three-stories-high house. PLATINUM AWARD '03. Or consider the smaller **Home Again, Home Again A-Frame** ($124), which can be enlarged with an add-on basement and stairs ($70). Also fun, a two-story **Backyard Clubhouse** with "cable car" that connects dollhouse to clubhouse. Multicultural families and interesting furniture collections available; and **Multimedia Mania** ($15 ●●●●) with a flatscreen TV, of course. (800) 421-4153.

■ My Dollhouse

(Alex $169 ●●●●●) Done in a bright-colored, pat-

terned palette, this house has three floors with 22 pieces of furniture. (800) 666-2539.

■ Smart Living Holiday Home 2006

(HaPe $79.95) A four-level build-your-own tower-shaped house with spiral staircases has an ultra modern look. Includes furniture and people; scaled for tight spaces. Final version not ready for testing. (800) 661-4142.

Dollhouse Accessories
■ Groovy Girls Minis 2006

(Manhattan Toy $4.99 & up ○○○○½) Best props for dollhouse play this season are long-term multi-ethnic favorites, Groovy Girls, now launched as "minis" in molded plastic with various hair-

dos, groovy clothes, pets, and funky home furnishings. These little 4" dolls can stand on their own two feet and are pose-able for active pretend. (800) 541-1345.

Other Pretend Settings
■ Plan Toys Stable Set

(Brio $30 ○○○○) Charming small stable with a red roof, two wooden horses (with movable heads), hay box, broom, and bucket. (888) 274-6869.

■ Ryan's Room Adventures Ahoy

(Small World Toys $99.99 ○○○○○) Yahoo! Get ready for imagination to set sail with Captain Hook and two of his mates aboard this magnif-icent wooden ship with working sails, rig-ging, hatches, anchor, crow's nest, and even a plank to walk! A stunning gift for years of dramatic play. 34" W x 24" H. Add-on sets with more figures available. 4–8. PLATINUM AWARD '05. Also great fun from the same line, **Lil' Fire Stoppers Main Station** ($75 ○○○○), a two-story firehouse has pole for fire-fighters to use along with furniture. 4 & up. (800) 421-4153.

Medieval Times
Maybe it's the popularity of the *Lord of the Rings* trilogy, but castles have made a comeback in toyland. Here are

two top picks:

■ Ryan's Room Majestic Castle & Mighty Knights

(Small World Toys $100 ●●●●●) A truly majestic wooden castle, 20" x 20", with working drawbridge, movable staircases, four towers, and walls that can be arranged in different configurations. Comes with four knights and a horse. Additional figures such as king, queen, jester, wizard, jousting knights, and dragon are available. Easy to assemble, this play setting might become an heirloom. 4 & up. PLATINUM AWARD '04. (800) 421-4153.

■ Folding Castle Play Set

(Melissa & Doug $70 ●●●●) An all-wood castle that measures 16" x 16" x 12" when closed, 31" x 16" x 12" when open. Comes with three human figures and a horse. (800) 284-3948.

■ Deluxe Tumble Treehouse & Skycoaster

(Maxim Enterprises $99 ●●●●●) One of our favorite pretend settings! With pulleys and stairways, this furnished treehouse has lots of pretend power and action. A Sky Coaster can be added for vehicles ($30). A gender-free setting that will mix well with block structures. An outstanding value! 4–8. Platinum Award '05. (888) 266-2946.

Trucks and Other Vehicles

Preschoolers are fascinated with all forms of transportation. The real things are out of reach and on the move, but toy trucks, cars, boats, jets, and trains are ideal for make-believe departures, both indoors and out. Choose vehicles with working parts to use with blocks, in the sandbox, or at the beach. BLUE CHIP choices such as Funrise's **Tonka Trucks** or Little Tikes' **Construction Trucks** are perfect gifts for now. So are **Matchbox** or **Hot Wheels** cars, which are now appropriate and often the first "collectible."

■ Automoblox 2006 PLATINUM AWARD

(Automoblox $32 each ooooo) A new collection of sleekly designed cars destined to be a bestseller in museum shops for their handsome design,, and a hit with kids for their playability. Each wooden car comes apart (making it part vehicle, part puzzle). The plastic connectors have shape receptors. For parents looking for "cool design" for the playroom, look no further. 4 & up. (973) 364-8090.

■ Bendos My First RC Buggies 2006 PLATINUM AWARD

(Kid Galaxy $19.95 each ooooo) Our testers loved this new line of remotes designed with preschoolers in mind. Choose a **Bumble Bee** or a spotted **Ladybug** with simple one-button control. These have plenty of action; even when the remote is not pressed, they spin. Still top rated, **Old Tyme R/C Bumper Cars** ($49.99 oooo½). (800) 816-1135.

■ Ramp Racer

(Maxim Enterprises $24.99 oooo½) A five-storey-high wooden raceway with double tracks so that you can race two cars at once. It will combine well with blocks. (888) 266-2946.

■ Rugged Riggz 2006

(Little Tikes $9.99 & 14.99 oooo) We're big fans of this updated collection of basic trucks. New for 2006 are a **Helicopter Hauler,** a **Sports Car Hauler** with two cars, and a **Garbage Truck.** Still top rated, **Motorcycle Hauler,** and the classics (**cement, dump,** and **hauler**). All are just right for the 3 & up crowd. (800) 321-0183.

First Trains and Track Toys

What They Learn

A nonelectric train is a classic toy that will keep growing in complexity as you add working bridges, roundhouses, and other extras. Note: Preschoolers are not ready for electric trains, except to watch!

Trains are really open-ended puzzles with no right or wrong answers. Making the track work often becomes more important to many kids than actually playing with the trains.

Many stores display their trains on tabletops with the track glued down, but much of the open-ended play value is lost when you do that at home. Making ever-changing settings is half the fun. Skip the table and invest in more tracks and bridges.

Editors' Note: First, we know from many testing families that toddlers are playing with wooden trains. Be forewarned that the trains have small parts and that many of the accessories are also very small and pose a choking hazard. Second, as a sign of the times, some of our four-year-old testers were overheard discussing that they don't want to play with the trains that they have to "push" (preferring the battery operated trains). Sad.

Wooden Train Sets

■ Sky Train Set

(Brio $40 ooooo) 24-piece set comes with two trains that run on elevated track with gondola-like wagons suspended beneath. PLATINUM AWARD '04. Also fun, a **Remote Control Sky Train** ($15 oooo). Still stop rated, **Zoo Set** ($50 oooo), a 35-piece starter set. 3 & up. (888) 274-6869.

■ Thomas & Friends Water Tower Figure 8 Set *2006*

(RC2/Learning Curve $39.99 oooo½) This 25-piece set is a great buy and gives beginners a great place to start. Includes Thomas, a cargo car, water tower, and stone bridge for a figure 8. For a larger set, consider **Down by the Docks** ($149.99/45 pieces ooooo) with **Sodor Bay Bridge, Lighthouse,** and **Crane.** PLATINUM AWARD '03. New for *2006*, a **Deluxe Aquarium** themed set ($299 oooo½). Call in the grandparents! (800) 704-8697.

Plastic Train and Track Sets

■ Thomas & Friends Interactive Railway

(RC2/Learing Curve $29.99 & up oooo½) Purists may not like this talking plastic railway system—we had some doubts ourselves. The good news is the mechanisms work well and all are compatible with wooden trains and tracks. Each set has an interactive mechanical prop that directs kids to find a specific color or to count out actions to load trains. True, the train directs some of the play; it does work well, however, and allows for open-ended play, as well. Our testers liked the **Lift'n'Load Crane Set** ($49.99 ●●●●) as well as the smaller **Barrel Loader** set ($29.99 ●●●●). 3 & up. (800) 704-8697.

■ GeoTrax Workin' Town Railway *2006*

(Fisher-Price $39.99 ●●●●) This 30-piece set comes with a bridge, station, and windmill. Our testers did notice that it is possible for the train to get caught in a loop. Fitting the tracks together is more challenging than wooden tracks, since these only fit right side up. That said, they liked the many features of this set and the flexibility of extending the system with other settings, such as the **GeoTrax Coastal Winds Airport** ($24.99 ●●●●½) with a plane that zooms around the control tower. Marked 2½—we'd say it's a true preschool set. (800) 432-5437.

■ Shake 'N Go Speedway *2006* PLATINUM AWARD

(Fisher-Price $39.99 ●●●●●) This is a closed system with looping tracks, but the upside is kids can use the cars off the track, too. Kids loves the two innovative cars in this racing set that have to be shaken to make them go. Does this mean no batteries? Sorry, Charlie! Still, this is going to make a memorable gift and a better choice than electric trains for this age. 4 & up. (800) 432-5437.

Best New Wooden Train Props

New accessories can inspire fresh layouts and keep interest chugging along.

■ Thomas & Friends Tidmouth Timber Yard *2006*

(RC2/Learning Curve $ 49.99 ●●●●) For older train players this is a must-have prop! The wood splits (courtesy of a plastic saw and magnets). The crane is then used to pick up the timber and load the trains that come by. Very, very neat but will be difficult for 3s to use independently— a better choice for 4s and up. Also great fun (and easier to operate), **Thomas & Friends**

Sodor Cement Works ($39.99 ●●●●)—"cement" drops down from the mixer onto the waiting train below. Fans of castles and trains will also enjoy the new **Rolf's Castle Bridge** ($44.99 ●●●●) with a castle wall that comes down and a moat below (of course!). (800) 704-8697.

■ Double Suspension Bridge

(Brio $25 ●●●●½) This is the longest bridge in the line—three and a half feet long! Can also be used side by side for two-way traffic. Also new, the **Speaking Station** ($30 ●●●●½) A smart station master speaks in English, German, or French, depending on the city shown above the ticket master's window. Our tester liked the new **Stop & Go Station** ($16.50 ●●●●); with a simple push button the train is locked into the station and then released to go. For the techno-minded engineer, there's a new sleek **Remote Control Express Train,** but it was not ready for testing. Still one of our favorites for drama on the tracks, the **Collapsing Bridge** ($20 ●●●●●) With a press of a button, the bridge really does collapse. Great for suspenseful train rides. PLATINUM AWARD '05. (888) 274-6869.

Construction Toys

If there's one toy no child should be without, blocks are it! Few toys are more basic. Stacking a tower, balancing a bridge, setting up a zoo—all call for imagination, dexterity, decision making, and problem solving. Built into the play are early math and language concepts that give concrete meaning to abstract words such as *higher, lower, same,* and *different.* Best of all, blocks are wonderfully versatile—they build a space city today, a farm tomorrow.

Kids will enjoy both wood and plastic types of blocks, which encourage different kinds of valuable play experiences. Choosing blocks depends largely on your budget and space. Although many of these sets are pricey, they are a solid investment that will be used for years to come.

Wooden Blocks

Unit blocks come in many shapes and lengths and should be carefully proportioned to each other. Many catalogs offer unit blocks in sets of different sizes. Parents are sometimes disappointed when kids don't use the small starter sets they buy. Keep in mind that kids really can't do much with a set of 20 blocks and no props. This is one of those items where the more they have, the more they can do.

COMPARISON SHOPPER
Unit Blocks

No two companies have the same number of blocks or shapes in any set, so there are small differences among all the sets listed. The cost of shipping will vary depending upon where you live and the weight and price of the item. Our best suggestion is that you call around and compare. Here's a sampling of what a good basic set will run:

Back to Basics set of 82 blocks in 21 shapes. #2728. $172.99 (800) 356-5360.

Constructive Playthings set of 82 pieces in 12 shapes. #KRP-U312L. $79.99 (800) 832-0572.

Small World Toys' IQ Preschool (120 pieces $120); New for **2006**, **IQ Preschool Block Party** ($30) a 60-piece set of small-scaled colorful wooden blocks. (800) 421-4153.

Props for Blocks

Providing a variety of props such as small-scale vehicles, animals, and people enhances building and imaginative play. Here are some props designed to inspire young builders. Our favorites:

■ **Bendos** **2006** BLUE CHIP

(Kid Galaxy $5 & up **ooooo**) Perfect for pretend, two new playsets: **King's Court** ($15) with throne, king, queen, jester, crowns, and coat of armor; and **Jousting Set** ($15) with two knights with horses, and plenty of armor.

These will appeal to older preschoolers and early school-age kids as well. These bendable action figures are also available as multiethnic athletes, community workers, and animals. They stand up with blocks, fit into vehicles, and satisfy young collectors. 3 & up. (800) 816-1135.

■ Flocked Animal Sets 2006

(Melissa & Doug $14.95 & up **oooo**) Set of nine **Barnyard Friends** (or nine **Prehistoric Pals,** or **Pasture Pals,** 12 different horses), are perfect for block play. Sets come in wooden display storage boxes that make order out of preschool chaos. 3 & up. (800) 284-3948.

■ Jumbo Farm Animals 2006

(Learning Resources $22.95 **oooo**½) Seven farm animals beautifully molded and colored and ready for years of pretend play action. They are in size proportion to each other and will fit into block settings. Set includes a horse, cow, pig, goat, sheep, goose, and rooster. 3 & up. (800) 222-3909.

■ Magna Morphs 2006

(Wild Republic $11.99 **oooo**½) These dinosaurs have interchangeable heads, feet, and tails that hold together with magnets buried inside the bodies and parts. A playful way to learn the names of the most familiar dinosaurs while developing part/whole relationships, dexterity, and dramatic play. 4 & up. (800) 800-9678.

■ Rescue Heroes

(Fisher-Price $7.99 each **ooo**) As a concept we like this multicultural collection of firefighter, construction worker, and police officer. Stay clear of the ones that have projectile parts, which pose a safety hazard to preschoolers. 3 & up. (800) 432-5437.

■ Windows and Door Blocks BLUE CHIP

(Constructive Playthings $16.95 **ooooo**) Scaled to standard unit blocks: a five-piece set of four windows and one door. #PCR-62L. (800) 832-0572.

■ Woody Click 2006

(HaPe $4.99 & up **oooo**½) Part construction, part pretend, the Woody Click line has many wooden vehicles, sold individually or as part of sets. They are ideally scaled for unit blocks, but will require adult assistance to assemble. Choose from colorful construction vehicles, fire trucks, and a helicopter with small flexible play figures. There are several pricey but handome mini-settings ($99 each) such as a hospital, fire station, and police headquarters. (800) 661-4142.

> **SMART PARENT TRICK: Playful Cleanup.** Preschoolers often need help cleaning up. You can get some learning in by saying, "I'll find the trucks, you pick up all the cars," or "Let's find all the smallest blocks first." Set up open shelves for blocks and baskets for props to avoid having a constant jumbled mess!

Plastic Blocks

Plastic building sets call for a different kind of dexterity. Here's what you should look for:

> Beginners are better off with larger pieces that make bigger and quicker constructions.

> Encourage beginning builders to experiment rather than copy or watch you build.

■ Mega Bloks BLUE CHIP

(Mega Bloks $10 & up oooo) These oversized plastic pegged blocks are easy for preschoolers to take apart, fit together, and assemble into B-I-G constructions with a minimum of pieces. Select a set with wheels and angled pieces for more flexibility. (800) 465-6342.

■ Kid K'nex Crimpy Critters *2006*

(K'nex $9.99 oooo½) These up-sized K'nex look related to your old Tinkertoys—our testers especially like the "crimpy pieces." Testers liked the larger **Wild Ones** kit ($14.95 oooo). We'd pass on the new **Story Book Pals** ($7.99 oo) with cheesy (very merchandisy) books (e.g., featuring Chicken Little made out of K'nex). Fitting the pieces together can be challenging and requires finger strength as well as visual discrimination. Marked 3 & up, but we'd say more like 4 & up. (800) 543-5639.

■ Legoville Fire Station 2006 PLATINUM AWARD

(Lego Systems $29.99 ●●●●●) A 58-piece fire station that can be built as a tower or horizontally. Comes with firefighters and great truck with ladder. Also a hit with testers, the **Big Farm Set** ($39.99 ●●●●½) with barn, tractor, farmers, and animals. Past winners include **Bob the Builder** and **Dora the Explorer** sets. We also highly recommend a big bucket ($19.95) for open-ended creations. 3 & up. (800) 233-8756.

■ Magneatos 2006 PLATINUM AWARD

(Guidecraft $30 & up ●●●●●) These primary colored plastic rods and balls are oversized, safe and easy to manipulate for preschoolers. Exactly right for small hands and big results! Comes in 36 pieces ($30), 72 ($50) or 144 pieces ($100). 2 & up. (800) 524-3555

Early Games

Preschoolers are not ready for complex games with lots of rules or those that require strategy, math, or reading skills. Best bets are games of chance such as lotto and picture dominoes, and classics such as Candy Land, where players depend on luck of the draw rather than skill. Taking turns is often hard, and so is the concept of winning or losing. We've selected games that can be played cooperatively and those that are quick and short so there can be lots of winners.

Active Games

■ Cranium Hullabaloo

(Cranium $24.95 ●●●●●) Players have to listen carefully to the electronic ringmaster that directs play among the 16 playmats. The player on the "lucky" mat when the ringmaster says, "Freeze!" is the winner. Will also be enjoyed by the next age group. PLATINUM AWARD '04. 4 & up (877) 272-6486.

■ Egg and Spoon Race 2006

(International Playthings $12 ●●●●½) Four big plastic spoons are loaded with bright eggs to balance as kids race for the fin ish line. But watch out—if you drop the egg, it cracks and a yoke falls out! A classic game with fabric yokes that are less messy, and no risk of salmonella! They say 3 & up, we'd say more like old 4s and 5–6s. Great for a party! (800) 445-8347.

■ Pin the Tail on the Donkey

(Eeboo $14 ●●●●) This classic game is printed on a sturdy reusable poster and comes with a bandanna blindfold and two sets of 16 self-adhesive tails—no tacks needed! A good party prop for several years of play. 4–8 (212) 222-0823.

Color, Counting, & Other Concepts

■ Dora the Explorer Candy Land ⬥2006

(Milton Bradley $9.99 ●●●●½) Fans of Dora will enjoy this variation of the classic color matching game that incorporates Dora and her friends. Still top rated, **Duck Duck Goose** ($19.99 ●●●●●) a fun, easy-to-learn color concept game. PLATINUM AWARD '05. (888) 836-7025.

■ Frog Hoppers ⬥2006

(International Playthings $5.95 ●●●●) We've seen a number of tiddlywink-style games this season (see Early School Years, p. 132.) This one is easy enough for beginners to play. Four sets of colored frogs are ready to hop back into the container as players spar off. No heavy rules to learn. A good game for learning about turn taking; requires some eye-hand coordination. They say 3 & up—we'd say more like 4–6. (800) 445-8347.

■ Sleepy Princess and the Pea ⬥2006

(Haba $24 ●●●●½) Kids who know the story of the Princess and the Pea will enjoy taking turns and adding a cushion, pillow, and comforter to the stack before it topples over! Quick to learn and lots of chances to win and lose, this calls for some dexterity. (800) 468-6873.

■ Zimbbos! ⬥2006

(Blue Orange Games $19.95 ●●●●½) Roll the die and stack the

number of elephants shown. Can you do it without having the pyramid fall? Oh, yes, if you roll a star you have to add a clown or a balance beam—not exactly easy. A fun way to work on simple counting skills and dexterity. Takes 5–10 minutes to play a round and plenty of chances to win and lose. 3–6. (800) 819-6264

Two recent winners not to be missed: **Cookin' Cookies** (Fundex $9.99 ●●●●●)—players get recipe cards and use their suction-cupped spoons to be the first to pick up all ingredients. But don't pick up a rotten egg or you have to start from scratch! PLATINUM AWARD '05. 4–7. (800) 486-9787. And **Cranium CariBoo** (Cranium $16.95 ●●●●●)—totally on the mark for preschoolers, this "treasure hunt" game introduces early color, letter, and number concepts. PLATINUM AWARD '03. (877) 272-6486.

Matching and Memory

Prereaders match pictures before they match words. These games provide playful ways to develop vocabulary, memory, and visual skills. While there are lots of choices, many sets either have too many images or are not sufficiently distinct for young players. We found the following to be graphically clearer for kids to follow. Here are our top picks:

■ I Never Forget A Face Memory Game

(eeBoo $12.95 ●●●●) Our almost-five-year-old tester proclaimed this the best memory and matching game ever (after resoundingly beating his grandma in several rounds). Features illustrated faces of kids from around the world. A classic concentration game for a new generation. 3 & up. (212) 222-0823.

■ Spinnerific Bye-Bye Balloons & Animal Pairs Games *2006*

(International Playthings $7.99 each ●●●● ½) Here is a new spin on concentration. Quick and easy to learn, each game comes with a deck of cards and a domed spinner. Push the dome and it tells what color balloon you must find. In **Animal Pairs** the spinner will tell you to turn 2, 3, or 4 cards over and find matching animals. Our four-year-old tester loved beating us every time, and wanted to play again and again . . . the best sign of success. 3–5. (800) 445-8347.

■ Hisss

(Gamewright $10 oooo) A fun, fast-paced, interactive game to reinforce color concepts. Comes with 50 snake tiles that picture parts of the snake (head, tail, body section). The object is to build and collect the most snakes for your snake pit. The cards are sturdy, and the graphics are colorful and not scary! 4 & up. (800) 638-7568.

■ WonderFoam Dominoes ★2006★

(Chenille Kraft $15.49 oooo) These oversized foam dominoes with traditional dots were a favorite of our testers. Our tester said: the "chunky play pieces were easy to pick up" and it "was a game he came back to again and again." (800) 621-1261. Also top rated, **Color** or **Candy Dominoes** (eeBoo $12.95 each oooo) This handsomely designed sturdy cardboard set of dominoes focuses on colors and matching shapes (stars, moon, train, heart, blueberries) rather than traditional numbers or dots. Our twin three-year-old toy testers enjoyed making up their "own game." 3 & up. (212) 222-0823.

A Word About Electronic Quiz Toys for Preschoolers

For the past few years, we have objected (loudly) to many of these platforms because they did not use real books as a foundation and because the games were really nothing more than drill and practice. We are happy to report that things are changing—you'll find that well known storybooks are now being used, and that the games are more open ended. These toys are attractive to preschoolers, who generally love pressing buttons, making things happen, and working on learning their numbers and letters. That said, preschoolers still learn best through concrete experiences and should have a rich diet of playing games, working on puzzles, and listening to great stories. Here are our top picks:

■ Fridge Phonics Magnetic Letter Set

(LeapFrog $17.99 oooo ½) For the 21st-century child, magnetic letters that talk! Put the "magnetic phonics reader" onto the fridge and play one capital letter at a time. They say and sing each letter's name and sing each letter's "sounds." Letters are raised to give kids the feel for their shapes. Also fun, **Fridge Farm Magnetic Animal Set** ($14.95 oooo ½), five animals, each in two pieces; match front and back, and they say their names. (800) 701-5327.

■ My First Leap Pad Bus *2006*

(LeapFrog $39.99 oooo ½) Three Dr. Seuss books have been adapted for this platform, which has been updated with a bus motif. You can listen to the story and/or play the games that extend the experience. Each page has items to find with a sensor pen. Comes with *Leap's Big Day*, with many basic preschool counting and language skills, not just the usual alphabet drill. Happily, there's a volume control, so it won't blast their ears. (800) 701-5327.

■ Read With Me DVD *2006* PLATINUM AWARD

(Fisher-Price/Scholastic $34.99/$14.99 each DVD ooooo) Nothing short of a breakthrough—because it marries technology with great storybooks! Kids interact with a wireless controller that allows them to play real picture books and games on your TV. The DVDs read stories or on play mode it interrupts the story to ask questions. Some of the workbook-ish games are rough going for 3s and 4s, but on target for 5s and up. That said, this is a story machine for younger kids and slow paced game machine for 5–7s. Packaged with *Where the Wild Things Are*, we suggest *The Little Engine That Could* and *Chicka, Chicka, Boom Boom!* as better choices for 3s and 4s. Does it replace reading with your kids? No. We applaud Fisher-Price for their great book selections. We hope they stay true to this mandate and stay clear of the usual diet of licensed characters and subpar books. 3–7 (800) 432-5437.

■ V.Smile *2006*

(Vtech $59.99 ooo) A console that also plugs into the TV and specializes in drill-and-review games that usually borrow from arcade formats. While seven-year-olds often enjoy reinforcing what they know, the pace of this product is way too fast to "learn" from and certainly way beyond the preschool crowd (its targeted audience). (800) 521-2010.

Puzzles

A word about puzzles: Preschoolers gradually move from whole-piece puzzles, to simple puzzles that challenge them to see how two or more parts make a whole. For kids with no previous experience, start with five to seven pieces in a frame. Children's skills vary, so take your cue from the child. Some 4s can handle 20 to 30 pieces, while others are still working on 10 to 15 pieces. Large pieces are easier for little hands. A word of warning: with some notable exceptions listed below, many of the wooden puzzles that came our way continued to be badly finished and were rife with splinters.

■ Alphabet Boat Puzzle 2006

(Infantino $12.99 ●●●●) Each boat being pulled by the Coast Guard boat has a letter in upper- and lowercase painted on the side and an object that starts with the sound of the letter. Also top rated, **I Spy My House Puzzle** ($12.99 ●●●●), with objects in the frame to "spy" in the puzzle, and **Town Heroes Puzzle** ($12.99 ●●●●). New for 2006 but not ready for testing, **When I Grow Up Alphabet Puzzle** (interesting circular shape featuring yoga teacher and zoo keeper as two possible careers). (800) 840-4916.

■ Baby Animals 2006

(eeBoo $14.99 ●●●●) Twenty puzzle sets of mother and baby animals done with charming illustrations that have a storybook quality. Ideal for working with your child on knowing and naming familiar animals such as *bear/bear cub*, *cow/calf*, and *kangaroo/joey*. We recommend starting out with five at a time. 3 & up. (212) 222-0823.

■ Beginner Pattern Blocks

(Melissa & Doug $19.99 ●●●●½) Ten wooden scenes are ready to fill with triangles, circles, squares, rectangles and ovals. Part puzzle/part shape sorter, all beautifully crafted with wooden storage box. 2½ & up. (800) 284-3948.

■ Lauri Puzzles 2006 BLUE CHIP

(Lauri $7.99 ●●●●●) Lauri's puzzles come with rubber pieces and a

pattern printed in the container/tray for beginners to follow. For building confidence, these are the perfect place to start. New for **2006**, a 13-piece **T-Rex** and a 16-piece **Farm Scene.** Past favorites include **Triceratops, Car, Birthday Cake,** and **Airplane.** 3–7. (800) 451-0520.

■ Magnetic Dinosaur Puzzle **2006**

(The Orb Factory $14.99 **○○○○**) Dino fans will love working with this circular puzzle with magnetic pieces featuring 15 dinosaurs. The puzzle board gives a little hint by showing the skeleton of the dino and the shape of the puzzle piece (a little creepy but a big hit with testers). Puzzle also comes with a huge dino poster full of info. (800) 741-0089.

■ Our World **2006**

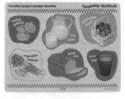

(Mudpuppy Press $15 **○○○○**) A satisfying oversized floor puzzle (24" x 36") with 24 pieces. Each of the continents is illustrated with animals, people, and landmarks. A good way to introduce the concept of the world to older preschoolers. Still top rated, this company's picturebook-inspired puzzles including **Richard Scarry's Busy House, Olivia,** and **Curious George.** They say 3, we'd say more like 4 & up. (212) 354-8840.

■ Puzzibilities Sound Puzzles **2006**

(Small World Toys $15 each **○○○○○**) Six raised pieces are easy to lift, and when they are put back in the puzzle board, each makes a rip-roaring sound. Choose **Wild Animals, Dinosaurs,** or **Under Construction.** 2½ & up. PLATINUM AWARD '05. New for **2006**, Bilingual puzzles: **Colors and Shapes** (**○○○○**), and **Count 1–10** (**○○○○**). The latter uses nontraditional forms of "9" and "4," which may be confusing for some beginners. Still top rated, **Puzzibilities** (**○○○○**) ninepiece puzzles with small red knobs (themes: transportation, snapshot wild animals, or community vehicles). (800) 421-4153.

Lacing Games

Kids dive right into lacing activities without knowing they're a great way to develop the fine-motor skills they'll need for writing. Our favorites:

Musical Friends and **Fairies of the Field** (eeBoo $14.00 each ooooo), beautifully illustrated sturdy cards that kids will love to work on. Marked 3 & up, but will be most enjoyed by 4s. (212) 222-0823. New for **2006**, **Seven Pets to Lace and Trace** (Lauri $6.99 oooo) are made of sturdy chipboard punched with holes that kids "sew" with colorful laces. (800) 451-0520.

Science Toys and Activities

Floating a leaf in a puddle, collecting pebbles in the park, making mud pies in the sandbox, watching worms wiggle—these are a few of the active ways children learn about the natural world.

■ Mighty Magnet

(Learning Resources $6.50 oooo½) A jumbo 8" horseshoe-shaped magnet that can hold up to four pounds! They also have a set of **Six Mighty Magnets,** 5" horseshoes that can be used for hunting up how many places kids can make them stick ($17.95 oooo). 4 & up. (800) 222-3909.

■ Live Butterfly Pavilion

(Insect Lore $29.95 oooo) Kit includes a 3'-long, wind-sock-like habitat where ten Painted Lady caterpillars (which they mail to you) are transformed. A coil allows the habitat to pop up, stand on a table, and fold away for future use. Take pictures of the metamorphosis, or encourage your child to draw the changes and keep a log. Great for preschoolers as well as early school years. Company also makes a **Ladybug Land** ($16.95 oooo) where you hatch ladybugs! (800) 548-3284.

SMART PARENT TRICK: Give your preschooler a magnet and a sheet of peel-off stickers to put on anything they find that the magnet sticks to. Or give kids a bag full of household items to sort into two baskets. Have them put all the things that are attracted to the magnet in one basket and all the rest in another.

Garden Work

Preschoolers love the magic of seeing things grow. If you're looking to get a young gardener started, we recommend plastic **Garden Tools** (Little Tikes $2 each for small tools/$13 for a set of three larger tools. (800) 321-0183). **WHAT TO AVOID:** For preschoolers, stay clear of metal tools. An accidental swing in the wrong direction with plastic will not mean a trip to the ER. They also don't have splintery handles as some metal tools do, and won't rust when they are inevitably left outside.

Sand, Water, & Bubble Toys

Sand and water are basic materials for exploring liquids and solids, floating and sinking, sifting and pouring. An inexpensive pail and shovel are basic gear along with a sand mill for sandbox or beach. Older preschoolers will be delighted with a set of turrets and tower molds for building beautiful sand castles—kids will add moat, imagination, and who knows what else! Some other sand tools are also worth considering.

■ Naturally Playful Sand & Water Table

(Step2 $70 ●●●●½) This oversized table is half for sand and half for water, with waterways for boats to travel. A terrific patio toy for stand-up digging and splashing. Comes with several boats, tools, and an umbrella for shade. As with all water toys, adult supervision is a must. 2½ & up. For a smaller table, consider their **WaterWheel Play Table** ($39.99 ●●●●), p. 42. (800) 347-8372.

■ Castle and Bucket Set

(International Playthings $12.99 ●●●●) A castle-shaped bucket doubles as a mold and comes with a watering can, three stout digging tools, and sand/water mill. 3 & up. (800) 445-8347.

■ **Car Wash** *2006*

(Alex $23.99 ●●●●½) After a day in the sandbox, it's tough to deal with the "don't wanna take a bath" preschooler. But this floating car wash with spritzer, conveyer belt, and turning gate might just change some minds. Comes with four little cars and miles of play power. Takes some hand strength and fine motor tuning to operate. 3 & up. (800) 666-2539.

Bubbles

Blowing bubbles has come a long way since the small plastic containers of pink liquid with the small, sticky wand. We recommend: **Little Kids' Super Size Bubble Wand** ($7.99 ●●●●) for super duper bubbles. (800) 545-5437.

FREEBIE: For superlarge bubbles, mix 1 cup of Dawn liquid detergent with 3 tablespoons of Karo syrup in 2½ quarts of cold water. Stir gently. Leftovers (if you have any) need to be refrigerated. Ideal for large groups.

Portable Pools and Sandboxes

See Toddlers chapter.

Active Physical Play

Active play builds preschoolers' big muscles, coordination, and confidence in themselves as able doers. It also establishes healthy active patterns for fitness, relieves stress, and provides a legitimate reason to run and shout. Agreeing on the rules of the game and taking turns promote important social and cooperative skills.

■ 2 in 1 Hitting Trainer Hit-a-Way Jr.

(Coop Kids $29.99 ●●●●) Our baseball players-in-training can work on their swing with the well designed low-tech hitting machine. The ball is tethered so that you don't have to run after every hit. Be sure to load the base with water for added stability. (760) 931-5733. For a T-ball that also converts into a battery-operated hitting machine, our testers gave high marks to the **Triple Hit Baseball** (Fisher-Price $20 ●●●●½). (800) 432-5437.

■ Crawl N Fun BLUE CHIP

(Playhut $25 ●●●●●) Testers giggled their way through this 6'-long tunnel as they crawled along! Also top rated: longer and more spacious **Yellow School Bus, Red Fire Engine,** and a blue **Deluxe Train** engine. These each easily accommodate two kids for pretend fun. 3 & up. New for **2006**, **SpongeBob Hot Shot** ($19.99 ●●●●) Pop this nylon & net basketball game up for slam dunk action. Like a skee-ball table, this has a basketball hoop with ball return. Sponge Bob decor. It is 30" x 30" x 40" high. 4 & up. (888) 752-9488.

■ Easy Score Basketball Set

(Little Tikes $29.99 & up ●●●●) Adjustable to six different heights, from 2½ to 4 feet, folds for storage, and has wheels for portability. Must be filled with sand to avoid tipping. 2½ & up. For big preschoolers consider the **Adjust & Jam** ($35 ●●●●), a hoop that starts at 4' and grows to 6'. (800) 321-0183.

■ Gertie Balls BLUE CHIP

(Small World Toys $4 & up ●●●●●) Preschoolers need soft, lightweight, easy-to-catch balls that will not bend back a finger or hurt when they hit. Gertie Balls are gummy and soft enough for kids who may be scared of big heavy balls coming toward them. New for **2006**, **Polka-Dot** or **Clear Bumpy Gertie.** 3 & up. Also fun, **Think Big Sports Balls** **2006** ($19.99 each ●●●●). Two feet in diameter, these inflatable vinyl balls are covered with a basketball, baseball, or soccer design. Be forewarned, they do get dirty. 4 &

up. (800) 421-4153.

■ Hopping Sport Balls

(Franklin $14.99 each **oooo**) Our testers liked the sports theme of these classic 18" ball hoppers. Comes as either a basketball, baseball, or soccer ball. Comes with its own air pump. (800) 225-8647. For bigger kids, consider **26" Hoppity Ball** (Small World Toys $19.99 **oooo**). (800) 421-4153.

■ Mini Golf

(Alex $19.99 **oooo**) Our four-year-old testers thought this circus-themed miniature golf set was loads of fun. Comes with two clubs (with foam heads); two balls; and 6 illustrated targets. 3 & up. (800) 666-2539. For a basic plastic set of clubs, **TotSports Golf Set** (Little Tikes $20 **oooo**) comes with a pull cart, two clubs, and three balls. Says 2 & up; we'd say 4 & up. (800) 321-0183.

☞ SAFETY TIP: Do little kids really need helmets? More than 500,000 people are treated annually in U.S. emergency rooms for bicycle-related injuries. Data shows very young riders incur a higher proportion of head injuries. A helmet can reduce risk of head injury by up to 85%!

Wheel Toys: Trikes and Other Vehicles

Preschoolers will still use many of the vehicles featured in the Toddlers chapter. Vehicles with no pedals remain solid favorites. Older preschoolers are also ready for tricycles and kiddie cars with pedals. The battery-operated vehicles that go 5 mph look tempting, but they won't do anything for big-muscle action. Here's what to look for in a three-wheel drive with pedal action:

⊛ Bigger is not better. Don't look for a trike to grow into. Take your child to the store to test-drive and find the right-size trike. Kids should be able to get on and off without assistance.

⊛ Preschoolers need the security of a three-wheeler,

which is more stable than a two-wheeler.

⊛ A primary-colored bike can be reused by younger sibs regardless of their gender.

⊛ See Safety Guidelines section for safety standards for helmets.

COMPARISON SHOPPER
Rocking Horses

Many of us remember the rocking horses from our own childhood. They are back, but not all winners. Our testers loved the Mamas and Papas horses that come in a variety of sizes. They are pricey but likely to become a family treasure. These are plush ponies with furry manes, tails, and leather saddles. For younger preschoolers, there's **Topaz** ($99/seat height 16" ⚬⚬⚬⚬⚬) or **Acorn** ($169.99/seat height 19" ⚬⚬⚬⚬⚬). For the biggest rider, consider the gliding **Patches** ($299/seat height 26" ⚬⚬⚬⚬⚬). (310) 631-2222. We found the new **Liberty** (Radio Flyer $120 ⚬⚬), a classic style spring rocker with plastic horse and yarn mane difficult to put together, and the frame was so big that you'd need to be more like six or seven to get on it without making a parent wince. Their smaller horse (with safety seat) requires a parent to lift the child in and out to ride and we found that the seat required a pretty slim child. (800) 621-7613.

Wheeled Toys
■ Fold 2 Go XL Trike *2006*

(Radio Flyer $60 ⚬⚬⚬⚬) Our tall four-year-old tester had trouble with her long legs on other trikes. According to her mom, "The minute I put her on this one, she took off. This one is easy for her to steer and pedal, it's stable because of the wide base at the back, and it folds up nicely . . . the best one yet!" She did note that the parent push bar was not as sturdy as the one on their **Ultimate Family Trike** ($80 ●●●●●) but her daughter found this one easier to ride! Also new for **2006**, the **Twist Trike** ($60 ●●●●) You can twist the body of this trike from trike to low-to-the-ground "chopper." Our tester enjoyed the dual mode of the trike, although her mom noted that the turning radius wasn't as good as other Radio Flyer trikes. (800) 621-7613.

■ Kiddo Supertrike

(Kettler $80 ●●●●) This gender-proof primary-colored trike has a stroller bar and high back bucket seat (seat belt available), storage bin, and air-filled tires. Well built, this has an adjustable four-position frame for growth. Kettler trikes tend to run small and fit younger preschoolers only. (757) 427-2400.

■ PlasmaCar **2006** PLATINUM AWARD

(PlaSmart $69.95 ●●●●●) Our testers from ages 4 to 12 could not get enough of this new ride-on which, according to the manufacturer, runs on "inertia, centrifugal force, and friction." Sounds like a lot of serious scientific principles—but this is sheer fun rolled up into one zippy vehicle! There are no pedals, or batteries needed. Rotate the steering wheel and you're off on any smooth surface. One mom suggested the manufacturer should add bumpers to the front and back to protect the walls. 4 & up. (877) 289-0730.

■ Scrambler Pedal Coupe **2006**

(Step 2 $70 ●●●● ½) Our testers really enjoyed this innovative little front-wheel-drive pedal car that has "center-pivot" steering in the handles on either side of the gender-free red vehicle. Kids use both arm and leg power. 2½ & up. New for **2006**, **Zip & Zoom Pedal Car** ($70), has a similar mechanism but with a more open design and promises to fit bigger kids. Was not ready for testing. (800) 347-8372.

■ Scream Machine Jr.

(Razor $99 ●●●●●) Remember your classic Big Wheels? Here's the updated version of that low-to-the-ground pedal toy. A junior model is smaller, but just as much fun as the original gleaming chrome version. We'd add a flag so vehicles can see riders low to the ground! PLATINUM AWARD

'04. 4–8. (866) 467-2967.

Stand-Alone Climbers

■ Little Tikes Playground Blue Chip

(Little Tikes $480 ●●●●○) This top-of-the-line climber is part playhouse, part climber. It does not provide the kind of big-muscle climbing, dangling, and jumping that classic monkey bars do, but kids had no complaints. They loved the multiple play areas with mini-tunnel, slides, and platforms for imaginative play. Expensive, but a solid investment. 3 & up. (800) 321-0183. For other climbers, see Toddler chapter.

> **SHOPPING TIP:** Little Tikes suggests using a little liquid detergent or cooking oil on the connecting pieces of their toys if you are having difficulty putting them together.

Playhouses

A playhouse is the ultimate toy for pretend that will be used for years of solo and social play. Kids as young as two love the magic of entering their own domain—being the owner of a space that's scaled to size. Children love opening and closing the door, looking out the windows, or playing with the toy kitchen (in some models). You'll find houses to fit a variety of tastes and budgets.

■ Naturally Playful Welcome Home Playhouse
2006 Platinum Award

(Step 2 $550 ●●●●○) This oversized 66" high house will accommodate growing children and has bay windows, full kitchen, doorbell, and room for multiple children. "She loves playing peek-a-boo and having her own special space," wrote our tester's mother. The smaller **Adobe House** ($299) is 55" high, has small kitchen, sand tones, red "tile" roof, and stucco adobe look. (800) 347-8372.

■ Endless Adventures Tikes Town Playhouse
2006 PLATINUM AWARD

(Little Tikes $200 ●●●●●) An innovative design with four different themed sides on this 55" tall structure (firehouse/schoolhouse, gas station, grocery store/bank with ATM machine (of course), and a sports wall complete with hoop. For grander housing, consider the **Playcenter Playhouse** ($499 ●●●●), 78" high with kitchen, bay window, deck, slide, and optional ($99.99) swing set. We do not suggest **ImagineSounds Interactive Playhouse** (●●) with motion sensors that trigger random messages such as "Open the windows!" or "Dinner's ready!" We think kids can do their own imagining! (800) 321-0183.

■ Jump 'n Slide 2006

(Little Tikes $200 ●●●●½) The neighborhood kids that tested this new inflatable toy had one word: "Great!" Ideal for the 2–5 year old range. (Older testers were disappointed that it didn't have enough bounce for them.) Parents liked the protective walls on the sides and loved the extra-wide slide. Great fun for a birthday party and just backyard fun, but does require parental supervision. Like an air mattress, it inflates quickly with the built-in pump (also a plus). 3 & up. (800) 321-0183.

■ Megahouse

(Playhut $39.99 ●●●●) This is one big fabric pop-up playhouse with a roll-up window and a doorway. Five feet tall and almost as wide, this is a big enough play setting for several kids to enjoy. Best suited for indoor use. A good gust of wind would send it flying! We couldn't put it back into its case. (888) 752-9488.

■ My Playhouse/Theatre BLUE CHIP

(Alex $200 ●●●●●) Here is imagination central! A giant 60" high combo playhouse, puppet stage, and store. Sure to be the focal point of any playroom, this sturdy wood-and-laminated play center is done in Maisy-like primary stripes and dots. It has a shelf for a puppet stage, side-window "ticket" office, front and back curtains, and a working door. 3 & up. PLATINUM AWARD '00. (800) 666-2539.

FREEBIE: For temporary indoor housing, don't overlook the charm of a big cardboard box with cutout windows and door or a tablecloth draped over a table for little campers to use as a tent. A great way to overcome rainy-day cabin fever.

Art Supplies

Markers, crayons, chalk, clay, and paint provide different experiences, all of which invite kids to express ideas and feelings, explore color and shapes, and develop the muscles and control needed for writing and imagination. A supply of basics should include

Big crayons	**Washable markers**
Glue stick	**Safety scissors**
Finger-paint	**Colored construction paper**
Tempera paint	**Plain paper**
Molding material such as Play-Doh or plasticine	

Paints and Brushes

Tempera paint is ideal for young children because of its thick, opaque quality. Watercolors are more appropriate for school-aged children. Young children will have more success with thick brushes than skinny ones, which are harder to control. To reduce the number of spills, invest in paint containers sold with lids and openings just wide enough for a thick paintbrush. Buying paint in pint-sized squeeze bottles is more economical than buying small jars of paint that will dry out. Look for both nontoxic and washable labels on any art supplies you buy.

■ Aquadoodle 2006

(Spinmaster $24.99 ●●●●½) Our four-year-old tester looked up and said, "Even if I get it on the floor, it won't show, will it?" Indeed, this is a mess-free and semi-magical oversized mat for drawing with water! Using the "water pen," blue

drawings appear on the surface and disappear once they are dry. Great for developing hand and arm movements needed for writing without restrictive lines. New travel version was not ready for testing. (800) 622-8339.

■ Crayola Color Wonder Paper & Markers

(Binney & Smith $8.99 ●●●●) Our three-year-old tester couldn't get enough of making pictures "appear"! These are washable markers sans color to stain wallpaper and clothing! We prefer the open-ended paper to the coloring book so kids can make their own designs. Forget the new "magic" finger paints; they don't work well because they require more pressure than kids can exert. 2 & up. (800) 272-9652.

■ Colossal Barrel of Crafts

(Chenille Kraft $39.99 ●●●●●) Like a giant jar of treats in an old-fashioned candy store, this huge plastic jar has a mammoth supply of pom-poms, craft sticks, beads and string, foam shapes, pipe cleaners, googly eyes, glitter, metallic spangles, cutters, and plasticine. Add glue, scissors, and imagination for many crafty sessions! 4–8. PLATINUM AWARD '02. (800) 621-1261.

■ Finger Painting Party **2006**

(Alex $20 ●●●● ½) Roll up those sleeves and get ready to make squiggles, swirls, and other delicious patterns with the tools that come in this bucket with six jars of fingerpaint. Assorted tools with chunky handles add new dimensions to the messy whole-hand fun of fingerpaints! Also fun, **Collage Party** (●●●●). 3 & up. (800) 666-2539.

■ Nature Barrel of Beads **2006**

(Bead Bazaar $19.99 ●●●●) A huge bucket of wooden beads that are big enough for small hands to string. Includes natural and colored strings, ten wooden charms, and rings for keychains. There are enough packets of colored beads for ten or more kids to use as an activity for a party. They say 3 & up; we'd say more like 4–7. (800) 838-1769.

■ Sir Steps-A-Lot

(imadethat $39.99 ●●●●) These carpentry kits are just right for parents who aren't particularly handy! The step-by-step instructions are clear and the small wooden hammer is just right for kids to use. Maybe they'll even brush their teeth longer if they stand on a step stool that they've made. Also, **Mr. Feet Table** ($49.99 ●●●●) will be just right for snacks and artwork, and you won't mind having it in your house. Paints sold separately. (877) 804-8004.

> **SMART PARENT TRICK: Magic Painting** is great fun. Have child draw on paper with a piece of wax or a white crayon. Then water down a bit of tempera and have child paint over invisible drawing. Abracadabra! The drawing appears!

Easels

A flat table may still be easier for young preschoolers, since the colors won't run. Older preschoolers are better able to adjust the amount of paint they load on brushes, and many enjoy painting at an easel. Avoid watering down paint; thicker paint is easier to control. Having an easel set up makes art materials accessible whenever the mood moves young artists.

Plastic Easels 2006

Depending on your space and needs, the following are top-rated choices: **Double Easel** (Little Tikes $50 ●●●●) or **Easel for Two** (Step 2 $35 ●●●●), both come with chalkboard on one side. The Step 2 easel comes with magnetic letters that attach to the magnetic board. You can't go wrong with either. Little Tikes (800) 321-0183/Step 2 (800) 347-8372. **Safety note:** While easels can be enjoyed by 2s, the magnets that come with this set are small and can come out of the plastic, so they are unsafe for kids under 3.

Wooden Easels

■ **Super Rolling Art Center**
    2006 PLATINUM AWARD

(Alex $129.99 ●●●●●) You need a lot of room for this generously sized art cart that has two easels and place for storing your child's creations and supplies in between. The wheels gives this good-looking piece of equipment some portability. It does require a fair amount of assembly which was not always easy. That said, it looks like it belongs in a Pottery Barn catalog. If space is an issue, consider the **BLUE CHIP Tabletop Easel** ($40 ●●●●●). Folds flat for convenient storage. (800) 666-2539.

Modeling Materials

These totally pliable, unstructured materials invite kids to use their hands and imagination to shape something from nothing. Fun for pounding, stretching, kneading, and rolling—three-dimensional experiences that preschoolers love. Older preschoolers may name what they make after the event. Few set out to design something in particular. The focus here is on the process, and not on making something realistic. Some of our favorite materials:

■ Dough Party *2006*

(Alex $17 ●●●●) Comes in a newly designed see-through canister with six bright colors, a roller, cutters, plus a mat to work on. If you prefer clay, consider their **Clay & Play Party** ($17 ●●●●). 4–7. (800) 666-2539.

■ Crayola Model Magic Bucket

(Binney and Smith $16.99 ●●●●) Our toy testers love working with model magic for school projects and just playing around. We recommend the bucket that comes with four 8-oz. packages. 2 & up. (800) 272-9652.

■ Play-Doh BLUE CHIP

(Hasbro $2 and up ●●●●●) Play-Doh is one of those products you either love or hate as a parent. We are long-time fans—the product can be used to build hand strength, and small pretend settings like this new farm are fun for pretend play as well. Classic **Play-Doh** ($2 & up ●●●●●) without the doodads is still our favorite since it is the most open-ended. Remember, this self-hardening dough dries out if left uncovered. 3 & up. (800) 327-8264.

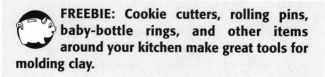

FREEBIE: Cookie cutters, rolling pins, baby-bottle rings, and other items around your kitchen make great tools for molding clay.

Music and Movement

Many instruments for children have such poor sound quality it's hard to call them musical. And kids at this stage are not ready for reading notation. It's more an exploration of sound, rhythm, and movement that makes good sense for preschoolers.

■ Lollipop Drum BLUE CHIP

(Remo $21.99 ooooo) Preschoolers can easily hold onto the handle of this 10" lollipop-shaped drum. Makes a pleasing sound, according to both kid and parent testers. Still top rated, **Maracas Shakers** ($5 oooo), small maracas with great sound and perfect fit for little hands. (800) 525-5134.

■ Woodstock Band *2006*

(Woodstock Percussion $29.99 oooo½) Beat out that rhythm with this six-piece set with wooden tambourine, recorder, maraca, egg shaker, castanet, and sleigh bell jingler with big wooden handle. Solid-sounding instruments. (800) 422-4463.

> **SMART PARENT TRICK:** Use a drum to beat out someone's first name. For example, Sa-man-tha would get three beats. Take turns guessing whose name is being marked.

Preschool Furniture Basics

Table and Chairs

These convenient pieces of basic gear will be used for artwork, puzzles, tea parties, and even lunch. You'll find many choices in both plastic and wood. This is a decorating choice as well as a functional one. **Super Art Table** PLATINUM AWARD '04 (Alex $179.99 ooooo) is an oval table outfitted with a roll of paper for painting, a chalkboard center, and wells for supplies, and comes with two long stools. For a smaller round table with same style, consider **My First Table** (Alex $100 oooo½). 3 & up. (800) 666-2539.

Best Travel Toys

Preschoolers can entertain themselves for short periods of time with toys and art supplies. A well loved soft doll or mini-setting with multiple pieces make sfor cozy pretend play. At this stage, a piece of home, whether it's a toy or a blanket, is still important. One of the best ways to make time fly is to bring along a tape player with favorite songs or stories to enjoy. For restaurant stops, pack a plastic baggy filled with simple games, cards, or crayons and paper to fill time before the bread basket arrives. Bring along a handful of paperbacks to share and for independent "reading." Here are some of our favorites:

■ Construction Activity Pack

(Lauri $14.99 oooo) Loaded for dramatic play, with lacing and tracing figures, workers and tools, 20 stringing pieces, dump truck, roadway and sawhorses. Plenty of activity here for developing fine motor skills along with pretend play. Also top rated, **Fire & Rescue** or **Space Odyssey Pack.** 4–7. (800) 451-0520.

■ Groovy Girl Trendy Traveler *2006*

(Manhattan Toy $36 oooo) Designed to carry four dolls and all of their clothes for on-the-go doll play. Our tester thought it was "amazing" and liked the wild groovy-licious colors. We liked the soft straps that won't cut into little shoulders. The cardboard **Groovy Girls Mini Pod** "dollhouse" looks like a great take-along for new mini-dolls, but wasn't ready for testing. ($16). (800) 541-1345.

■ Play Scene: A Day At the Zoo

(Mudpuppy $10 oooo) A sturdy zoo scene opens like a book with 50 reusable animal and people stickers to arrange. A good choice for story telling, dramatic play and language development. Small sticker pieces take some dexterity, but this is the sort of toy that engrosses a preschooler. 3 & up. (212) 354-8840.

■ Woodkins

(Pamela Drake $12–$25 **○○○○**) These wooden "paper" dolls come with fabric choices that stay in place with a "frame" that lifts and closes over the edge of the doll. Also fun, a charming collection of fairies to dress in gossamer and glittery fabrics plus a necklace for the "designer." Perfect for quiet pretend time. 4 & up. (800) 966-3762.

Best Third and Fourth Birthday Gifts for Every Budget

Big Ticket $100 Plus	**Set of wooden blocks, trains, playhouse,** or **dollhouse** (various makers), **table and chairs**
$100 & under	**Wooden train set or easel** (various makers) or **Ultimate Family Trike** (Radio Flyer) or **Color Pixter** (Fisher-Price)
Under $75	**Lila** (Corolle) or **Leapster L-Max** (LeapFrog) or **Stroller** (American Girl) or **Supersized Groovy Girl** (Manhattan Toy)
Under $50	**Train Accessories** (various makers) or **Mr. Feet Table** (imadethat)
Under $40	**Automoblox** (Automoblox) or **Colossal Barrel of Crafts** (Chenille Kraft) or **Pretend & Play Teaching Telephone** (Learning Resources)
Under $25	**Collapsing Bridge** (Brio) or **Pretend & Play Doctor Set** (Learning Resources) or or **Lollipop Drum** (Woodstock Percussion)
Under $20	**Bendos My First RC Buggies** (Kid Galaxy) or **Our World** (Mudpuppy Press) or **WonderFoam Dominoes** (Chenille Kraft)
Under $15	**Rugged Riggz** (Little Tikes) or **I Never Forget A Face Memory Game** (eeBoo)

Under $10   **Bendos** (Kid Galaxy) or
Birthday Cake Puzzle (Lauri) or
Dora the Explorer Candy Land
(Milton Bradley) or **Model Magic** or
Color Wonder Paper (Crayola) or
Super Size Bubble Wand (Little Kids)

Under $5   **Gertie Ball** (Small World Toys) or
Hot Wheels Cars (Mattel)

4 • Early School Years
Five to Ten Years

What to Expect Developmentally

Learning Through Play. During the early school years, as children begin their formal education, play continues to be an important path to learning. Now more-complex games, puzzles, and toys offer kids satisfying ways to practice and reinforce the new skills they are acquiring in the classroom.

Dexterity and Problem-Solving Ability. School-age kids have the dexterity to handle more-elaborate building toys and art materials. They are curious about how things work and take pride in making things that can be used for play or displayed with pride.

Active Group Play. These early school years are a very social time when kids long for acceptance among their peers. Bikes and sporting equipment take on new importance as the social ticket to being one of the gang. Children try their hand at more-formal team sports where being an able player is a way of belonging.

Independent Discovery. Although these are years when happiness is being with a friend, children also enjoy and benefit from solo time. Many of the products selected here are good tools for such self-sufficient and satisfying skills.

⚙ BASIC GEAR CHECKLIST FOR EARLY SCHOOL AGE

✓ Sports equipment   ✓ Dolls/soft animals
✓ Craft kits   ✓ Board games
✓ Musical instruments   ✓ Tape player and tapes
✓ Water paints, markers, stampers
✓ Two-wheeler with training wheels
✓ Lego and other construction sets
✓ Electronic game/learning machines

🚫 Toys to Avoid

These toys pose safety hazards:

✓ Chemistry sets that can cause serious accidents
✓ Plug-in toys that heat up with lightbulbs and can give kids serious burns
✓ Audio equipment with volume controls that cannot be locked
✓ Projectile toys such as darts, rockets, B-B guns, or other toys with flying parts that can do serious damage
✓ Superpowered water guns that can cause abrasions
✓ Toys with small parts if there are young children in the house

The following is developmentally inappropriate:

✓ An abundance of toys that reinforce gender stereotypes; for example, hair play for girls and gunplay for boys

Pretend Play

School-age kids have not outgrown the joys of pretending. They like elaborate and realistic props for stepping into the roles of storekeeper, athlete, or racing-car driver. For some, mini-settings such as puppet theaters, dollhouses, and castles are a preferable route to make-believe. This is also the age when collecting miniature vehicles and action figures can become a passion. Such figures generally reflect the latest cartoon or movie feature. Nobody needs all the pieces, although many kids want them all. At this stage, owning a few pieces of the hottest "in" character represents a way of belonging.

Dollhouses, Castles, and Other Pretend Environments and Props

Kids are ready now for finer details in house and furnishings. Specialty dollhouse shops and craft stores sell prefabs and custom houses for all budgets. Some of the settings recommended here require construction skills and a great deal of adult involvement. Anticipate that you'll be doing most of the constructing, but then you have a wonderful playsetting for your child.

 COMPARISON SHOPPER
Dollhouses **2006**

For premade dollhouses, see Preschool Chapter, p. 82. For houses you have to construct, Playmobil offers several models: The new **Grande Mansion** **2006** **PLATINUM AWARD** ($129.99 ooooo) has two stories and a usable attic; this yellow house has an old world charm; Playmobil's **Family Vacation House** ($49.99 oooo), smaller than other houses, relatively easy to put together. Playmobil's **Modern House** ($119.99 ooo) did not test well; the roof collapses easily! (800) 752-9662.

PLAY TIP: Build these large structures on a board or table that they can remain on. Moving them later is an impossible dream!

COMPARISON SHOPPER
Castles **2006**

Playmobil's **Knights' Empire Castle** **2006** **PLATINUM AWARD** (Playmobil $179.99 ooooo) uses the company's new SystemX, which is designed for shorter assembly time and durability. Comes with a working gate and dungeon and looks like the classic friendly Playmobil settings of years past. By comparison, **Rock Castle** ($79.99 oooo) has a more sinister feel to it. Suggested add-on, the **Red Dragon** (because you always need a dragon), is sold separately. Projectile cannons sold separately. Also darker in feel than their previous castles is Lego's new **Vladek's Dark Fortress** ($99 ooo), which comes with catapults. Most kids love the action of projectiles until one hits them. 8–12. (800) 233-8756.

■ Lego Pirate Ship 🏆2006 PLATINUM AWARD

(Lego Systems $39.99 ooooo) We tested this with 4- and 5-year-olds and they all loved it, even though most needed help putting it together. While one parent wrote that the "pictorial directions were (blessedly) easy to follow," another complained that their 4 year-old son had a hard time conceptualizing the 3-D instructions. That child put the ship together with his Dad and he liked the poster and extra pieces. "This has been front-and-center since the 5 year-old put it together and is used for storing pirate treasure." Marked 4 & up but will need assistance. (800) 233-8756.

■ Zoo

(Playmobil $99.99 ooooo) "The Zoo took a long time to build but has plenty of play value" wrote our adult tester. PLATINUM AWARD '05. New for 🏆2006, a **sea lion pool** ($16.99 oooo). For construction-minded kids, check out the incredible, large **Crane** PLATINUM AWARD ($69.99 ooooo) that moves up, down, and around! One of the coolest toys around. Previous award-winning **Airport** ($54.99 ooooo) and **Fire Station** ($69.99 ooooo) have been scaled down in price and size. 5 & up. (800) 752-9662.

Props for Pretend

See Preschool chapter for this year's best costumes.

■ My Picnic Basket

(Alex $20 **oooo**) We liked the sturdiness of this
18-piece set that comes with blue enamelware
including plates, cups, spoons, forks, and tablecloth. Great for real picnics or pretend tea parties.
Also, **Play Bakeware** (Alex $20 **oooo**), now
updated with stainless steel pots and pans. (800)
666-2539.

Money, Money, Money

Teaching kids about money will cost you . . . . Here are our
favorites:

■ YOUniverse ATM Machine ⭐*2006*

(Summit Inc. $39.95 **oooo**½) After setting the
ATM with your name and PIN, you can make
deposits and withdrawals and check your balance. The machine recognizes the coins and
adds them to your total automatically.
Depositors need to let the bank know how many
bills they are putting in or withdrawing. We also
love the less complicated **Amazing Money Jar** ($12.99 **oooo**)—
coins only, but still very neat. (205) 661-1174.

■ Teaching Cash Register

(Learning Resources $44.95 **ooooo**) A clever
way to combine math skills with pretend play!
When kids play store with this smart new reg-
ister they learn to use a calculator, make
change, use coupons and charge cards,
and even check the customer's credit!
It has a pretend scale plus a three-level coin game
that asks kids to deposit specific amounts. PLATINUM AWARD '04.
(800) 222-3909.

Dolls

Now's the time when girls often get heavily invested in dolls
with tons of paraphernalia. Although 5- and 6-year-old boys

often find ways to play with a cousin's or sister's doll or doll-house, they are more likely to choose action figures for this kind of play. Both boys and girls continue to enjoy soft stuffed animals, the zanier the better.

For many years, the only kinds of dolls around were blonde with blue eyes but, happily, more manufacturers today are creating dolls that reflect our cultural diversity. Here are some of the best:

■ American Girl Elizabeth 2006 PLATINUM AWARD

(American Girl $87 doll w/book ○○○○○) The American Girl collection of dolls each comes with a book that introduces girls to a bit of history through stories. Elizabeth is an English girl from a prominent Loyalist family (and best friend of well-known Felicity). She's 18" tall with long blond hair and blue eyes. Still top rated, **Nellie O'Malley** (Samantha's best friend). PLATINUM AWARD '05. 7 & up. (800) 845-0005.

■ Barbie 2006

(Mattel $15.99 & up) Our testers all wanted the new **American Idol Barbie with Karaoke Machine** (○○○) but found the clothes particularly difficult to put on and take off. They also wished that the doll sang more than a part of a song. Also among this year's crop: **Fairytopia Barbie** (with light-up wings ○○○○); and **Fashion Fever** (with really neat clothes that come on little mannequins ○○○○). (800) 524-8697.

■ Les Cheries

(Corolle $35 each ○○○○○) Fourteen-inch dolls that are purposefully not fashion dolls; they are meant to look like girls of today. Think Olson twins before they discovered make-up. 4–8. PLATINUM AWARD '03. See preschool chapter for new **Lili** dolls that were a hit with early school girls, as well. (800) 668-4846.

■ Only Hearts Club Collection 2006 PLATINUM AWARD

(OHC Group $15 each ○○○○○) These 9" dolls have bendable bodies, delicately etched faces, and charming accessories, as well as small books that relate to typical problems of girlhood. Girls will need considerable dexterity to get the little shoes and clothing on and off. Unlike most fashion dolls today, these have outfits that would be acceptable to well-heeled parents and grandparents. They are dressed like girls—not funky streetwalkers in training. Our testers were thrilled with the **Ballet Studio Theater** ($50 ●●●●●) and **Stable** ($75 ●●●●●)—both are PLATINUM AWARD winners. (805) 456-0241.

■ Teen Trend 2006

(Mattel $39.99 each ●●●●) Courtney ("modern prepster"), Deondra ("sporty girl"), Gabby ("girly girl") and Kianna ("the rocker") all look as if they walked off a WB show. While we think their classifications are silly and Kiana's lipstick and hair are a little much, these are stylish, as opposed to the street-walker look of the Bratz line. (800) 524-8697.

COMPARISON SHOPPER
What's in a Head? 2006

If your child is into serious hair play, here's a dream gift (although it might creep other family members). Corolle's **Hairstyling & Make-Up Head** ($29.95 ●●●●) is just the head and shoulders of a beautiful blond doll with plenty of hair to brush and style. Kit also comes with make-up for the doll (of course). (800) 668-4846. If you're looking for a more grown-up head of hair (with really bad chunky highlights), consider **Barbie Fashion Fever Styling Head** (Mattel $19.99 ●●●). (800) 524-8697. (*Editors' note:* We're not big on hair play as a pre-occupation, but these styling heads might help encourage good grooming and reduce the common hassles over real hair care.)

Puppets and Puppet Stages

Puppets provide an excellent way for kids to develop the language and storytelling skills that are the underpinning of reading and writing. Kids who can tell a story have less trouble writing a story. Many of the puppets and stages in the Preschool chapter will get lots of mileage now. Older kids may also become interested in marionettes or making shadow, stick, or hand puppets of their own.

■ Royal Treatment Theatre Set

(Manhattan Toy $35 **oooo**) A royal blue brick velour tabletop stage has a foldout platform on which finger puppets can perform. Or consider **Puppettos Theatre Stage** (same idea but done in teal with a red curtain—not our favorite color combo, but that's a personal preference). Top-rated puppets include **Metropolicity Community** worker types, **Birthday Belles,** and, still wonderful, **Royal Rumpus Finger Puppets.** 4 & up. (800) 541-1345.

■ Puppet Palace

(Enchantmints $100 **oooo**) Built for hand puppets or marionettes, this wooden 42" x 36" tabletop theater is laminated with graphics, and has six backdrops and a curtain that hides stand-up puppeteers. A handsome choice for 7 & up. (888) 440-6468.

Favorite Hand Puppets

■ Polar Bear 2006

(Folkmanis $36 **oooo**½) Polar bears are beloved in our office. This is a formidable bear. On a more domestic scale, there is also a new adorable 13" brown **Tabby Cat** ($22 **oooo**), the favorite of one of our toddler testers! Also interesting, dragon puppets that sit on a shoulder and are operated with a hand lever. Not ready for testing. Still charming, a 30" honey-colored **Golden Retriever** ($60 **oooo**). (800) 654-8922.

■ Emergency Rescue Squad Puppets BLUE CHIP

(Learning Resources $19.95 set of 4 **ooooo**) Multicultural workers—doctor, paramedic, police officer, and firefighter—with vinyl heads and cloth bodies. 4 & up. (800) 222-3909.

■ Farm Puppets Lacing Craft Kit 2006

(Lauri $12.99 **oooo**½) The latest in the wonderful collection of pre-cut felt puppets (among other themes: bunnies, bugs, circus animals).

Kids lace them up and use them for storytelling. Kits come with yarn and big plastic needle for sewing (which develops fine-motor skills kids need for writing). 5 & up. (800) 451-0520.

■ Magical Mystique Puppets ✦2006✦

(Manhattan Toy $10 each **oooo**) These hand puppets are perfect for fairy tales: a splendid new dragon, a unicorn, and a pup who's dressed as a wizard. Still top rated, **Knightingtales Puppets** ($10 each). You need all five fingers to make the most of these velour royals—a king, queen, and knight. (800) 541-1345.

Electric Train Sets

Many train buffs will tell you that this is the stage when their romance with trains began. Select HO gauge for beginners. Smaller tracks can be frustrating to put together. Larger-gauge sets take up a tremendous amount of space, so you generally end up with just a boring circle of track. **Safety note:** Since trains are plug-in electrical items, they are labeled for 8 & up. Younger children may enjoy them, but only with adult supervision.

Remote Control Cars and Other Vehicles

■ Air Hogs R/C Wall Racer ✦2006✦

(Spinmaster $59.99) Just what you always wanted, a gravity-defying vehicle that kids can drive up the walls. Yes, a Humvee that will climb your freshly painted living room . . . but can it do wallpaper? We mean, what will it do to your wallpaper! Not available for testing. 8 & up. (800) 622-8339.

■ Mgears Remote Control Racers

(Learning Resources $29.95 **ooooo**) Our testers liked the speed they got with this 213-piece **Grand Prix Racer.** The base comes with the wheels already on (one year we had trouble getting the wheels on!). "The directions sometimes have too many steps in them—they should be more like Lego's." "It really works, the gears move when you make the car go." "Much better than last year's tethered remote control; it goes much faster, too." 7 & up. PLATINUM AWARD '05. (800) 222-3909.

■ **Morphibians** 2006

(Kid Galaxy $24.99 ●●●●½) These snappy vehicles run on land and water! With one-button full-function radio control, these are less complex than some of the larger RC's and have the added fun of float-abllity. 5 & up. (800) 816-1135.

■ **Roboraptor** 2006

(WowWee $100 ●●●●) As friendly as Robosapien was last year, **Roboraptor** is scary. A 32"-long white robotic dino, he acts like a pred-ator! His sensors allow him to react to his envi-ronment which sometimes means he'll hiss, snap, and generally creep you out. For our older toy testers this was cool. (Some little siblings may truly be freaked out by his aggressive nature). Easy to control, although "running" mode looks more like a fast walk. Also new for 2006, **WowWee Alive Chimpanzee** ($130) is a chimp head with "facetronics" that come alive with motion and sounds. Talk about creepy! Prototype was amazing, but it was not ready for testing. 10 & up. (800) 310-3033.

■ **Robosapien V2** 2006

(WowWee $250) Building on the success of last year's PLATINUM win-ner, the **Robosapien V2** is 22" tall. He can see, hear, and speak. Not only that—he can sit, lie down, and get up, and he has articulated fingers—the better to pick up after you! Not ready for testing, but last year, our testers were thrilled with the 14" programmable **Robosapien** ($99 ●●●●●) (now available in colors and glow-in-the-dark) that walks, dances, picks up and tosses objects! Not designed for instantaneous gratification—there's a manual that involves reading and thinking to make things happen. Marked 6 & up, we'd say better for 9 & up. PLATINUM AWARD '05. (800) 310-3033.

■ **Solar Racers** 2006

(Uncle Milton $9.99 & up) We sure hope these cars work because they looked so cool. They're only 2" long and with a built-in solar cell, promise to be great fun when used outside. Were not ready for testing. 6 & up. (800) 869-7555.

Construction Toys

What Kids Learn from Construction Toys

Builders learn to follow directions and develop dexterity, problem-solving skills, and stick-to-itiveness. Success is not always instant. Updated classics such as **Lincoln Logs** and **Tinkertoys** are more appropriate for this age even though they are labeled for preschoolers. **Glueless Snap Models** are also a good place to start for beginning model builders.

What You Should Know Before You Buy:

As their dexterity develops, kids can handle smaller pieces and more-complex building sets.

A variety of building sets is better than just one because building with Legos and K'nex, for example, involve different, but equally valuable, skills.

Open-ended sets that can be built in multiple ways are a great place to start. As your child becomes a more confident builder, move on to small models.

Age labels on most building sets are not accurate. If the box says 5 & up and your 5-year-old needs a lot of assistance, the problem is with the label, not your child.

Working on one of these sets together can be rewarding. Be careful not to take over; break the project into doable parts to build confidence.

Less can be more, which is helpful to keep in mind. Start with smaller doable sets that help your child learn particular building strategies.

Girls as well as boys need to develop spatial/visual skills that are built into construction toys.

■ B.C. Bones Empire State Building

(Toysmith $19.99 & up oooo) Our office is decorated with these stunning wooden structures that include the Eiffel Tower and Golden Gate Bridge. Our complaint with these beautiful sets is that there are no clear directions. The company insists that they make "puzzles," not construction sets. We suggested they put a cheat sheet up on their website. Good parent–child projects. 9 & up. (800) 356-0474.

■ City *2006*

(Lego Systems $19.99 & up) The consensus from our builders this year was, "no way a 5 year old could do this." That said, our older testers enjoyed the city-themed sets that include a **Fire** and **Construction** set. Our 8-year-old tester enjoyed building and playing with the **Fire Truck** ($19.99/214 pieces oooo) that comes with a movable ladder, two firefighters, and a boat for sea rescues. The same family had more difficulty with the **Fire Station** ($29.99/260 pieces oooo). One tester's parent commented that it's "like a boy's ultimate dollhouse," but the 6-year-old builder had trouble following the directions and the lift in the station "did not work well." Once assembled it was enjoyed as a pretend setting. Marked 5 & up, but most 5s will need assistance. (800) 223-8756.

■ Erector

(Brio $25–$200) One tester told us that the starter set was hard but "awesome," while another said it was "way too frustrating." That's how it is with Erector sets—you either love 'em or you don't. That said, your best bet is to try a smaller "starter" set. **Design Set 1** (oooo½) builds three different motorcycles. As much as we love the look of the **Landmark of the Worlds** (oo) models, even our most hard-core builders gave up in frustration. 10 & up. (888) 274-6869.

■ Flex K'nex Construction Squad
2006 PLATINUM AWARD

(K'nex $19.99 & up ooooo) An innovation this year—build the model flat on top of the instruction schematic, then "flex" it up into a three-dimensional form. Comes with instructions for four models, including a helicopter with a working pull string propeller and a truck. Our testers enjoyed making a hybrid of the two. Our tester noted that "the directions were much easier than the usual K'nex." Also new for **2006**, **Pirate Ship Park** ($49.99) Over two feet tall, this motorized kit can build three different amusement park-style rides with screaming sounds and swinging action. Not available for testing. Still top rated, last year's PLATINUM AWARD-winning **Big Air Ball Tower** ($99.99 ●●●●●)—a five-foot-tall ball run with 1350 pieces, so it's not for meek builders! We preferred this to the new version, **Loopin' Lizard** ($49.99 ●●●), with needlessly ugly-looking claws and toothy lizard head with open mouth. 10 & up. (800) 543-5639.

■ Gears! Gears! Gears! BLUE CHIP

(Learning Resources $20/$40 ●●●●●) These open-ended sets develop problem-solving skills as kids make their own moving machines with plastic gears. Our testers preferred the big set of gears to many of the newer themed sets. New for **2006**, **Wacky Wigglers** ($39.95 ●●●½). Got high marks from our 6-year-old tester who loved its big teeth, motorized glowing parts, and glow-in-the-dark eyeballs. He loves how it moves! We found it quite ugly. 5 & up. (800) 222-3909.

🛍 COMPARISON SHOPPER
Magnetic Building Sets **2006**

We love these open-ended magnetic sets. Put one on the coffee table and everyone will take a turn! Shop around because we found prices do vary. You want to bring home at least a medium-sized set (they range from $25 to $35). You won't go wrong with any of the basic sets of the following brands:

Magz-x (Progressive Trading ●●●●) Our testers gave high marks to their unique "x" design. (800) 903-6249.

Magbots Scorpion (Mindscope $19.95 ●●●●●) **2006** PLATINUM AWARD, a magnetically assembled robotic scorpion, was "awesome." "This is totally different from anything else," noted our tester. The embedded magnets make putting together this 96-piece futuristic scorpion a unique building experience. (800) 903-6249. **Geomag** (Ekos ⦿⦿⦿⦿)—new this year, gender-specific pastels (not our thing but if they get girls building, it's a plus). (888) 450-9858. **Supermag** (Plastwood ⦿⦿⦿⦿) has thinner and more tapered rods than most. Our testers, at first excited by their new model sets, gave them a so–so review: "Once you built the Ferrari the wheels really didn't work well enough to drive around and it felt like it was going to fall apart. We like the originals better!" (800) 770-9550. **MagStruction** (Educational Insights ⦿⦿⦿⦿) These sets come with plastic panels (similar to last year's Geomag panel set but with greater variation in sizes and shapes). 6 & up. (800) 933-3277.

■ Quadrilla 🏆*2006* PLATINUM AWARD

(HaPe $30 & up ⦿⦿⦿⦿⦿) A new line of imported marble run toys caught our attention for their design (they are beautiful). An unusual funnel-shaped piece is the center post of both the **Basic Set** ($49.95) and the big **Twist Set** ($149.95). Their **Rail Set** ($129.95) is also a beauty, with releases that add surprise motion. The first batch of these sets had some rough pieces that impeded the marble from rolling, but this issue has been addressed. If you got one of the old sets, exchange it. (800) 661-4142. (800) 654-6357.

■ Wild Hunters 🏆*2006* PLATINUM AWARD

(Lego Systems $29.95/630 pieces ⦿⦿⦿⦿⦿) The lion that you can make with this designer series set looks like it came from one of the Lego Parks. Designed with moving features, this is a lengthy and satisfying project for an experienced Lego builder. Marked 6 & up, we'd say more like 8 & up. Also top rated, **Star Wars ARC-170 Starfighter** 🏆*2006* PLATINUM AWARD ($39.99/ 396 pieces ⦿⦿⦿⦿⦿). Some of the best Lego sets this year came from the Star Wars line. Top marks went to this new fighter featured in the last film. Our testers also enjoyed the **Wookiee Catamaran** ($49.99 /376 pieces) which comes with Jedi lightsabers that really light up (very cool). 8 & up. **Editors' note:** Also noteworthy—**Lego Factory,** where you build your own creations online at lego.com and then they ship you the parts. (800) 223-8756.

Games

Classic and New Games

Now's the time when kids really begin to enjoy playing games with rules with both friends and family. Of course, winning is still more fun than losing, and playing by the rules isn't always easy. That's the bad news. The good news is that many of the best board games are both entertaining and educational. Many games can improve math, spelling, memory, and reading skills in a more enjoyable way than with the old flash card/extra workbook routine. Game playing also builds important cooperative social skills.

For 5s and 6s, now's the time for classic Blue Chip games such as:

Parcheesi	**Dominoes**	**Chutes and Ladders**
Checkers	**I Spy Bingo Lotto**	**Pick-up-Sticks**
Uno	**Trouble**	**What's My Name?**
Connect 4	**Lite-Brite**	

For 7s, 8s, and up, try classics such as:

Battleship Bingo	**Boggle**	**Chess**
Chinese Checkers	**Clue**	**Life**
Mancala	**Monopoly Jr.**	**Operation**
Othello	**Pictionary Jr.**	**Scattergories Jr.**
Scrabble	**Sorry**	**Twister**
Upwards Quarto!	**Yahtzee**	

For electronic games, see pp. 141, 159, 160, 289.

■ Bumparena 2006

(Cranium $16.95 **oooo** ½) Assemble the plastic sloped playing board and get ready to place "bumpers" that will divert or block your opponents' balls from reaching the scoring pit! There's strategy involved, as well as reading the visual symbols. "This was one of the best games that we ever played! We really liked it because it was different from any other game that we have ever seen," wrote one family. One mom complained about storing the game. For 2–4 players. Fun for 7 & up. (877) 272-6486.

■ Castle Keep 2006 PLATINUM AWARD

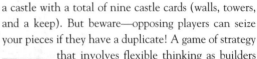

(Gamewright $11.99 ●●●●●) The object is to be the first to complete a castle with a total of nine castle cards (walls, towers, and a keep). But beware—opposing players can seize your pieces if they have a duplicate! A game of strategy that involves flexible thinking as builders must match geometric and color attributes. 8 & up. For younger players, **Leaping Lizards** ($9.99 ●●●●) is also an attribute game. The novel "game board" is actually a long shoestring and beads. With each turn players choose a "lucky" picture token that will help determine how many spaces they can move. Watch out, if you roll a sad face you move backwards! This can be frustrating for younger players. With adult participation, 5s & up. (800) 638-7568.

■ Charoodles 2006

(ThinkFun $24.99 ●●●●) Our families with older kids, 8 to 12, really enjoyed this new version of Charades that includes "props" (a foam ball, tube, square, and plastic cup) for acting out one of the 3,000 charades on the play cards. Timer included. A good choice for a family party. (800) 468-1864.

■ Make 'N' Break 2006

(Ravensburger $29.99 ●●●½) Players pull a card and must reproduce block structures within the time limit set on a timer. Our 9- and 10-year-old testers found the game to be too easy, but it was challenging for 7s. The game, however, is marked 8 & up. "More complicated cards would be a plus." 8 & up. (800) 886-1236.

Tiddlywinks, Anyone?

We have never seen so many variations on Tiddlywinks! Here are our favorites:

■ Alfredo's Food Fight 2006

(Fundex $19.99 ●●●●½) Set up Alfredo the chef with his Velcro plates and apron; push the button on the base and he turns. while players use "forks" to launch meatballs covered with yarn spaghetti strands that stick. Our school-aged testers thought this was pure "silliness" and fun to play. For 2–4 players. 5 & up. (800) 486-9787.

■ Bialo 2006

(HaPe $14.95 oooo½) Beautifully crafted with bamboo wood, the object here is to launch your wooden play piece into one of the colored circles (this determines how you move around the board). First to complete the outer circle wins. Requires finesse rather than strength. 5 & up.

Two other notable sets: **Frog Hoppers** (International Playthings $5.95 oooo), easiest of the new crop. See p. 93 for full review. **Ants in the Pants** (Hasbro $9.99 oooo) —same concept with a SpongeBob theme. (888) 836-7025.

■ Storefront Bingo 2006 PLATINUM AWARD

(eeBoo $14.99 ooooo) Each playing board is a different store. Dealer draws a picture tile and names object; player who has the store for that item calls out name of store. Winner is first to match and fill card pictures. Also new, **Life on Earth Matching Game** ($14.99 oooo), a concentration-style matching game with pleasing images of birds, snakes, kangaroos, and other earthly creatures. Also top rated, **Candy Matching** ($12.95 oooo) with yummy-looking candies to match. All 5 & up. (212) 222-0823.

■ Da Vinci's Challenge 2006 PLATINUM AWARD

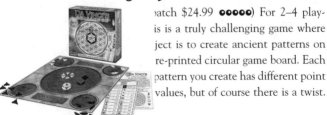

...atch $24.99 ooooo) For 2–4 play-...is is a truly challenging game where ...ject is to create ancient patterns on ...re-printed circular game board. Each ...pattern you create has different point ...values, but of course there is a twist.

Your opponents can block your patterns. "The game became more interesting as more pieces were put on the board and sometimes a bigger pattern emerges when you're not paying attention!" They say 8 & up, we'd say more like 10 & up. The connection to Da Vinci? He studied the Egyptian symbol called the Flower of Life. (800) 232-7427.

■ The Family Fun Game 2006

(Cranium $19.95 ●●●●½) Designed for teams of grown-ups and kids to play together, players use visual memory, creativity, factual information, cooperation, and communication skills to win. For example, with timer going, a player must sculpt a turtle of clay; or recall sequence of a pattern without looking; or name five zoo animals, each new one beginning with letter of last one named. There's plenty of thinking, doing, and laughing, too! 7 & up. Still top rated and geared for younger kids, PLATINUM AWARD-winner **Balloon Lagoon** ($19.99 ●●●●● 5 & up) and **Cranium Cadoo for Kids** ($19.99 ●●●●●) are similar to the new game but this one is played by kids with other kids. 7 & up. (877) 272-6486.

■ Groovy Girl Pet Show Game 2006

(Briarpatch $19.99 ●●) Our 8- and 9-year old Groovy Girl fans found the instructions confusing and the game play boring. We had similar complaints about the directions for last year's **Groovy Girl Sleepover** game. Similar poor results for clarity of directions and game play for new **Scooby Doo Coolsville 500 Game** and the really neat looking **Robot!** game. 6 & up. (800) 232-7427.

■ Raceway 57 and Chaturanga
2006 PLATINUM AWARDS

(Front Porch Classics $74.95 ●●●●●) Our older testers loved both of these new games, **Chaturanga** ($44.95 ●●●●●), an Indian game, is said to be the earliest form of chess. It's a strategy game with an element of chance, as players roll wooden dice and play one on one or in teams. **Raceway 57** has a handsome track, mini-cars, and metallic playing boards. Players race to be the first to finish three laps without running out of fuel, tires, and suspension. They say 8 & up— we'd say more like 10 & up. (206) 826-3202.

■ Pandabo *2006* PLATINUM AWARD

(HaPe $9.95 ●●●●●) Beautifully crafted, this is a balancing game with a wooden panda holding up round, half-round, and square rods. Fine motor skills help as players take turns trying not to be the one who upsets the stack. They say 4 & up, we'd say most fours will have trouble doing this. More like a good choice for 5–8. Also clever, **Cagola** ($9.95 ●●●●), another balancing game with a swinging "boat" and small pieces that fall overboard! We like them both, but Pandabo is better. (800) 661-4142.

■ Poppin' Puzzlers *2006*

(International Playthings $17.99 ●●●●½) This is a new twist on your old game of Perfection. Only two players use separate sections of the board to try to be the first to put all their playing pieces into the slots before the timer pops the playing pieces. Winner is the one with the fewest playing pieces left. 5 & up. (800) 445-8347.

■ Pretty Pretty Princess Cinderella Game *2006*

(Milton Bradley $12.99 ●●●●) The playing board fits together like a puzzle and girls play to "win" necklaces, rings, and tiaras from the jewelry box in the middle. Kids loved wearing their winnings and the only problem was keeping the game pieces for the next game. 5 & up. (888) 836-7025.

■ Star Wars *2006*

(Milton Bradley $15.99 & up) In honor of the last installment of the series, Hasbro has brought out several classic games with a SW theme. The **Star Wars Saga Edition Monopoly** ($29.99 ●●●●½) is great fun with features that span the series including Darth Maul, Darth Vader, Yoda. The board takes you through the galaxy. For parents who enjoyed **Stratego** ($15.99 ●●●●) or **Risk** ($24.99 ●●●●), your kids will enjoy these versions with characters from all six movies. We'd skip the **Chess Set** ($29.99 ●●); the pieces are too difficult to distinguish for young chess players). (888) 836-7025.

■ Toot and Otto Game

(Thinkfun \$9.99 ●●●●½) A simple strat-
egy game with twenty-four plastic tiles,
with "O"s and "T"s. One player must spell
Toot, the other *Otto* as they take turns
dropping letters into the game
tower to block their opponent and spell out their name. Quick and
easy to learn. 5 & up. (800) 468-1864.

■ Who? What? Where? Jr. 2006 PLATINUM AWARD

(Pazow \$19.95 ●●●●●) Each player takes a *who*, a *what*,
and a *where* card, which combine to ask you to draw a cer-
tain image—Abraham Lincoln fishing in Paris, for example. Players get points for guessing each other's
drawings. A fun family game for 7 & up. A
follow-up to last year's PLATINUM AWARD-
winning game for 12 & up. (415) 885-5006.

■ Zig Zag 2006

(Educational Insights \$19.99 ●●●●) The object
here is to get four of your pegs in a row. Of
course that's easier said than done, since your
opponent will also be trying to stop you with a
variety of road blocks that will make you zigzag!
Marked 7 & up, yet our tween and adult testers found
this to be a high strategy game that they wanted to play repeatedly.
(800) 933-3277.

Word Games
■ 4-Way Spelldown!

(Cadaco \$19.99 ●●●●●) Roll the two "letter" dice
and then try to make a word with the letters thrown
and as many of the 10 letter keys already on the play-
ing board. For example, if you roll a "t" and an "o," and you have a "y"
and an "s," you can spell "toys." The first to flip all of
their keys wins. Marked 6 & up, but we'd say more like
8 and up. PLATINUM AWARD '05. (800) 621-5426.

■ Maya & Miguel Word Scramble 2006

(Briarpatch \$19.95 ●●●●) Like last year's **I Spy
Word Scramble,** this has a big game board with
sliding tiles. Players take turns drawing a card,

choosing a letter or image on the card, and spelling that word by sliding letters before the timer runs out. Inspired by the PBS TV show, this game can be played both in Spanish and English. 7 & up. (800) 232-7427.

Top-Rated Card Games

Aside from a deck of cards for a fierce game of Rummy, War, or Old Maid, don't overlook deck-specific classics such as **Uno** or **Mille Bourne.** Here are other card games to play that are fun and quick and even have some learning power built in:

■ There's a Moose in the House

(Gamewright $9.99 ооооо) One of the most innovative card games we've played in years. The cards have pictures of empty rooms, doors, and moose in the same rooms. The object is to place as many moose as possible in your opponents' house of cards. The player with the fewest moose at the end of the game, wins. Easy to learn and a lot of fun to play! 2–5 players. 15 mins. 8 & up. PLATINUM AWARD '05. (800) 638-7568.

■ Whoonu *2006* PLATINUM AWARD

(Cranium $16.95 ооооо) It's all about knowing the people you are playing with; players take turns at being the "whoozit" and others get points by guessing what objects named on the playing cards the "Whoozit" likes best. Even testers who do not like board games love this card game for three or more players. Still top-rated, **Zigity** ($12.95 оооо). Visual discrimination and word and number play are all part of the fun. 8 & up. (877) 272-6486.

Geography Games

■ Map Tangle *2006*

(Borderline Games $24.95) Think Twister, but here the play mat is 6' x 5'5" with a marvelous map of the world! We really love the design of the giant playing mat and the idea of cooperative play by teammates who help each other find the two locations they must stand on while avoiding a "Map Tangle" and falling down! This came too late to test with families and we are not sure if the game play is going to be satisfying. We suspect kids will be making up their own rules. Still top rated, **Borderline** ($9.95 ●●●●). Whether you play with the USA or new World Edition, here's a painless way to make maps fun! The object is to get rid of all your cards, but you can only put cards down on a card that "borders" the state, body of water, or country in your hand. If you don't know, flip your card for a map that shows the borderlines. A no-tears-or-fears geography game! 8 & up. (973) 761-6260.

■ Great States

(International Playthings $20 ●●●●) This U.S.A. map game includes a board and cards that help young readers learn their state capitals, birds, flowers, and landmarks. What we really liked is that you use the map to find the answers—you're not expected to know them all already. Older players will enjoy playing with the timer, but it's not essential. 7 & up. We'd pass on the Junior edition, which doesn't work as well as the original. (800) 445-8347.

■ The Scrambled States 2 *2006*

(Gamewright $6 ●●●●) There are 50 state cards, each with four different attributes for that card (region, population, land mass, and color). Fifteen cards are placed face up, one card from the draw pile is turned over. The first player to "slap" one of the 15 cards that has a shared attribute with the face card, wins that round. A fun way to introduce kids to geography. Some parents may find it light on content, but it's a good way to get the subject introduced in a nonthreatening manner. 6 & up. Still recommended, the board edition. (800) 638-7568.

■ This Land Is Your Land USA Map

(eeBoo $16 ●●●●) Hang this handsome laminated picture map in your family or child's room. It comes with 50 stickers that kids use to mark places they have visited or locations where friends and family live. (212) 222-0823.

Math Games and Equipment

■ Buy It Right Shopping Game

(Learning Resources $19.95 ●●●●½) Making change is not always easy for kids who don't get to handle more than their milk money. This game involves a lot of buying and selling and some flexible thinking. Kids roll three numeral dice and decide whether they want to call a 4, 2, 1, \$4.21, or \$1.24 . . . a choice that depends on whether they are buying or selling. Unlike most shopping games, which are aimed at girls, this is a gender-free game. 6 & up. For working on simple addition and subtraction, **Sum Swamp** (\$14.95 ●●●●); for working on place-value skills, **Operation Space Chase** (\$13.95 ●●●●); for help with fractions, **Pie in the Sky** (\$12.95 ●●●●); and for telling time, **Tick, Tac, Tock!** (\$14.95 ●●●●). 7 & up. (800) 222-3909.

■ Dot 2 Dot Dinosaurs *2006*

(Lauri \$11 ●●●●½) Six dinosaur cards that kids lace by the numbers. These are sequenced from 1to 26; **Farm Animals** go from 1 to 22; wild animals in the **Animal Alphabet** set go from A to Z. These will appeal to both genders and develop sequencing skills as well as fine motor skills. Marked 4 & up, but we'd say more like 5 & up since the numbers go into the teens. (800) 451-0520.

■ 4-Way Countdown

(Cadaco \$19.95 ●●●●●) This PLATINUM AWARD winner just got more interesting. The object is to be the first player to turn over all ten of your pegs by rolling dice. Players may add, subtract, multiply, or divide the numbers they roll in order to get the number they need. 6 & up. New for *2006*, **Count Across** (●●●●), toss the dice and add or multiply. Cover the matching numeral on the playing board. Winner is first to get four in a row. (800) 621-5426.

■ Mad Math BLUE CHIP

(Patrix \$22.95 ●●●●●) If math facts are a source of tension in your house, here are two games for working on those skills. Mad Math is a board game that has addition facts on one side and multiplication on the other. The goal is to get three pawns in a row on the board. You collect spaces by rolling the dice and finding the corresponding math fact on the playing board. The board is self-correcting, which is a plus. (888) 834-2380.

■ Maya Madness

(Gamewright \$12.99 ●●●●) A great game for working on negative and positive numbers. To claim their "secret" number token, players must add and subtract numbers on the draw pile to reach their number. So, if your token is a 2 and the card showing is a 6, you could play a 4 card to claim your token. First player to claim five tokens wins. (800) 638-7568.

■ Old Century Shut-the-Box

(Old Century $49.95 ●●●●●) Here's a handsome wooden chest with numbered tiles that players flip after they roll the big wooden dice. Object is to turn over all the tiles or to have the lowest number of points left when you can no longer make a move. There's room for flexible thinking here since a roll of 7 and 2 means you can flip any combination of 9. Fun for reinforcing addition and place value. Pricey, but the kind of game you'll want to leave out in your living room. 8 & up. PLATINUM AWARD '04. (206) 826-3202.

■ Rapido 2006

(HaPe $14.95 ●●●●½) An elegant sequencing game. Players compete to pick up colored wooden marbles in special cylinders matching the pattern on their playing paddle. Seeing the pattern and responding quickly calls for good eye-hand coordination and memory. Fun quick rounds for 2–4 players. They say 4 & up, but we'd say more like 5–8. (800) 661-4142.

Math Manipulatives

Concrete materials give kids a greater understanding of counting and calculating. Don't rush to take these materials away from kids. They help make the transition to abstract thinking easier. A BLUE CHIP choice is **Unifix Ready for Math Kit** (Didax $12.95 set of 100 ●●●●●). Beginning math students use these cubes, book, and stickers for understanding early math concepts. We'd recommend pairing them with their activity books. (800) 458-0024.

■ Talking Clever Clock

(Learning Resources $34.95 ●●●●½) Hands down, the best electronic clock for teaching kids how to tell time. Our nine-year-old tester had given up on ever learning how to tell time—but within minutes he was having fun using the clock that has self-checking features with both digital and analog clock faces. 5 & up. (800) 222-3909.

Math Electronic Quiz Machines

Most math-quiz machines are like electronic flash cards—good for picking up speed, but if your child doesn't have the basic concepts down, these machines won't help. **What to Avoid:** many machines require that two-digit answers be entered with tens first. This is contrary to the way kids are taught, especially when regrouping is involved, so machines may be confusing. Our best advice: try them before you buy.

■ Talking Math Mat Challenge

(Learning Resources $29.95 ●●●●½) Kids step on this talking mat to answer math quizzes programmed at two levels of difficulty. Level One asks kids to find the numeral named and do simple addition and subtraction. More fun than flash cards, but not that different in content. It's for kids who are ready for drill. Labeled 4–7, most fours will do only the numeral game. Far more appropriate for mid-first and second graders. Forget the newer **Factor Frenzy (●●●)** and **Light 'N Strike Math (●●●).** Both require too many steps to enter an answer—totally frustrating. We passed on the new-for-**2006 Alpha-Bug Step 'n Spell (●●●)** that became too difficult too quickly and was not especially responsive. (800) 222-3909.

Other Electronic Equipment and Learning Tools

■ FLY 2006 PLATINUM AWARD

(LeapFrog $99 ●●●●●) Truly an innovation in electronic learning toys! FLY is a computer in a pen that works with special paper to create a variety of options: a working calculator that you draw, a translator (great for beginner language students), and we loved the musical keyboard you can draw and then play on your paper. There are also games that involve special baseball trading cards. All very George Jetson . . . will appeal most to tweens. (800) 701-5327.

■ Leap Pad Plus Writing Learning System

(LeapFrog $39.99 ●●●●) We were delighted that many Dr. Seuss classics, such as *Fox in Socks* and *One Fish Two Fish*, have been adapted for this platform or the Leap Pad. Unfortunately, this year there were only new licensed titles (**Bratz, Madagasacar,** etc.). We still believe this is a lost opportunity of bringing great literature together with innovative technology. Kids who are learning to write their letters and numbers will like this electronic workbook with stylus that really writes. Although the toy is marked 3 & up, the skills are more appropriate for 5s & up. (800) 701-5327.

 COMPARISON SHOPPER
Talking Globes

Although less expensive than they used to be, they don't work as well. Why ask questions that can't be answered by looking at the globe? Our testers liked pushing the buttons but quickly felt frustrated. The LeapFrog **Explorer Smart Globe** (LeapFrog $99 ⊙⊙) comes with a sensor pen and lots of information (the pace is frenetic). (800) 701-5327. The **GeoSafari World** (Educational Insights $59.95 ⊙⊙⊙) has 5,000 questions, but again you'd need an atlas to answer many of them. (800) 933-3277.

Puzzles

Putting jigsaw puzzles together calls for visual perception, eye-hand coordination, patience, and problem-solving skills. During their early school years, kids should build puzzles from 25 pieces to 50- and 100-plus pieces.

Beginners' Puzzles—Under 50 pieces

■ **A–Z Panels BLUE CHIP**

(Lauri $9.99 ⊙⊙⊙⊙⊙) Not only does fitting the rubbery letters in and out of the puzzle frame help kids learn to know and name the letters, but handling the 3-D letters also gives kids a feel for their shapes. Also, **Kids Perception Puzzle** ($7.99 ⊙⊙⊙⊙⊙); figures in slightly different poses that help kids look at small differences, just as they must when reading words that look almost alike, such as *cap* and *cup*. 4–7. (800) 451-0520.

■ **Alphabet & Number Puzzle Pairs** *2006*

(eeBoo $14.95 ⊙⊙⊙⊙) A handsome set of two-piece puzzles with easy-

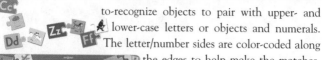

to-recognize objects to pair with upper- and lower-case letters or objects and numerals. The letter/number sides are color-coded along the edges to help make the matches. Illustrated by Saxton Freymann, well-known artist of *How are You Peeling?* and *Food for Thought*. These can be used for simple games or solo puzzle play. (212) 222-0823.

■ Parquetry Blocks Super Set BLUE CHIP

(Learning Resources $26.95 ○○○○○) Thirty-two geometrically shaped tiles are arranged on top of 20 colorful patterns. Advanced players can use tiles without the patterns. Develops skills in matching and sequencing patterns—skills that are needed in putting letters together to make words. 5–8. (800) 222-3909.

Intermediate & Advanced—
50 &100+ Pieces and Shaped Puzzles

■ Bug Tumble *2006*

(The Orb Factory $14.99 ○○○○) The graphics of this box don't do justice to the stunning puzzle inside. Much like a DK book, the collage of bugs, worms, and other creepy things will appeal to bug-fascinated kids. While there are 48 pieces, it is still a very challenging puzzle with a pleasing oversized 2' x 3' size. Puzzle comes with a big poster chockful of info on the creepy crawlies in the puzzle. Marked 4 & up, but we'd say most 6s will find it challenging. Really depends on the child. (800) 741-0089.

■ Jumpers & Crawlers *2006*

(Ravensburger $10 ○○○○) Look carefully at this 60-piece puzzle and you'll see all kinds of creatures sitting in and slithering along the branches and leaves of the jungle. Also special, **Wildlife in Africa (○○○○)**. And for a challenge, **3x49 Puzzles** ($8.50 ○○○○), three 49-piece puzzles (which you sort out first by using the different patterns on the puzzle backs). Our testers liked the dinosaur and jungle motifs. (800) 886-1236.

COMPARISON SHOPPER
USA & World Map Puzzles

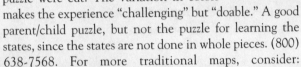

The Scrambled States of America ~~2000~~ (Ceaco $9.95 oooo): Our testers loved the unusual ways the pieces of this 150-piece puzzle were cut. The variation in colors makes the experience "challenging" but "doable." A good parent/child puzzle, but not the puzzle for learning the states, since the states are not done in whole pieces. (800)

638-7568. For more traditional maps, consider: **Puzzibilities USA Puzzles** (Small World Toys $20 oooo), a classic wooden version with landmarks, capitals, and a vinyl sheet for arranging pieces out of the frame, is a good choice. 6 & up. (800) 421-4153. **Wonderfoam Giant USA Puzzle Map** (Chenille Kraft $44 oooo): testers enjoyed putting together this giant-sized (4' w x 2½' h) floor puzzle with 73 thick foam pieces. State names are printed on the map with 16 landmarks (state capitals marked by a star but not named—you might want to add the capitals with a marker on the back of each state). Also, **Wonderfoam Giant World Puzzle Map** ($44 oooo). (800) 621-1261. (800) 284-3948.

Activity Kits and Art Supplies

For school-age kids, art class is seldom long enough. Besides, such classes are usually teacher directed, with little chance for kids to explore their own ideas. Giving kids the tools and space for art projects at home provides more than pure entertainment. Art helps kids develop their ability to communicate ideas and feelings visually, to refine eye-hand skills, and to learn how to stick with a task.

> ### ☼ BASIC GEAR CHECKLIST
> ### FOR EARLY SCHOOL YEARS ARTISTS
>
> ✓ Crayons, chalk, colored pencils, and pastels
> ✓ Watercolor and acrylic paints
> ✓ Watercolor markers
> ✓ Paper for origami   ✓ Loom (weaving, beads)
> ✓ Sewing supplies   ✓ Sand art supplies
> ✓ Lanyard kits   ✓ Colored wax
> ✓ Rug hooking supplies   ✓ Needlepoint supplies
> ✓ Woodworking supplies   ✓ Cutting/pasting supplies
> ✓ Flower press   ✓ Fabric paints
> ✓ Stamps   ✓ Air-hardening clay

Activity and Craft Kits

Again this year there seemed to be more craft kits than ever before. We had our network of testers get to work—with a mixed bag of results. Some kits that looked fantastic were disappointing; others were surprisingly good. Our testers complained that the packaging was deceiving, making products look bigger than they actually were. Both boys and girls love making things they can play with, wear, or give as gifts. Many require adult assistance. Here's a sampling of our testing. For even more reviews, visit our website.

Drawing, Painting, Coloring, and Gluing
■ Ceramic Allowance Bank

(Creativity for Kids $14.99 ●●●●) A chubby white ceramic pig ready to paint and hold spare change or allowance. It has an easy-to-pull-out rubber stopper, so kids don't need to break the bank when they want to spend some of their savings! Includes a "chores" booklet with star stickers . . . the idea being that they earn their allowance. We have mixed feelings about paying kids for chores . . . but we do like the idea of encouraging them to save their pennies. Also top rated, **Wake Up! Alarm Clock** ($17.99 ●●●●½)—a perfect back-to-school present! Both 7 & up. (800) 311-8684.

■ Fast Car Race Cars *2006*

(Creativity for Kids $14.99 ●●●●) Comes with three wooden cars with pull-back mechanisms that kids can paint (our kids used markers so that they use the cars sooner). Some of the included stickers did not stay put, but our testers still found these satisfying to use. Set up a roadway with some empty small boxes for simulated crashes and road races. (800) 311-8684.

■ Monster Art Center 2006

(Alex $69.99 oooo½) Imagine the thrill of opening this double-hinged art center with trays to the right, trays to the left, and trays below! It comes loaded with 30 fine-tip markers, 28 colored pencils, 26 crayons, 24 oil pastels, 12 watercolors, brushes, pencil, glue, and palette. The crayons aren't as juicy as Crayola, but the materials and kit would be a dream gift to most art-minded kids! They say 4 & up, we'd say this is more like a gift for 6 & up. (800) 666-2539.

■ Beaded Dresser Set 2006

(Creativity for Kids $14.99 oooo) Set comes with a small mirror set in wood, a ceramic heart frame and heart-shaped box, pastel colored beads, ribbons, and glue. A straightforward project that requires kids to spread the glue out and then spill beads onto the glue for decoration. The light beads have a "princess/fairy" look to them and will appeal to younger girls. 6 & up. (800) 311-8684.

■ My Star Box 2006 PLATINUM AWARD

(Balitono $19.95 ooooo) Our tester painted and then gave this star-shaped box as a gift for Mother's Day. A real hit! A keepsake for any gift giving season. Also new, **My Pinball Game Kit,** ($19.95 oooo½). Finding kits that will appeal to boys as well as girls is not always easy. This one was a hit with our eight-year old tester. Okay, it won't compete with the electronic versions, but it will be unique! Also fun for dramatic play, **My Doghouse Kit** ($19.95 oooo), with pooch, house, and feeding bowl. Still top rated, **My Horse Stable & Corral Kit** ($25 ooooo). PLATINUM AWARD '05. (609) 936-8807.

■ Paint & Play Dino Set 2006

(Wild Republic $12.99 oooo) Four detailed white plastic models come in this painting kit. Our eleven-year-old tester took pains to do all kinds of details. Our five-year-old ran out of paint! Once complete, they are ready for play or display. Also nice, an African set that includes an elephant, lion, giraffe, and leopard. Marked 3 & up—we'd say this is a better choice for older children. (800) 800-9678

■ Scrapbook and Memory Box Gift Set

(Creativity for Kids $28.99 ●●●●●) Scrapbook fans are going to love this commodious box with picture-frame cover that holds a spiral-bound scrapbook plus 16 sheets of patterned paper, stickers, stencil, scalloped scissors, paper punch, stamper, pens, glue stick, and great ideas. This will appeal to older girls ready to memorialize a school year, trip, or big event. Marked 7 & up, but was coveted by our 10- and 11-year-old testers. PLATINUM AWARD '05. New for **2006**, **It's My Life Soccer Scrapbook** ($19.99 ●●●●) comes with velvet art embellishment and themed stickers. 7 & up. (800) 311-8684.

■ Ceramic Swirl Art **2006** PLATINUM AWARD

(Alex $24.99 ●●●●●) Classic spin art type toys are one of our all-time favorites so you can imagine how excited we were to find this new "spin" that includes ceramic plates and tiles that attach to the platform. You can set your designs by baking them. Adult supervision a must. Also fun and messy, **Tie Dye Party** ($19.99 ●●●●) but we'd skip **Plaster Caster** ($44.99 ●●), which looked amazingly cool but we could not get a figure to form that wasn't cracked. 8 & up. (800) 666-2539.

Candles, Cooking, and Mixing

■ Beeswax Candles BLUE CHIP

(Creativity for Kids $16 ●●●●●) The best candle making kit—fun to do and makes great presents. Comes with five sheets of colored wax that you can cut to make different-sized candles. 6 & up. (800) 311-8684. We'd skip Alex's **Candle Painting** set, which our testers found disappointing—"my candle doesn't look like the box." 6 & up.

■ Crayola Gadget Headz Robot Lab 🏷️*2006*

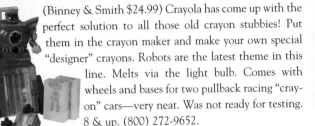

(Binney & Smith $24.99) Crayola has come up with the perfect solution to all those old crayon stubbies! Put them in the crayon maker and make your own special "designer" crayons. Robots are the latest theme in this line. Melts via the light bulb. Comes with wheels and bases for two pullback racing "crayon" cars—very neat. Was not ready for testing. 8 & up. (800) 272-9652.

■ Wax Works BLUE CHIP

(Chenille Kraft $5.49 **ooooo**) These waxy sticks can be twisted and shaped into free-form sculptures. Great for developing fine motor skills. 5 & up. (800) 621-1261.

Beads, Jewelry, & Accessory Kits

Using beads is more than engaging in a creative craft; it's helping kids develop fine-motor skills.

■ Funky and Inspire Bead Chests
🏷️*2006* PLATINUM AWARDS

(Bead Bazaar $19.99 **ooooo**) A dream gift for a beader! **Funky Bead Chest** is a tall, brightly painted wooden chest with three lined drawers comes topped with a juicy collection of wooden beads, charms, and colorful string to match. Equally neat, **Inspire Bead Chest (ooooo)**, same idea with words on the front of the box. If you're having a party, consider **Totally Fun Beads** ($18.99 **oooo**½); comes with 30 charms, 1000+ of beads, and 30 strings. Plenty for a group! Our testers also raved about this company's **Hemp** and **Mystic** bead kits ($9.99 **oooo**) that will appeal to tweens, teens, and their mothers! (800) 838-1769.

■ Comfy Chic Flip Flops 🏷️*2006*

(Creativity for Kids $17.99 **oooo**) Set comes with two pairs of flip flops (sizes 11–2 and 4–7). The project is fun to do. One set comes with chenille yarn, the other with confetti ribbon that you simply wrap around the upper part of the flip-flop. "We got our yarn tangled up but it still came out fine"—then you paste a flower to the top and you're done. (Be forewarned—the flip-flops and yarns are not

identical, which can create a problem with some siblings/friends).
(800) 311-8684.

■ Sand Bands 2006

(Alex $14.95 ●●●●) "Not for beginning
beaders" noted one parent. Kit comes with
a variety of seashells, beads, and hemp
string for making ten bracelets and rings to
wear with your beachy outfits! Marked 8 & up, more like 10 and up.
Bead Bash ($13.99 ●●●) & **Just Pearls** ($13.99 ●●●) got mixed
reviews. These kits would fare better if they told kids to put nail polish on the beading string, which frays otherwise (the most common
complaint). (800) 666-2539.

■ EZ 2 Quikrochet 2006 PLATINUM AWARD

(The Bead Shop $15.99 ●●●●●) Remember as a kid making yarn
snakes with a wooden spool knitter? This kit updates that craft by

including beads to work into your creations. Comes with four pastel sets of
elastic and a plentiful supply of glass
beads. Also new for 2006, **Wish
Weaver** ($9.99 ●●●●) Use hemp or
colored twine to braid with glass beads
for making 20+ bracelets. Fine motor
skills, following directions, and patience are rewarded with good-
looking payoffs. **World Colors** ($19.99 ●●●●) is a more advanced
kit with four colors of hemp to weave with a generous supply of shells,
bells, wooden beads, and painted beads for bracelets, necklaces, and
rings. *Editors' Note:* All of these new kits are marked 8 & up, but
we found that kids often needed help getting started. Past favorites
that are also easier to do: **Alphadot Bracelet Kit** ($19.99 ●●●●●),
with 85 Alphadot beads that slide onto three thin watch-like bands;
Ribbon Raps ($14 ●●●●●), has beads to string on gossamer ribbon;
and **Mystix** ($16 ●●●●), which includes semi-precious stones. 8 &
up. (800) 492-3237.

■ Clikits 2006

(Lego Systems $11.95 & up ●●●●●) We found a real age divide with
Clikits this year. Younger girls love them, but our 9-year-olds felt the
kits were "too young looking." That said, Clikits are great for developing fine motor skills along with creativity. Flower-shaped beads snap
together with larger cutout flowers and leaves. New for 2006, our
tester's favorite is the **Pretty in Pink Beauty Set** ($19.99 ●●●●½)

with customizable mirror, brush, comb, cases, picture frame, bracelets, and holders for dressing table. 7 & up. (800) 223-8756.

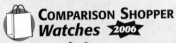

COMPARISON SHOPPER
Watches 2006

Watch It! 2006 **PLATINUM AWARD** (Alex $24.95 ●●●●●) —technically not much of a craft kit, but a huge hit with our testers. The kit comes with a watch and seven different colorful ribbon bands. 6 & up. For older girls who can tell time (the watch has numbers only on the quarter hours) will enjoy **Charm Watch** (Klutz $21.95 ●●●●), a silvery linked bracelet that comes with charms and beads to attach. Requires a great deal of fine-motor skill to do. 12 & up.

■ **Musical Jewelry Box** 2006 **BLUE CHIP**
(Alex $19.99 ●●●●●) This is the quintessential jewelry box with spinning ballerina. Comes with sparkling gems to glue on top and a frou-frou tutu of pink tulle on a hot pink ribbon to attach to the box. A very girlie-girlie gift, but likely to win the oo-ooohs and ah-h-h-hs of beginners. The box is finished in pink so there's not a lot to do, but it's showy and quick. 6 & up. (800) 666-2539.

COMPARISON SHOPPER
Retro Jewelry 2006

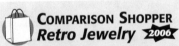

Both The Bead Shop and Alex came out with plastic jewelry that you paint. These throwback kits got rave reviews from Moms and so-so reviews from kids. With both the **Paint Ice Jewelry** (Alex $13.99 ●●●●) and **Pop Art Painted Jewelry** (The Bead Shop $16 ●●●●) you get an assortment of chunky rings and bracelets that you paint from behind. The paint in the Alex kit is more vibrant but our testers also liked the nail polish that comes with the Pop Art kit. All moms agreed that they would use the jewelry even if their daughters did not. Marked 8 & up, but maybe it should be 30 & up! Alex (800) 666-2539/The Bead Shop (800) 492-3237.

■ Friendship Wheel 2006

(Alex $13.99 oooo) Remember braiding friendship bracelets in multicolored threads? Well, they are back, only now there is a weaving wheel that guides the process and takes just a few minutes to master. Kit comes with enough for 10 bracelets and two wheels. Kids can pass the wheels around and help make all of them, or bring home a wheel for each guest. Also a great choice for playdates or keeping hands busy on a trip. (800) 666-2539.

Knit One, Purl One— Knitting & Crocheting 2006

Knitting continues to be a big trend for adults and kids. While we believe that nothing replaces a real instructor for knitting, these kits will appeal to kids. Here are our top picks:

I Knit this Poncho! (The Bead Shop $16 oooo½) This is a simple knitting project for the fashion conscious tween. Knitters make two panels with the basic garter stitch and then put them together following the simple instructions. Comes with one set of thick needles and heavy yarn. (800) 492-3237.

Knitting Circle (Alex $39.99 oooo½) Designed for four kids, this includes four pairs of chunky wooden knitting needles, funky colorful thick yarn, and directions for 6-foot-long scarves and fluffy little hats. There are easy-to-follow directions and results are quick since the needles and yarn are big! 7 & up. Also top-rated, **Granny Squares Crochet Activity Kit** 2006 (Alex $19.95 oooo) Somehow this kit makes doing Granny Squares look new and cool. It must be the brightly colored yarn and the really neat lunch box-style box. Their **Hip Hoop Knitting** ($15.95 ooo), however, with super-sized hoop did less well—our testers found that the included thick yarn kept getting caught in the hoop. 8 & up. (800) 666-2539.

Weaving

■ Weaving Fashion Weaving Loom 🏷2006

(Alex $18 ●●●●) Cleverly packaged with very current chunky, fluffy yarn, this kit gives weaving an updated look. Our testers gave high ratings to both this kit and the **Giant Weaving Loom** ($29.99 ●●●●). Must be threaded but easy to use. (800) 666-2539.

■ Potholders & Other Loopy Projects

(Klutz $16.95 ●●●●●) Don't look any further, this is the best potholder set on the market. The supplies are vibrant and inviting and the book really does explain what to do. Weaving not only develops eye-hand coordination, it also involves following patterns and problem solving. Marked 6 & up, we'd say more like 7 & up. PLATINUM AWARD '04. (800) 737-4123.

Musical Instruments

■ Barbie "Jam with Me" Guitar 🏷2006

(Kid Design $39.99 ●●●½) We sent this guitar to a family of professional musicians. "It's actually a fairly musical toy. The sounds aren't bad (often toys like these have really tacky, cheesy sounds). Not all of the samples are great, but enough are pleasant and cool-sounding to make it fun. The microphone on the headset isn't that powerful, but it does work, and has an echo available, which is cool. This isn't a toy for someone who is serious about music or learning. But it is fun for a child who enjoys music, and gives them a chance to dabble and pretend." Another test family agreed on all points above, including the size of the headset. 4 & up. (888) 867-8697.

■ Chimalong & Mini Chimalong BLUE CHIP

(Woodstock Percussion $20 & up ●●●●●) The tone of this metal-chime xylophone is lovely, and it can be played by number/color or musical notation. Reinforces reading from left to right. Mini version is not as sweet sounding. Marked 3 & up; we'd say 4–8. New for 🏷2006, a **Concertina** ($29.99 ●●●●) that makes real music. Kids need big enough hands to use the buttons to play the notes and a stick-to-it mindset to figure it out. 10 & up. (800) 422-4463.

■ The Flea Ukulele 🏷2006

(Magic Fluke Co. $144 ●●●●½) Here's a handsome four-string sopra-no-size ukulele with a solid musical sound. Perfect for beginners and

available in multiple colors. The back is made of plastic
and the top is wood. It comes with a storage bag and
instructions. (800) 459-5558.

■ Kids' Tom Tom

(Remo $53 **oooo**) If you're lucky, they'll let you play this col-
orful drum while they dance! Comes with mallets, but
testers say that tones are better when played by hand.
Also terrific: a **Kids' Konga Drum** ($63 **oooo**) and
Two-Headed Bongo ($50 **oooo**). Their new line of
less expensive instruments does not have the same rich
sound. (800) 422-4463.

■ Music Maker Harp BLUE CHIP

(European Expressions $32 **ooooo**) No electronic sounds here. This
is a cross between a zither and an autoharp, but much easier to learn
to play. Slip one of 12 follow-the-dot song sheets under the strings
and pluck. Has a soft and lovely tone. Includes folk, Beatles, and classical music sheets. 6 & up. (800) 779-2205.

Active Play

Young school kids are often more eager than able to play many
games with rules. Sometimes the real equipment is too heavy for
them to use. Balls that are softer don't hurt as much and promote
kids' confidence. The same is true of scaled-down bats, rackets,
and other equipment.

■ Backyard Flyer 2006 PLATINUM AWARD

(Kid Galaxy $14.95 **ooooo**) "One of the best
toys of the year" was the consensus among our
tween testers. They were thrilled with this small
blue and yellow plane that is launched by using the
battery-powered hand-held launcher. It kept our testers
(parents included) well occupied for part of an afternoon—even
when it went flying into the neighbor's backyard! A great toy for the
price. (While our testers gave rave reviews to this product, they found
the company's remote control plane very difficult to make work.)
(800) 816-1135.

■ Beamo

(Stuff Design $25 **ooooo**) We really
wish that we had had one of these when
we were young! These fabric discs are about two feet wide
and have a foam outer core that doesn't hurt as much as a

regular frisbee if you miss! Great for multi-generational play. 6 & up. PLATINUM AWARD '04. (888) 946-7464.

■ ESPN Game Station *2006*

(Fisher-Price $179 ●●) We worry when a toy comes with a warning not to return the toy to the store, but to call the help line. The thick instruction book and three hours of assembly are ridiculous for a $179 toy. Proceed at your own risk with this 6-in-1 play center for soccer, basketball, golf, hockey, football, and baseball games. 5 & up. New for *2006* ,
ESPN Shot Block Basketball ($69.99) was not ready for testing but we hope it's not as complicated to put together. (800) 432-5437.

■ Fun Roller *2006*

(Small World Toys $33.99) Looks like a prop for a circus clown. After inflating the big circle (four-foot diameter), kids can walk forward on it and make it go. Will require a certain level of coordination and balancing skill. Lots of fun, but is too small for taller 5s and 6s. (800) 421-4153. 4 & up.

■ Hopscotch *2006*

(Alex $24.95 ●●●) A brightly colored board that comes in big foam pieces that fit together well like a puzzle. When put together it measures 23" x 81" and comes with a carry-along bag. Early sets with disks to throw tend to roll (a big drawback); the company is replacing disks with beanbags (make sure you get one of these sets!). Ideal for outdoor fun or a rainy day. Marked 3 & up, but really need to be more like 5 to play. (800) 666-2539.

■ Play Sports Croquet Set

(Small World Toys $50 ●●●●) This nifty updated croquet game comes with two mallets, six balls, two tees, and nine bendable, weighted foam wickets. Better than the old metal wickets that used to rust, this will survive the elements. (800) 421-4153.

■ Wet Head *2006*

(Imagination $19.99 ●●●●) On a hot day, this water roulette toy is the perfect outdoor game. After you fill the hat's reservoir with water, each player takes a turn wearing the hat and having the other players pull one of the water plugs on the hat.

Watch out, one of them will release all the water! (310) 395-1354.

Wheel Toys
Shopping Checklist

Fives will continue to enjoy many of the wheel toys in the Preschool chapter.

By 6 or 7, most kids are ready and eager for a two-wheeler with training wheels. Steer clear of bikes with gears or hand brakes. Learning to balance is a big enough deal.

Tempting as it may be to surprise your child, your best bet is to take your child to the store.

Buy a bike that fits, rather than one to grow into. When kids straddle a bike they should be able to put a foot on the ground for balance.

Budget and size will dictate the choices. **Schwinn, Huffy,** and **Razor** ($100 & up) offer solidly built 16" bikes with adjustable training wheels and an assortment of accessories.

Helmets do help! According to the Consumer Product Safety Commission, one in seven children suffers head injuries in bike-related accidents. While studies show that wearing helmets reduces the risk of injury by 85 percent, the sad fact is that only 5 percent of bike-riding kids actually wear helmets. See Safety Guidelines for helmet standards.

■ Green Machine

(Huffy $100 ❍❍❍❍❍) You'll want a turn on this truly innovative ride-on. Steer the two chunky rear wheels by moving the two hand levers (one also has a brake). Solidly made even for bigger kids (and small adults!). PLATINUM AWARD '04. (800) 872-2453.

■ Flying Turtle

(Mason Co. $69.95 ❍❍❍❍) Low to the ground, this seat on skate wheels zips along on any smooth surface by twisting the handlebars from side to side. No pedals, no batteries, no motor! This is kid powered and fun for kids up to 150 pounds. One test family keeps this indoors and claims that all visiting kids from 4–12 enjoy it! (800) 821-4141.

■ **Trikke 5**

(Trikke Tech $139 ●●●●●) Our testers wrote: "A HUGE HIT! The kids love this! It works well, and looks super cool, too. It operates much like the flying turtle." Designed for kids 7–11 with a maximum rider weight of 150 lbs., the three-wheeled scooter will go where the rider leans. The company sells bigger models for teens and grown-ups but we did not test them. 8 & up. PLATINUM AWARD '05. (877) 487-4553.

Science Toys and Equipment

COMPARISON SHOPPER
Hydroponic Gardens **2006**

Maybe it's that ride at Epcot, but growing plants without soil has always fascinated us. Our testing families were equally intrigued. They tried both Discovery Kids' **Aqua Garden Fountain** ($40 ●●●) and the **Uncle Milton Hydroponic Garden** ($55.95 ●●●). Both got similar so-so marks mainly because both kits came without seeds and other items such as distilled water or liquid nutrients (there is no warning on the box about additional purchases). Testers wrote, "It was a little irritating since we were all ready to start and we looked through the box and through the manual before we realized we needed to go out and get stuff to set it up. However, once we got the seeds going they grew quickly and the little plants are thriving." Another tester told us that the Aqua Garden fountain and lights make this noisy; it runs 24/7, making it a poor choice for a child's bedroom. Due to the electrical aspect of this toy, it is not intended for kids under 8.

■ **Tabletop Greenhouse**

(Creativity for Kids $24.99 ●●●●½) This decidedly low-tech greenhouse comes in natural wood with plastic windows and it is ready to decorate with paints. Put it in a sunny location and get small plants started that can be moved to your garden. We suggest herbs that can be used in the kitchen. An opportunity for kids to see not just how the plants grow, but how the moisture from the soil and plants recycles itself. (800) 311-8684.

■ Box of Rocks

(GeoCentral $21.99 ●●●●) If you have a young rock hound in the family, this box with 16 specimens and an informative booklet will be a hit and may inspire further discoveries. **Activity Rocks** ($5.25 ●●●●) has four specimens—including one that floats! (800) 231-6083.

■ Discovery Awesome Avalanche Kit

(Discovery Kids $19.95 ●●●●½) At first glance this looks like most of the volcano kits you may have seen—a five-minute wonder. But our 11-year-old tester liked painting the model of Mt. Everest, reading the excellent booklet about avalanches, and the "insta-snow," white polymer that comes with the kit. Add water, and "Watch out below!" Adult supervision suggested. 8 & up. (800) 938-0333.

■ I Dig Treasures: Dinosaurs and Mysteries of Egypt Excavation Adventure

(Action Products $24.99 each ●●●●) Both boy and girl testers enjoyed playing archeologist with these sets that require patience to unearth treasures from pebbly bricks. We rate them higher than other similar kits, since these come with digging goggles. (800) 772-2846.

■ Perfumery *2006*

(Scientific Explorer $20 ●●●●) Lots of perfume kits come with such cheap-smelling scents that we usually pass on them. This is the exception. It really is a chemistry kit with directions to read and recipes to stir up—with pleasant payoffs that kids can use or give as gifts. 8 & up. (800) 900-1182.

Nature Houses & Lodges

■ My Birdhouse Kit

(Balitono $19 ●●●●) One of the best outdoor crafts is to prepare a birdhouse for backyard visitors. This wooden house is pre-constructed (7½" x 5½" x 6½") with drainage holes, removable roof, and a ventilation slot for added comfort! Kids can enjoy painting the house. We'd recommend pairing this kit with a bird guidebook, a pair of binoculars, and a log. Also for the outdoors, **Spiral Windchime Kit** ($17 ●●●●½). 7 & up. (609) 936-8807.

■ **Hanging Bird Feeder** and **Bird Houses Kits**
(TWC of America $17–$20 ●●●●) If you'd like to build your own birdhouse, these beautifully crafted pine kits come with rounded edges and predrilled holes, making them the best kids' kits on the market. Adult assistance required. Also, **Deluxe Clear-View Nature House** ($17.99 ●●●●½), a sturdy hut-shaped wooden house, half see-through, half screened, with sliding door; a perfect temporary habitat for observing bugs and small critters. 6 & up. Also, **Soil Dweller Nature House Kit** ($20 ●●●●) for making a wooden-framed house for earthworms. 8 & up. (800) 301-7592.

The Scoop on Scopes
■ Discovery Kids SL-70 Telescope

(Discovery Kids $149.95 ●●●●●) With many of the same features usually found on expensive adult models, this is a terrific value. Includes precision ground lenses, an erecting prism, and universal 10mm and 25mm Kellner eyepieces. Comes with a tripod that extends to 55" viewing height and a padded shoulder carry bag—the whole kit (tripod, scope, bag) weighs just 16 lbs. Ultra neat are the illuminated night-vision dials. PLATINUM AWARD '04. 7 & up. (800) 938-0333.

■ **ETX 105PE Telescope** *2006* PLATINUM AWARD
(Meade $699 ●●●●●) Our reviewers gave high marks to this model because it comes with the Autostar computer controller (usually found only on much more expensive models). The Autostar allows the viewer to find celestial objects by using the handheld automated controller. The model also comes with a tripod. We would recommend this model for tweens and up. A worthy investment for a family of stargazers! Still top rated, **ETX 90AT** ($595 ●●●●●), PLATINUM AWARD '04. Both 10 & up. (800) 626-3233.

Best Travel Toys and Games

As kids get older they enjoy traditional games such as I Spy, Twenty Questions, Geography, or Facts of Five. They are also ready for word games and travel books. While we don't recommend plugging your kids into electronics for long stretches of time, there are times when everyone needs some down time! **Leapster, Pixter,** and **Gameboy** are among our testers' favorites. Be sure to bring along some story tapes (see Audio chapter). Here are some neat take-alongs:

■ 20Q *2006*

(Radica $9.99 **ooooo**) How does it know? Play twenty questions with this handheld machine and it really seems like magic! The programmed answers also have a sense of humor. PLATINUM AWARD '05. New for *2006*, a bigger desktop version, **20Q Challenge** ($22.95 **ooo**). We prefer the portability and price of the original. (800) 803-9611.

■ Fashion Angels Fashion Design Sketch Book *2006*

(The Bead Shop $13.95 **oooo**) Design enthusiasts will love this lit-

tle portfolio sketchbook that comes with a flip-book full of style choices (everything from necklines and pants to jackets and shoes). Our testers loved learning the difference between Palazzo and Gaucho pants. 8 & up. (800) 492-3237.

■ Leapster L-MAX *2006* PLATINUM AWARD

(LeapFrog $99 **ooooo**) We told you about the Leapster last year. It's still a great travel toy, but now there's a simple cable connection that will put Leapster games on your TV screen, so it can be used either way. Now it's a good take-along that can also be plugged in at Grandma's. Without the usual frenetic pace, these respond to your child and are more than just zap-and-blast games. If you have been looking for a handheld game machine that's more age-appropriate than Gameboy, look no further. Billed as a learning machine, it's a lot more playful than most. The games and skills are well targeted to older preschoolers and early school-age kids. It has a larger screen and games that can be played at three levels of difficulty. There are math, phonics, reading, and spelling games, as well as an art program that takes some help to learn how to use. We really liked **Letters on the Loose** but we'd skip the **Batman** cartridge (too scary looking for the age group).4–8. (800) 701-5327.

■ Love Mini Piccolo Bead Kit *2006*

(Bead Bazaar $9.99 **oooo**) Perfect for throwing into the suitcase, our testers loved the tiny case that comes with wooden bead, heart-shaped charms, and string. The Daisy version comes with plastic/metallic beads and charms. Ideal for some downtime fun at the beach or in the hotel. (800) 838-1769.

■ Crazy Faces *2006*

(eeBoo $8 **oooo**) Saxton Freymann's wonderful fruit and veggie faces are the art for these oversized crazy eight cards. Players match pictures, numbers, or card suits in order to be the first to cast off all their cards. They say 3 & up; we'd say more like 5 & up. (212) 222-0823.

■ Magnetic A to Z *2006*

(Klutz/Chicken Socks $12.95 **oooo**½) A new collection of books for younger kids from Klutz includes some good choices for travel. There's a good parent-child activity book with magnetic letters and steel pages that ask kids to find objects that begin with several different letters and then put magnetic letters on the objects. Testers liked **Hand Art** ($12.95  **oooo**), a pack of crayons, paste, and pompoms for making creatures by tracing your hand! Also fun, **How to Make Pompom Animals** ($12.95 **oooo**). Late arrival, **Shadow Games** ($12.95 **oooo**), a flashlight and book full of activities that would be fun in a motel room or at Grandma's house. (800) 737-4123.

■ Magnetic Checkers & Slides & Ladders *2006*

(eeBoo $12.95 each **oooo**) Packed in their own carrying bag each of these traditional games is done with magnetic playing pieces and a playing board that opens like a book. Charming illustrations give these classic games a new and lively look. Still top rated, **Travel**

Bingo ($10 ●●●●), with four bingo pads and four pencils. Objects to look for include stop signs, bikes, flags, cows, railroad crossing signs, etc. 4 & up. (212) 222-0823.

■ Pixel Chix *2006*

(Mattel $29.95 ●●●●) Watch a 2-D image of a girl move about in her house. Help her pick what's she going to do (rollerblade vs. watch TV), what she's going to eat or wear. There are five different levels of play and, like a Tamagochi, she' ll let you know if she's happy or sad. The coolest feature: you can connect two houses together and the chix will visit each other. A little noisy at times but will fit in a backpack. (800) 524-8697.

■ Pixter Multi-Media *2006*

(Fisher-Price $84.99) A handheld, no-mess art platform that allows kids to create countless combinations of designs with the easy-to-use stylus on the touch-sensitive back-lit screen. This PLATINUM AWARD winner is being retooled but was not ready for testing. An interesting cartridge, **Symphony Painter** ($19.99), allows kids to draw and experiment with composing music. Will work with both the new and old models. (800) 432-5437.

■ Power Brain YoYo *2006* PLATINUM AWARD

(Hasbro $10.99 ●●●●●) We wish we had had this yo-yo when we were kids! While some purists may think of it as the yo-yo for dummies, we love the fact that it knows how to come back up with its "auto-return technology." It also makes doing tricks such as "walk the dog" that much easier! (800) 327-8264.

■ Road Trip Activity Journal

(Mudpuppy Press $10 ●●●●) There's lots to keep a tween busy with this clever activity journal that has a place for addresses, bingo, lots of other games, and space to write and draw as they travel. 9 & up. (212) 354-8840.

■ Wig Out

(Gamewright $5.99 ●●●●) The object is to match all of your wig cards to those on the table. Be fast . . . there are no turns here. Everyone is

trying to do the same thing, whether it's matching ponytails, beehives, or mohawks! First player to get rid of all her cards wins. Still top rated, **Hocus Focus** ($5.99 ○○○○○), where the object is matching wizards (harder than Wig Out), PLATINUM AWARD '04; and **Stampede** ($5.99 ○○○○), where the player with the most complete hippos, rhinos, and elephants before the deck runs out wins. 6 & up. (800) 638-7568.

Best Birthday Gifts for Every Budget

Big Ticket $100 plus	**Telescope** (various makers) or **Castle** (Playmobil) or **Trikke5** (Trikke Tech) or **Robosapien V2** (Wow Wee)
Under $100	**The American Girls Collection Doll** (American Girl) or **Leapster L-MAX** or **FLY** (LeapFrog) or **Pixter Multi-Media** (Fisher-Price) or **Robosapien** (WowWee)
Under $80	**Lili** (Corolle) or **Color Pixter** (Fisher-Price) or **Monster Art Kit** (Alex)
Under $40	**Lego Pirate Ship** or **Star Wars ARC-170 Starfighter** (Lego Systems) or **YOUniverse ATM Machine** (Summit)
Under $30	**Mgears Remote Control Racers** (Learning Resources) or **Scrapbook and Memory Box Gift Set** (Creativity for Kids)
Under $25	**Morphibians** (Kid Galaxy) or **Magnetic Building Sets** (various makers) or **DaVinci's Challenge** (Briarpatch)
Under $20	**Bumparena** (Cranium) or **My Pinball Game Kit** (Balitono) or **Alfredo's Food Fight** (Fundex)
Under $15	**Bialo** (HaPe) or **Puzzles** (various makers) or **Bead Kits** (various makers) or **Bingo** (eeBoo) or **Backyard Flyer** (Kid Galaxy) or **Power Brain YoYo** (Hasbro)
Under $10	**Wig Out** (Gamewright)

II • Books

Reading to children is more than a great way to entertain them. Studies show that young children who are read to every day learn to read earlier and with greater ease. But quite aside from the academic benefits, sharing books with children is one of the pleasurable ways of being together. With books we can share the thrill of adventure, the excitement of suspense, and the warm satisfaction of happily-ever-afters. Through books we can help children find answers to their questions about real things and how they work. Books give grown-ups and children a ticket that transports them from everyday events to a world of faraway, long ago, and once upon a time.

You'll find useful lists of BLUE CHIP Classics for each age group as well as reviews of the best new and recent award winners. Many classic picture books can also be found in the Audio and Video chapters.

Books are primarily arranged by age groups. "Coping with Life" and holiday-book sections include books for mixed ages. You'll also find recommended reference books and encyclopedias for mixed ages at the end of the section. An "also" after a review indicates other recommended titles by that author, or other related books.

Babies and Young Toddlers

At this stage, books are not merely for looking at. Babies and toddlers tend to taste, toss, and tear their books. Even sturdy cardboard books may not survive this search-and-destroy stage. Cloth and vinyl make good chewable choices. The mechanics of turning pages, pointing to pictures, and even listening make books among baby's favorite playthings and a key to language development.

TEN BLUE CHIP BOOKS EVERY BABY AND YOUNG TODDLER SHOULD KNOW

✓**Baby Animal Friends,** by Phoebe Dunn
✓**Baby's First Words,** by Lars Wik
✓**I See,** by Rachel Isadora
✓**Spot's Toys,** by Eric Hill
✓**This Is Me,** by Lenore Blegvad
✓**Tom and Pippo series,** by Helen Oxenbury
✓**Pat-a-Cake,** by Tony Kenyon
✓**What Do Babies Do?** by Debby Slier
✓**What Is It?** by Tana Hoban
✓**My Very First Mother Goose,** edited by Iona Opie

Cloth, Vinyl, and Board Books for Babies and Toddlers

Choose books with round corners and clear pictures of familiar things to know, name, and talk about. For the littlest reader, single images on a page are easier to "read." There may be one word or no words on the page, but you can use many words as you talk about the familiar objects and relate them to baby. Older babies will like pointing and finding the red cup that's full of milk or the sweet yellow banana. Little stories that center on the child's world are most appropriate for young toddlers. Here are some favorites:

■ Animal Talk *2006*

(by Dawn Sirett, et al., DK Books $4.99 ⊙⊙⊙⊙½)
Go ahead and ham it up as you introduce baby to these familiar animals who are seen in full-body photos and then in close-ups as you lift the flaps and make their animal sounds. Also in the same series, **Noisy Trucks,** illustrated with colorful toy vehicles.

■ Fluffy Chick and Friends *2006* PLATINUM AWARD

(Priddy Books $8.95 ⊙⊙⊙⊙⊙) A fabric book with interesting textures on every page that introduce familiar animals. Small rhyming couplets tell about a rooster, duck, sheep, horse, cow, goat, pig, and goose . . . each with a special texture to explore. A well crafted book that is both safe and entertaining, and keys into baby's sensory learning style. 6 mos. & up.

■ Playtime Peekaboo! *2006* PLATINUM AWARD

(by Dawn Sirett et al., DK $6.99 ●●●●●) A small clue, such as a toy elephant's trunk, is revealed behind each of the flaps and, once found, there is also a texture to explore. Featuring a cast of multi-cultural babies, familiar toy animals, and the favorite game of peek-a-boo. Also in the same series, **Bathtime Peekaboo!**

■ What's that Sound? *2006*

(Soft Play $17.95 ●●●●) Ernie wants to know what to call each of the items that makes a special sound in this cloth book. There's a squeaky duck, a ringing phone, a choo-choo train, a boing-boing ball, a chirping bird, a mooing cow, and a big bus that says beep! An interactive book that adults will need to activate at first. A good take-along travel toy. (800) 515-5437.

■ Who Loves Baby? *2006*

(Sassy $6.99 ●●●●½) Refreshed in new colors, this vinyl book has no text. It has pockets where you put photos of the people who love baby inside. A great take-along for little ones going off to daycare or for stay-at-home tots, as well.

Resources for Parents

■ Head, Shoulders, Knees and Toes

(by Zita Newcome, Candlewick $15.99 ●●●●●) More than fifty hand-clapping, finger-snapping, action games and rhymes wonderfully illustrated with close-up directions for motions and jolly looking toddlers. PLATINUM AWARD '03. 2 & up.

■ A Treasury of Children's Songs

(Metropolitan Museum/Henry Holt $19.95 ●●●●½) A collection of 40 classic children's songs paired with artwork from the Metropolitan Museum. Each song is complete with easy piano arrangements and guitar chords. Still top rated: **Lullabies: An Illustrated Songbook** BLUE CHIP (Metropolitan Museum $23 ●●●●●): words and music for 35 memorable lullabies illustrated with works of art from the Met. PLATINUM AWARD '98.

■ **My Mother Goose Library**

(edited by Iona Opie/illus. by Rosemary Wells, Candlewick $40 ⦿⦿⦿⦿⦿) Both PLATINUM AWARD volumes come in a handsome gift set or in board books for tots to enjoy ($8 each) with the same delicious art.

Older Toddlers

Toddlers are ready for new kinds of books. Just as they can understand almost anything you say, they can also follow books with small stories that center on their familiar world.

They like playful language with rhythm, rhyme, and repetitive lines they can chime in on. They enjoy stories about children like themselves, and playful animal stories in which a dog or a bear is really a "child in fur." Toddlers also love books about real things, such as colors, caterpillars, and cars. Choose books you really like, because toddlers like to hear their favorites again and again!

TEN BLUE CHIP BOOKS EVERY TODDLER SHOULD KNOW

✓**Goodnight Moon,** by Margaret Wise Brown
✓**Jamberry,** by Bruce Degen
✓**Wheels on the Bus,** adapted by Paul Zelinsky
✓ **Polar Bear, Polar Bear, What Do You Hear?** by Bill Martin Jr.
✓**Sheep in a Jeep,** by Nancy Shaw
✓**Where's Spot?** by Eric Hill
✓**The Little Red Hen,** by Byron Barton
✓**You Go Away,** by Dorothy Corey
✓**When You Were a Baby,** by Ann Jonas
✓**The Very Hungry Caterpillar,** by Eric Carle

First Little Stories, Adventures, and Mysteries

■ **I Love You Through and Through** *2006*

(by Bernadette Rossetti-Shustak/illus. by Caroline Jayne Church, Scholastic $8.95 ⦿⦿⦿⦿ ½) A valentine for the littlest love in your life. "I love your inside and outside, your happy side and sad side." Not much of a rhyme here, but a sweet book that talks to unconditional love with lively illustrations all on sturdy cardboard pages. 2 & up.

■ Mouse's First Snow *2006*

(by Lauren Thompson/illus. by Buket Erdogan, Simon & Schuster $12.95 ●●●○) Mouse and his Poppa enjoy the magic of a snowy day doing all the things father and child might do, including making a marvelous snow mouse friend. 2–5.

Rhythm and Rhyme and Repetitive Lines

■ I Went Walking *2006*

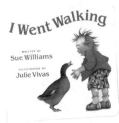

(by Sue Williams/illus. by Julie Vivas, Harcourt $10.95 ●●●●●) Reintroduced in a very large 10" square board book format, this is a BLUE CHIP animal and color identification book with repetitive lines. Because of its size it is heavy to handle, but otherwise still a fine read-aloud favorite of toddlers. 2 & up.

■ Little Yoga *2006*

(by Rebecca Whitford/illus. Martina Selway, Holt $9.95 ●●●● ½) Whether you are doing yoga or not, this is an appealing little book that invites active doing—stretching like a cat, wobbling like a bird, crouching like a frog—among other things. Clear illustrations include boys and girls as well as lively animals. 2 & up.

■ Mama Loves You *2006*

(by Caroline Stutson/illus. by John Segal, Scholastic $6.99 ●●●● ½) Charming mother-and-child pairs, from polar bears to buzzing bugs, are introduced with four lines of verse that capture their loving unconditional connections. 2–5.

■ More Fun With Maisy! *2006*

(by Lucy Cousins, Candlewick $4.99 ○○○○½)
A lift-the-flap book with a repetitive refrain
that reinforces the idea that lots of things are
fun and even more fun when you do them
with someone else. A very pro-social book
with peek-a-boo surprises under the flaps.
Also cute, **Ha Ha, Maisy!** 6 mos. & up.

■ Quack! *2006* PLATINUM AWARD

(by Phyllis Root/illus. by Holly Meade,
Candlewick $6.99 ○○○○○) Mama Duck calls,
"Quack, quack, quack!" and five baby ducklings hatch with a crack, crack, crack! Tots
will enjoy the rhythm of this short celebration
of ducklings as they flap their wings, wibble
and wobble and splish, splosh, splash! 6 mos.
& up.

■ Zoo's Who? *2006*

(by Robert Tainsh, Priddy Books $8.95 ○○○○) Too
often textured books have doo-dads that fuzz and
tear loose. This handsome board book holds
together physically and has full-color photos of wild
animals with cutout parts where the textures are
revealed.

Slice-of-Life Books

■ Baby Bear's Chairs *2006*

(by Jane Yolen/illus. by Melissa Sweet, Harcourt
$16 ○○○○½) Picking up on the Three Bears'
chairs, this is a cozy ode to Papa Bear. Our
favorite line . . . "My papa's lap is just for me till
I'm as big a bear as he!" Sweet's cozy images are
a picture-book-perfect match for Yolen's warm
words. 3 & up.

■ Piglet and Mama *2006*

(by Margaret Wild/illus. by Stephen M. King,
Abrams $14.95 ○○○○) Piglet has wandered off
and lost her Mama. One by one the animals
she meets try to console her and find a way to

entertain her. But alas, no one will do but Mama. While Piglet is looking for Mama, Mama, happily, has been looking for Piglet. A reassuringly happily-ever-after story. 2½ and up.

Coping with Life's Little Ups & Downs

■ It's Quacking Time! 2000

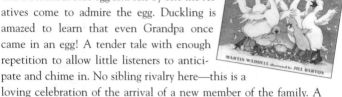

(by Martin Waddell/illus. by Jill Barton, Candlewick $15.99 **oooo**½) Mama Duck has laid a beautiful blue egg and one by one the relatives come to admire the egg. Duckling is amazed to learn that even Grandpa once came in an egg! A tender tale with enough repetition to allow little listeners to antici-pate and chime in. No sibling rivalry here—this is a loving celebration of the arrival of a new member of the family. A keeper! 3 & up

■ Za-Za's Baby Brother

(by Lucy Cousins, Candlewick $6.99 **oooo**) If there's a new baby in the family, big brothers and sisters will relate to the problems Za-Za is having. Life is not the same for poor Za-Za, who has to share everyone's attention. Using a "zebra" fami-ly takes this one step away from reality and may help older sibs talk about their feelings. 2–5.

Potty Corner (Results not Guaranteed!)

■ Going to the Potty BLUE CHIP

(by Fred Rogers/photos by Jim Judkis, Putnam $5.95 **oooo**) In his usual reassuring way, Mr. Rogers talks with children about using the potty. This photo essay reinforces the idea that using a potty is another step toward growing up. Also excellent: **Your New Potty,** by J. Cole, Morrow. 2 & up.

■ My Big Boy/Girl Potty

(by Joanna Cole/illus. by Maxie Chambliss, HarperCollins $5.95 **oooo**) If you're introducing the concept of potty training, you can make a gender-specific choice with either version of this little book that makes the transition from diapers to potty sound "doable"—let's hope! We find this more age-appropriate than the "What to Expect for Kids" book on the same subject. 2 & up.

■ Big Girls/Big Boys Use the Potty *2006*

(by Andrea Pinnington, DK $6.99 ●●●●) Choose the gender-specific version of a small board book in which the toddler also gets a favorite teddy bear involved. This comes with 80 reward stickers—if you think that will help. 2 & up.

Sweet Dreams—Bedtime Books

■ Cornelius P. Mud, Are You Ready For Bed?
2006 PLATINUM AWARD

(by Barney Saltzberg, Candlewick $15.99 ●●●●●) Want to hear your child say "Yes, yes, yes," even if it is bedtime? With Mom offstage, Cornelius P. Mud, a playful pig, is not entirely honest about his bedtime progress! Little listeners are sure to enjoy answering for Cornelius and having the vicarious thrill of his naughtiness all the way through this bedtime romp. 2½ & up.

■ Goodnight Moon BLUE CHIP

(by Margaret Wise Brown/illus. by Clement Hurd, HarperCollins $6.95 ●●●●●) Happy news! This bedtime classic is available in a sturdy board book that toddlers can enjoy without ripping. 18 mos. & up.

Early Concept Books— Color, Counting, and More

■ Animal Babies *2006*

(by Vickie Weber, Kingfisher $6.95 ●●●●) Handsome full-color photos of animal babies and their mothers light up the pages of this sturdy board book. Each animal is introduced with a partial view and some hints as to its identity, as in "an animal that goes 'Oink' and has a curly tail." The turn page shows the whole animal and its mommy and the baby's proper name, as in "piglet."

■ Do Gloves Go on Feet? *2006*

(DK $6.99 ●●●●) Newest in a fun series that invites children to give their favorite answer of "NO!" to some fairly obvious questions. This book is all about clothes and their connections to the seasons. 2 & up.

■ Duckie's Ducklings: A One-to-Ten Counting Book 2006

(by Frances Barry, Candlewick $7.99 ●●●●½) Mama Duck only looks ahead, so she fails to see all of her ducklings who appear one by one behind her in this beginner's counting book with cutaway pages. 2–4.

■ Food for Thought 2006 PLATINUM AWARD

(by Saxton Freymann, Scholastic $14.95 ●●●●●) Fruits and veggies have been transformed into amusing creatures that have been photographed and grouped to introduce basic concepts. There are pages devoted to counting, colors, shapes, letters, and opposites. Big sturdy pages make this a treasure children will go back to again and again. 2 & up.

■ Hooray for Fish! 2006 PLATINUM AWARD

(by Lucy Cousins, Candlewick $14.99 ●●●●●) A big book of deliciously colorful fish. A delightful introduction to the many different shapes and looks of life under the sea. Also, **Maisy Goes to the Library** ($12.99 2006 ●●●●). Young book lovers who are ready for their first library card will enjoy Maisy's trip to the library. 3 & up.

■ 10 Little Rubber Ducks 2006

(by Eric Carle, HarperCollins $19.99 ●●●●) This is not so much a counting book as another one of Carle's glorious knowing and naming books. Ten little toy ducks fall off a container ship and meet a variety of ocean-going creatures along the way. Ends with an electronic squeak that little listeners will love to anticipate and activate. 2 & up.

■ My Car 2005 BLUE CHIP

(by Byron Barton, HarperTrophy $6.99 ●●●●●) If you have a toddler obsessed with cars, here's the perfect book. Clear illustrations that are all about cars and transportation. A reissue of one of our old favorites in a larger format. 2 & up.

■ Teeth Are Not for Biting

(by Elizabeth Verdick/illus. by Marieka Heinlen, Free Spirit $7.95 ●●●●) A message book that may be helpful for toddlers who use their teeth when they get angry or frustrated. It's a little off, semantically—we do use our teeth to bite—but the repeated refrain, "Ouch! Biting hurts!" might be useful as a reminder. Also highly rec-ommended: **Hands Are Not for Hitting** (by Martha Agassi/illus. by Marieka Heinlen ●●●●●) PLATINUM AWARD '03. 1½–3.

Books to Sing

■ He's Got the Whole World in His Hands 2006

(by Kadir Nelson, Dial $16.99 ●●●●½) Except for the cover, we loved the illustrations of this spiritual. Following an African-American boy and his family through day and night, rain and shine, Nelson enlarges the joy and comfort of these familiar words.

■ If You're Happy and You Know It!
2006 PLATINUM AWARD

(by Jane Cabrera, Holiday House $16.95 ●●●●●) A favorite song that invites movement along with singing. Jane Cabrera gives this old song new life with a cast of delightful creatures stamping their feet, clapping their hands, and flapping their arms. A playful way to combine animals' names, body parts,, and action. 2 & up.

■ Wheels on the Bus BLUE CHIP

(by Paul Zelinsky, Dutton $17.99 ●●●●●) For the traditional song in a delightful, though very rippable pop-up format, bring home Zelinsky's version, but save for parent/child together times. 2 & up.

Preschool Books for Threes and Fours

Preschoolers delight in books of all kinds. They enjoy longer sto-ries about real kids like themselves and animal stories that are really about "kids in fur" with whom they can identify. Folktales and fantasy are fine as long as they're not too scary. Kids like the rhythm and rhyme of verse as well as prose that touches their hearts and funny bones. Eager to learn, they like playful counting and alphabet books. Kids are also interested in true facts about real things that satisfy their curiosity about the world.

BLUE CHIP BOOKS
EVERY PRESCHOOLER SHOULD KNOW

✓ **Caps for Sale,** by Esphyr Slobodkina
✓ **Curious George,** by H. A. Rey
✓ **If You Give a Mouse a Cookie,** by Laura J. Numeroff
✓ **The Little Engine That Could,** by Watty Piper
✓ **Make Way for Ducklings,** by Robert McCloskey
✓ **Mama, Do You Love Me?** by Barbara Joosse
✓ **Millions of Cats,** by Wanda Gag
✓ **The Nutshell Library,** by Maurice Sendak
✓ **Olivia,** by Ian Falconer
✓ **The Tale of Peter Rabbit,** by Beatrix Potter
✓ **The Runaway Bunny,** by Margaret Wise Brown
✓ **A Snowy Day,** by Ezra Jack Keats

Great New Read-Alouds for Preschoolers
■ Big Little Elephant 2006

(by Valeri Gorbachev, Harcourt $16 ○○○○)
Learning how to be a friend is not always easy. Preschoolers will relate to Little Elephant's problem with being too big for many things and wanting to be accepted. 4–7.

■ Carl's Sleepy Afternoon
2006 PLATINUM AWARD

(by Alexandra Day, Farrar Straus $12.95 ○○○○○)
This mostly wordless book is just begging for a child storyteller to interpret the illustrations and tell the story of Carl's very busy afternoon when he did everything but sleep. Wordless books like this are perfect for the beginning storyteller. It is not likely to be told twice in the same words and each time the story is apt to grow fuller. 4–8.

■ Duck Skates 2006

(by Lynne Berry/illus. by Hiroe Nakata, Holt

$15.95 **oooo**) A lively romp as five little ducks wake up to find a snowy day. Told in zippy rhyme, this captures the flavor of a winter day of fun topped with cups of cocoa and a cozy ending. 3 & up.

■ Ella Takes the Cake 2006

(by Carmela & Steven D'Amico, Scholastic $16.95 **oooo**) Eager to help, Ella finds her big chance and runs into some tense moments when it seems that cake is destined to smash! A suspenseful adventure that will satisfy those seeking independence—if only vicariously. 3 & up.

■ The Fairy Tale Cake 2006

(by Jonathan Langley/illus. by Mark Sperring, Scholastic $15.95 **oooo**½) Imagine if every character from your favorite nursery tales got together to make a special cake for your birthday! It's fun to study the pages of this charming book looking for old favorites such as "The Three Little Pigs," "The Gingerbread Boy," and "The Three Bears," to mention just a few. This is more about the pictures than the story, but when there's a birthday cake at the end, it's likely to please—especially if you sing "Happy Birthday" to finish it off! 4–8.

■ The First Day of Winter 2006

(by Denise Fleming, Holt $15.95 **oooo**) Based on *The First Day of Christmas*, this is a cumulative tale that involves building a perfect snowman. Fleming's art captures the fun of snow and the delight of building a snowperson. 3–5.

■ Tacky and the Winter Games 2006

(by Helen Lester/illus. by Lynn Munsinger, Houghton Mifflin $16 **oooo**) Everybody's favorite penguin is back. This time, Tacky is a member of a team trying to get in shape. But Tacky has his own idea of how to do that and the results are not exactly what his teammates had in mind. Lively language and images—with silly antics that make up for the lackluster ending. 4 & up.

■ How Do Dinosaurs Eat Their Food? **2006**

(by Jane Yolen/ illus. by Mark Teague, Scholastic $15.99 ●●●●½) For a funny take on table manners, what could be better than some dinosaurs dining? Sure to please as much as the earlier winners in this playful series. 4 & up.

■ If You Give Pig A Party
2006 PLATINUM AWARD

(by Laura Numeroff/illus. by Felicia Bond, HarperCollins $15.99 ●●●●●) Once again, this award-winning team has come up with a universal theme and what one expects will be predictable outcomes—but soon after the balloons, the book takes a left turn as Pig and her friend go looking for Pig's friends and end up at a street fair. One surprise follows another in this newest addition to a fine series. 4 & up.

■ Leonardo the Terrible Monster
2006 PLATINUM AWARD

(by Mo Willems, Hyperion $15.99 ●●●●●) Once again, Mo Willems brings his own special brand of tongue-in-cheek humor to a weird world of his own creation. Like his big-mouthed pigeon, this time he's created a monster who turns out to be kinder than expected. As monsters go, this is a pretty benign fellow, milder mannered than those Wild Things. 4 & up.

■ Skating with the Bears **2006**

(by Andrew Breakspeare, Dutton $15.99 ●●●●) Tim can't skate until one night he awakes from his sleep and learns to skate from some magical bears. A small fantasy for beginners. 4 & up.

■ The Wild Little Horse **2006**

(by Rita Gray/illus. by Ashley Wolff, Dutton $15.99 ●●●●) Little horse takes off on a lively adventure into the big world, racing with the wind. Told in lyrical verse and illustrated with Wolff's bold strokes, this tale of independence ends at the edge of the sea where the wild little horse is lost and found. 4 & up.

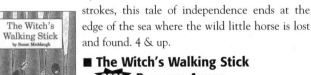

■ The Witch's Walking Stick
2006 PLATINUM AWARD

(by Susan Meddaugh, Houghton Mifflin $16

ooooo) With an economy of words and lively illustrations, the creator of Martha, the talking dog, has created a new cast of winning characters: a nasty witch who gets her comeuppance, and a little sister who teaches her older siblings a few lessons. Meddaugh takes familiar fantasy material and makes it fresh with her own brand of humor. Her art and wit make her a worthy successor to William Steig. 5 & up.

■ The Quangle Wangle's Hat *2006*

(by Edward Lear/illus. by Louise Voce, Candlewick $15.99 oooo ½) Unlike Dr. Seuss's, Lear's nonsense verse has no message to deliver. It's all about the sheer pleasure of the words and the playful rhymes about made-up characters that never were and never can be. Voce's art adds to the fun. 4 & up.

All in the Family
■ Because Your Daddy Loves You *2006*

(by Andrew Clements/illus. by R.W. Alley, Clarion $16 oooo ½) How refreshing! A Daddy book that follows a patient and loving daddy through the day. Dad avoids saying the typical critical remarks, but Clements has it both ways; he says what the daddy didn't say and then what he really does say as he kindly makes a day at the beach a happy time together. In a way, Clements models some great parenting strategies along with a pleasing story. 3–5.

■ Here Comes Grandma! *2006* PLATINUM AWARD

(by Janet Lord/illus. by Julie Paschkis, Holt $12.95 ooooo) It doesn't matter if Grandma has to hike, bike, drive, or fly— she's coming to see her darlings! Charming illustrations of an old-fashioned babushka's granny who is thoroughly modern and ready to rumble if it

will lead to her darling grandchild! 3 & up.

■ Mama Panya's Pancakes, A Village Tale from Kenya *2006*

By Mary and Rich Chamberlin/illus. by Julia Cairns, Barefoot Books $16.99 oooo) Adika seems to be two steps ahead of his Mama as he invites too many people to join them for pancakes for dinner. Set in a village in Kenya, with many sights to see, this charming storybook unfolds its tale of generosity being rewarded. You can identify animals in the glossary or whip up a batch of pancakes with Mama Panya's recipe. 4–8.

■ McDuff's Wild Romp 2006

(by Rosemary Wells/illus. by Susan Jeffers, Hyperion $9.99 ●●●● ½) McDuff goes visiting with his family to Aunt Frieda's where one nasty old cat named Purlina gets dear little McDuff in all sorts of trouble. If you don't know McDuff from earlier adventures, you should. He's a lovable storybook character. 2–5.

■ My Mom 2006

(by Anthony Browne, Farrar Straus & Giroux $16 ●●●● ½) With just enough tongue in cheek to make you smile and a rich dollop of non-sticky sweet affection, here's an ode to the Mom everyone should have! 3 & up.

■ No Place Like Home 2006

(by Jonathan Emmett/illus. by Vanessa Cabban, Candlewick $15.99 ●●●●) An old-fashioned and rather predictable story about a little mole who decides he'd like a new home. Each animal he meets has another place to show. But each of these places has something wrong with it. Finally Mole leads all of them to the source of the title, where Mole finds contentment. 3 & up.

■ Not Norman, A Goldfish Story 2006

(by Kelly Bennett/illus. by Noah Z. Jones, Candlewick $15.99 ●●●●) Like most kids, the boy in this story wanted a pet other than Norman, a boring fish that just swims 'round and 'round. But as the story unfolds, both boy and goldfish are transformed. A tad unbelievable but surely satisfying for those who cannot have furry or feathery pets for any number of reasons. 4 & up.

■ Piggy and Dad Go Fishing 2006

(by David Martin/illus. by Frank Remkiewicz, Candlewick $14.99 ●●●● ½) If you've ever had trouble putting a worm on a hook or wanted to throw back any poor fish that made the mistake of

getting caught, you'll love this father and son pair of pigs who end up feeding the fish instead of eating them! A great catch. 4–7.

Separation
■ Yoko's World of Kindness *2006*

(by Rosemary Wells, Hyperion $19.99 **oooo**) Six little stories about going to school and getting along with others. The first is about Yoko's problem with letting Mama leave. Marked 5–7, but these are stories that will have meaning to preschoolers as well. 4 & up.

■ When I Miss You

(by Cornelia Maude Spelman/illus. by Kathy Parkinson, Albert Whitman $15.95 **oooo**) Knowing that your parent will come back is a big step to a happier separation. Told through animals, this is a good talking book for reassuring your child that you miss them when you're apart and that you look forward to seeing them too! 3 & up.

Bedtime
■ Humphrey's Bear *2006*

(by Jan Wahl/illus. by William Joyce, Hyperion $16.95 **oooo**) Dad thinks Humphrey may be too old for sleeping with his teddy bear. But Humphrey rushes off to bed and his adventure with bear. His dad later remembers how much he too enjoyed sailing off with this very same bear. 4–8.

■ Sleep Tight, Little Bear *2006* PLATINUM AWARD

(by Martin Waddell/illus. by Barbara Firth, Candlewick $15.99 **ooooo**) Little Bear has decided to move into a little house of his own. Big Bear not only helps, he brings Little Bear supper and tucks him in. But as night comes, Little Bear worries that Big Bear will be lonesome. As always, Waddell tells a tender story and Firth makes the images that make it even better.

Concept Books—
Numbers, Letters, Words, and More

■ Animal Antics A to Z 2006

(by Anita Lobel, Greenwillow $15.99 ●●●●)
Bouncing bears, happy hippopotami, romping rab-
bits—to name just a few of the playful pairs Lobel
has chosen to illustrate in this menagerie. Some of
the choices are a little esoteric… as in "impish ibex-
es" and "exuberant xenopus." 4–8.

■ Babar's World Tour 2006

(by Laurent de Brunhoff, Abrams $16.95 ●●●● ½)
Babar takes older fans on a grand tour of the world,
where they learn to say key phrases in every language and learn a little about each culture, along
with a dollop of wit and whimsy. The Babar-
shaped iceberg is totally cool! Still top rated,
Babar's Book of Colors, PLATINUM AWARD '05.
4–7.

■ Click, Clack, Quackity-Quack 2006

(by Doreen Cronin and Betsy Lewin, Atheneum
$ 12.95 ●●●●) From the creators of **Clack,
Clack, Moo,** this is a lively alphabet book with
many of the barnyard gang rushing off to a picnic. There's not a lot of story but the action
words and lilting language are one way to turn
young listeners' attention to the A, B, C's.

■ Daisy Gets Dressed 2006

(by Clare Beaton, Barefoot $15.99 ●●●●) Beaton's fabric collages are
designed as an "I Spy" game. Children must hunt for a piece of clothing with a particular pattern to help Daisy get dressed. 3 & up.

■ Opposites 2006

(by Robert Crowther, Candlewick $12.99
●●●● ½) Sturdy pages with pull tabs and
turning wheels that reveal clear pairs of
opposites. Bold colors and illustrations
showing dynamic motion add much to the
meaning of pairs of opposites, such as a
rollercoaster seen going up and then one
going down; a glass of juice full, and then

empty; a sandwich thin, and then and thick; an alligator's mouth open and then shut. These are just a few of the delightful illustrations. 3 & up.

■ Tall 2006 PLATINUM AWARD

(by Jez Alborough, Candlewick $15.99 ooooo) From the author of *Hug*, another very simple concept book that is told largely through illustrations and next to no words. This time a little chimp discovers that *tall* and *small* are really only a matter of perspective as the tall animals of the jungle keep giving Chimp a new way of seeing himself and others. 2½ & up.

■ Time to Say Please! 2006

(by Mo Willems, Hyperion $15.99 oooo½) Good manners are more fun when they are stirred up with a touch of humor—one of Willems's specialties! He didn't forget the thank-you part of the equation, either!

■ What Does Bunny See? 2006

(by Linda Sue Park/illus. by Maggie Smith, Clarion $15.00 oooo½) Bunny hops through the garden discovering a world of colors. Smith's flowers are lush and reinforce color concepts within the context of a small story. 3–6.

Young Science
■ Bugs Pop-Up

(by Sally Hewitt/illus. by Chris Gilvan-Cartwright, Abrams $14.95 oooo) With a playful rhyme about each of the creatures, this is a spectacular pop-up book with giant faces of a wasp, bee, and other creepy crawlers that almost leap off the pages! A memorable novelty book. 3 & up. Also ideal for bug fans, **Big Bugs! Giant Creepy Crawly Pop Ups** (by Keith Faulkner/illus. by Stephen Holmes & Jonathan Lambert, Scholastic $10.95 oooo) with big foldouts that answer riddles posed on each page. 3 & up.

■ Eye Guess 2006

(by Phyllis L. Tildes, Charlesbridge $9.95 oooo) Eight different animals are introduced with close-up images of their eyes and a riddle. Open the flap to discover the whole animal in its habitat. 4 & up.

■ Hamsters to the Rescue 2006

(by Ellen Stoll Walsh, Harcourt $16 oooo) once again Walsh introduces young children to some science concepts through a small story. Two Hamsters find a feather and try to return it to Seagull. Along the way they meet a hermit crab who is trying to avoid Seagull and some cranky crabs. From the creator of Mouse Paint. 3 & up.

■ Mister Seahorse

(by Eric Carle, Philomel $16.95 ooooo) Get ready for a Johnny Carson "I did not know that" kind of moment when you share this handsome early science book. Carle visits the important role of fathers in the sea. Male seahorses carry the eggs in their pouch and male tilapia carry their eggs in their mouth. Lift-up see-through pages add visual surprises. PLATINUM AWARD '05. 3 & up.

■ One Smart Goose 2006

(by Caroline Jayne Church, Orchard $16.95 oooo) One little goose manages to outfox the big bad fox that chases all the other geese. Knowing how to disappear is the Smart Goose's secret that leads to a merry chase. Undergoose wins! A happy solution in a world where the small are not usually mighty. An introduction to the concept of camouflage in nature. 3–6.

■ Watch Me Grow Farm Animals 2006

(by Lisa Magloff et al., DK Books $7.99 oooo) Clear photos and simple text introduce young readers to animals on the farm. Also in the series, **Puppy,** from closed-eye puppy to wide-eyed pooch.

■ We've All Got Bellybuttons! 2006 PLATINUM AWARD

(by David Martin/illus by Randy Cecil, Candlewick $15.99 ooooo) Toddlers and young preschoolers will enjoy the repetitive questions and active replies built into this jolly romp of a book. A playful book that introduces a big concept, namely that we all have a lot in common—hands for clapping, feet for kicking, and belly buttons for tickling. 2–5.

■ Winter's Tale `2006` PLATINUM AWARD

(by Robert Sabuda, Simon & Schuster $26.95 ●●●●●) Save this to share together—little hands are apt to destroy it—as they will be thrilled with the stunning pop-ups that glitter with scenes of winter and white owls, bunnies, bears, deer, and a fabulous moose! Enjoy this with and without the words; with large and small pop-ups on every fold, it's a double "oooh!" through and through! All ages.

Starting to School

■ Bunny School `2006`

(by Rick Walton/illus. Paige Miglio, HarperCollins $15.99 ●●●●) Charming illustrations of bunnies in preschool give little ones a preview of things to come. Rhyming text and typical activities of the day make this a reassuring guide to starting preschool. 3 & up.

■ When an Elephant Comes to School `2006`

(by Jan Ormerod, Orchard Books $16.95 ●●●●½) Though Elephant seems rather large to be starting school and though he is a bit unsure of how school will be, in no time at all Elephant and his classmates and teacher are having a wonderful time! A happy romp that makes school look too good to miss! 3–6.

■ Super Sue at Super School `2006`

(by Cressida Cowell/illus. by Russell Ayto, Candlewick $8.99 ●●●●) A novelty pull-the-tabs book for those who may be feeling a bit shy about saying good-bye. Let's hope they all have the good fortune of Super Sue who bounces through that first day of school and makes a good friend, too! 3 & up.

Early-School-Age Children

During the early school years, as kids become readers and not just listeners, keeping them "in books" is a challenge. Reading is something they should do for pleasure, not because it's "good for them." By bringing home a rich variety of books—fact and fantasy, science and history, humor and adventure, read-alouds, and read-alones—you will be building a link to a lifetime of pleasure found in books.

BLUE CHIP BOOKS EVERY EARLY-SCHOOL-AGE KID SHOULD KNOW

✓ **Alexander and the Terrible, Horrible, No Good, Very Bad Day,** by Judith Viorst

✓ **Amazing Grace,** by Mary Hoffman

✓ **Amos and Boris/Sylvester and the Magic Pebble,** by William Steig

✓ **Martha series,** by Susan Meddaugh

✓ **Jolly Postman books,** by Janet and Allan Ahlberg

✓ **Magic Schoolbus series,** by Joanna Cole

✓ **Olivia** and **Olivia Saves the Circus,** by Ian Falconer

✓ **Ramona series,** by Beverly Cleary

✓ **Tar Beach,** by Faith Ringgold

✓ **The True Story of the Three Little Pigs,** by Jon Scieszka

✓ **Where the Wild Things Are,** by Maurice Sendak

Great Read-Alouds for Older Listeners

■ Diary of a Spider
2006 PLATINUM AWARD

(by Doreen Cronin/illus. by Harry Bliss, HarperCollins $15.99 ●●●●●) Like her amusing *Diary of a Worm*, this new diary gives us an inside view of the eight-legged world of a young spider who has an unlikely friend, Fly. Not quite as funny as the original, but likely to amuse young readers. 4 & up.

■ The Dog Who Cried Wolf ✦2006✦ PLATINUM AWARD

(by Keiko Kasza, Putnam $15.99 ●●●●●) Moka is a dog who loves his girl, Michelle, until she reads a story about wolves that inspires Moka to run away and be free. In his adventure with independence, Moka discovers real wolves and that home is not as boring as he thought. 4–8.

■ Granite Baby 2006

(by Lynne Bertrand/illus. by Kevin Hawkes, Farrar Straus $16 ●●●●) In the tradition of the tall tale, this story of a wailing baby is likely to amuse big sisters and brothers who have endured the endless cries of a new baby. Kevin Hawkes' art gives this yarn a giant-sized lift. 4–8.

■ The Knight Who Took All Day 2006

(by James Mayhew, Scholastic $15.99 ●●●●) In this spoof, a not-so-gallant knight seems more concerned with his appearance than in saving his kingdom from a fiery dragon. It is a young princess who tames the dragon and goes off with the patient young squire to live happily ever after! Though some might wonder why. 4–8.

■ Mutt Dog 2006

(by Stephen M. King, Harcourt $16 ●●●●½) A homeless dog takes the reader to the underside of life in the city. He ends up in a shelter where he is at least accepted, but not for long. A tender story that might help adults talk with children about homelessness and how one person's kindness can make a difference. 6 & up.

■ Pig Tale 2006

(by Helen Oxenbury, Simon & Schuster $16.95 ●●●●½) Bertha and Briggs wished for money and riches and by a stroke of good fortune they dug it up. But, alas, after getting all they wished for, the two lucky pigs discover that money doesn't really buy happiness. Oxenbury's verse goes along with her merry illustrations. 4–7.

■ Pirate Girl 2006 PLATINUM AWARD

(by Cornelia Funke/illus. by Kerstin Meyer, Scholastic $15.95 ●●●●●) When Captain Firebeard captures a little red-headed girl named Molly, he thinks he will get a huge ransom for her. But, alas, the joke's on Redbeard when Molly's mom comes to the rescue. "The Ransom of Red Chief" it's not, but it's a good yarn for young pirate lovers. 4–8.

■ Terrific 2006

(by Jon Agee, Hyperion $15.95 ●●●●½) Eugene wins a cruise to

Bermuda and it's all downhill from there. As each mishap occurs, Eugene pronounces it "terrific" until his ship sinks. There on a deserted island he meets an injured parrot who does indeed turn out to be terrific. A funny yarn with enough repetition to invite and delight young listeners. 4–8.

■ Upstairs Mouse, Downstairs Mole *2006*

(by Wong Herbery Yee, Houghton Mifflin $16 oooo½) There are several connected stories about these two neighbors, Mouse and Mole, that play on the theme that we don't all enjoy the same things—yet we can be friends. Learning that others have different tastes and needs for their comfort is a giant idea to children who are struggling with being and making friends. 4–7.

Families Then and Now

Kids love stories about families like their own as well as those that are totally different. We've chosen family stories about kids today and those who lived in the past. The historic settings and figures offer kids a glimpse into another time and place. Past or present, good stories speak to kids about human experiences.

■ Are You Going to be Good? *2006*

(by Cari Best/illus. G. Brian Karas, Farrar Straus $16 oooo½) Great-Gran Sadie is about to celebrate her 100th birthday. Young Robert not only has to dress up (which he likes), he is warned about so many rules of behaving that it's bewildering. But, in true form, there's one person who understands well when Robert starts dancing. Charming and often true—young and old often understand each other well. 5 & up.

■ Game Day *2006*

(by Tiki and Ronde Barber/illus. Barry Root, Simon & Schuster $16.95 oooo½) Twin brothers, who happen to be NFL Superstars in real life, give young readers a story about their earlier years. A solid story about being a team player. A not-too-heavy-handed message in a win-

win sports story. 7 & up.

■ Kamishibai Man 2006

(by Allen Say, Houghton Mifflin $17 oooo) Based on his childhood in Japan, Say recalls the kamishibai man who used to come to the neighborhood (much like the Good Humor Man) to sell candies along with cliffhanger stories that grew each day. TV finished this old tradition, but here the kamishibai man returns to his old neighborhood and is received lovingly by his former children and a new generation. As always, the art is splendid, while the story may interest adults more than children. 7 & up.

■ Lizzie Nonsense, A Story of Pioneer Days 2006

(by Jan Ormerod, Clarion $15 oooo½) Here is Little House in the Outback . . . a charming picture book set in pioneer days in Australian bush country when Papa needs a week to travel fifty miles. That leaves Lizzie, her mom, and baby sister alone in an isolated place where dingoes howl at night, along with other dangers. But Lizzie's imagination turns out to be just the right kind of "nonsense" to carry them through. 5 & up.

Legends, Bible Stories, and Folktales

■ Cinderella 2006

(Retold and illus. by Barbara McClintock, Scholastic $15.99 oooo½) After a trip to Paris, the artist used Versailles and the Paris Opera as the inspiration for the Prince's palace, and the costumes and hairdos are from the time of Louis XIV. 5 & up.

■ Honey... Honey... Lion! 2006

(by Jan Brett, Putnam $16.99 oooo) An African folktale about a honeyguide bird and a honey badger who usually work together. But one day the badger fails to share and the next day the clever bird leads him to a less-than-sweet treat. 4 & up.

■ Little Bear, You're a Star! *2006*

(by Jean Marzollo, Little Brown $12.99 ○○○○½)
With a Greek chorus of birds running along the
bottom of the pages, here is an amusingly light
and airy spin on the Greek myth of Callisto and
Arcas, and how the constellations Ursa Major
and Minor came to be. As in her collection of
Bible stories, Marzollo introduces children to
some of the big stories with child-sized versions
that are entertaining and memorable. 5 & up.

■ The Wolf's Story *2006* PLATINUM AWARD

(by Toby Forward/Izhar Cohen,
Candlewick $15.99 ○○○○○) Maybe
you think you know what happened
to Little Red, but here is the wolf's eye
view of that old story! Of course, he
meant no harm! Told with great good
humor, this is a perfect tale for ham-
ming it up! 5 & up.

Alphabet Books

■ A Apple Pie *2006*

(illus. by Gennady Spirin, Philomel $16.99 ○○○○) Merry illustrations
give a new look to this classic ABC that dates back to the 1600s and
is written in flowing script. Both printed and script letters are shown
on each page along with multiple objects that start with the given
letter. 5 & up.

■ A Was Once an Apple Pie *2006*

(by Edward Lear/illus. by Suse MacDonald, Scholastic $12.99 ○○○○
½) Readers and listeners are going to enjoy
the nonsense rhyme of this playful alphabet
book. The cut-paper illustrations may also
inspire young artists to make up their own
bold images for original alphabet books with
alliterative rhymes, as in, "R was once a little ring . . . ringy, springy, lingy, dingy,
ringalingy little ring!" 5 & up.

Information, Please:
Science, History, Art, and More

School-age kids have an appetite for information about the real world. They want to know where things come from, how they are made, and how they work. Though they live very much in the present, they are curious about the past and how things were. Such information used to be found only in encyclopedias or dull textbooks. Today there are gloriously beautiful and lively nonfiction books for young readers.

Science

■ Birds *2006*

(by Philippe Dubois and Valerie Guidoux/photos by Gilles Martin/drawings Jean Chevallier, Abrams $18.95 ০০০০½) Stunning photographs and beautiful drawings fill this oversized book about birds. This is more of a coffeetable book to dip into for short but informed pieces about the origin of birds, their social habits, their songs, and other unusual facts. A gem for "birders" young and old. 6–66.

■ Smithsonian Rock & Fossil Hunter *2006*

(by David Burnie, DK $9.99 ০০০০) One of an excellent new series designed for young readers. There are activities to do as well as foldout covers with clear images of typical rocks and fossils to spot. An informative and inviting format for young science explorations. Also in the series, by various authors: **Star Gazer, Bird Watcher, Bug Hunter.**

■ Prehistoric Actual Size *2006*

(by Steve Jenkins, Houghton Mifflin $16 ০০০০½) It isn't about the facts, though this is a picture book crammed full of facts and tidbits of information. In this case, it's far more about the wonder of these amazing specimens, shown in their actual size. Though they can't fit in their entirety, Jenkins show you enough of a detail to deliver the big ideas. Imagine a dragonfly with wings more than two feet across, or a

terror bird large enough to eat a horse! Of course, we do not know how large or small horses were in those days. Also top rated, **I See a Kookaburra!** Introducing animals from differing habitats. 6 & up.

■ Scholastic Atlas of Space *2006*

(edited by Caroline Fortin et al., Scholastc $17.95 ●●●●) An introduction to the solar system with handsome illustrations and readable chunks of information for beginning star gazers.

■ Volcanoes: Journey to the Crater's Edge

(by Philippe Bourseiller/adapted by Robert Burleigh, Abrams $14.95 ●●●●●) Stunning photographs give armchair travellers a sense of the drama that erupts in so many different ways from volcanoes around the world. PLATINUM AWARD '04. A worthy sequel to PLATINUM winner **Earth From Above** (by Yann Arthus-Bertrand/Robert Burleigh, Abrams, $12.95 ●●●●●). 8 & up. New for *2006* in this handsome collection of books about our earth, **Philip Plisson's Lighthouses** (by Francis Dreyer ($18.95 ●●●● ½) A history with drawings and splendid photographs of lighthouses all over the world, from ancient Egypt to today.

■ Why? *2006*

(by Lila Prap, Kane/Miller $14.95 ●●●●) Why do hyenas laugh? In bold print around the amusing illustration, there are all sorts of silly answers. But to the right a scientific explanation tells all. A collection of questions about animals such as the zebra, kangaroo, monkey, and many more are answered in the same way. Kids might enjoy making up more Q & As to go with other animals. 6 & up.

People and Places in History

■ Egypt: In Spectacular Cross Section *2006*

(by Stephen Biesty, Scholastic $18.99 ●●●● ½) Stunning illustrations fill this oversized view of ancient Egypt. He shows us an 11-year-old boy and his father on a 30-day journey up the Nile to the Valley of the Kings. Miniatures to study in cutaway views and text that explains the details.

■ From Rags to Riches: A History of Girls' Clothing in America *2006*

(by Leslie Sills, Holiday House, $16.95 ●●●● ½) Future clothing and costume designers or those keen on clothes will enjoy this pictorial history. 8 & up.

■ The Patchwork Path, A Quilt Map to Freedom *2006*

(by Bettye Stroud/illus. by Erin S. Bennett, Candlewick $15.99 ●●●●) A father and daughter attempt to escape the plantation in this handsomely illustrated work of historic fiction. Using quilt patterns that were really messages, escaping slaves found help along the way on their journey to freedom. 7 & up.

■I Could Do That! *2006*

(by Linda Arms White/illus. by Nancy Carpenter, Farrar Strauss $16 ●●●●) Esther Morris was a determined young girl who always felt she could meet whatever challenge came her way. In time, she not only moves to the frontier, to the Wyoming Territory, she also manages to become the first woman elected to public office in the United States, and gets the vote for Wyoming women! 7 & up.

■ Memories of Survival *2006*

(by Esther Nisenthal Krinitz & Bernice Steinhardt, Hyperion $15.99 ●●●● ½) Embroidered panels are done by a survivor of the Holocaust in Poland and are accompanied with her own words and a commentary by her daughter. Stunning! 10 & up.

■ Our Eleanor *2006*

(by Candace Fleming, Atheneum $19.95 ●●●● ½) You can read this from front to back or dip into the one- and two-page sections that address a particular moment in Eleanor Roosevelt's remarkable life. There are tons of pictorial materials, photos, newspapers, cartoons, and letters that fill in this "scrapbook" and give young readers a sense of Eleanor's life as she grew from lonely child to greatly admired leader in a time when there were few such women in the world. 10–14.

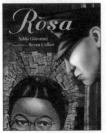

■Rosa *2006*

(by Nikki Giovanni/illus. by Bryan Collier, Holt $16.95 ●●●● ½) With quiet strength and dignity, Rosa Parks led people to stand up for their rights just as she refused to give up her seat on the bus. Beautifully crafted, the story builds as it tells of those who changed the law; the foldout pages show the many people who followed her lead and walked instead of riding the buses in Montgomery. 7 & up.

■ So You Want to be an Explorer 2006

(by Judith St. George/illus. by David Small, Philomel $16.99 **oooo**) A bit less focused than this team's **So You Want to be President?**, this is an interesting concept book that introduces young readers to certain commonalities that explorers through the ages share, such as being curious, adventurous, and determined. They are also risk-takers who respect native people they meet along their way. This will not replace the encyclopedia for school assignments, but rather will address the spirit of exploring in ways that the facts in encyclopedias sometimes forget. 8 & up.

■ Twenty-One Elephants and Still Standing 2006

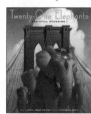

(by April Jones Prince/illus. by Francois Roca, Houghton Mifflin $16 **oooo** ½) We had a similar story based on true events last year. In that version the child storyteller is at the center of the story and longs to go on the newly built Brooklyn Bridge. In this one, it's P.T. Barnum who comes up with the solution. Either way, it's a great story and speaks to the fears people have of most new things. 7 & up.

Dinosaurs

■ Boy, Were We Wrong About Dinosaurs! 2006

(by Kathleen V. Kudlinski/illus. by S.D. Schindler, Dutton $15.99

oooo ½) A refreshing look at dinosaurs, con-trasting what we used to think we knew, with what we think we know now. As interesting as the information is in this book, it's the bigger idea that wins the day by helping young people see that our body of knowl-edge is not fixed and closed, but rather is ever-growing and often changing. 7 & up.

■ Encyclopedia Prehistorica Dinosaurs 2006 PLATINUM AWARD

(by Robert Sabuda & Matthew Reinhart, Candlewick $25 **ooooo**) There are several pop-ups on almost every page of this amazing book. And on flaps and lift-up sections of the pages, there is more information than most pop-up novelty books usually provide. The paper engineering is highly detailed with smaller and more intricate pop-ups than the typical full-page ones for younger audiences. This is likely to become a collector's item—for those who love dinosaurs or pop-ups, this is a must-have gift!

The Human Body and Reproduction

■ Hello Benny!

(by Robie H. Harris/illus. by Michael Emberley, McElderry Books $16.95 ●●●● ½) The lively illustrations and narrative tell the story of how it feels to be a baby. Each big idea is further explained with scientific explanations that are easy to understand. For example, Benny is shown smiling at himself in a mirror and enjoying playing peek-a-boo with Grandma. Stranger-anxiety is explained in 50¢ words instead of the $5 variety. 4–8.

■ How Are Babies Made?

(by Alastair Smith/illus. by Maria Wheatley, Usborne $7.95 ●●●●) Simple, clear text and illustrations on flap pages give children an intro to the facts of life. 5 & up. Also top rated, **How You Were Born** (by Joanna Cole/photos by Margaret Miller, Morrow).

Sports

To get reluctant readers to pick up a book, try a topic they have a lively interest in. Reading about sports is a key for some kids. Older readers will enjoy both the *Eyewitness* books on different sports and Matt Christopher's many sports-centered chapter books.

■ I Love Tennis 2006

(by Naia Bray-Moffatt, DK $12.95 ●●●● ½) Kids who are taking tennis lessons will dive right into this book with clear photos and a cast of multicultural boys and girls. We know "how-to" books do not substitute for hands-on play, but this one may just give young players a chance to reflect and recall some of the fast-paced advice they get in class. 7 & up.

■ Joe Louis: America's Fighter 2006 PLATINUM AWARD

(by David A. Adler/illus. by Terry Widener, Harcourt $16 ●●●●●) Adler has taken a huge story and given young readers a true sense of the highlights, and the ups and downs of a man who changed the world of boxing. The story of Joe Louis, an American icon, is told with suspense as well as compassion. 8 & up.

Art and Art History
■ Art in a Box *2006*

(by Sarah Richardson, Abrams $19.95 ○○○○ ½) You don't need to get to the Tate in London to enjoy these activity cards. Each has a work of art on one side, and suggestions and questions for looking at the details of the art on the reverse. But this is more than an exercise in art appreciation; each card has open-ended art activities that relate to the art, creative exercises that kids (and adults) are likely to enjoy together. 7 & up.

■ The Usborne Complete Book of Art Ideas
2006 PLATINUM AWARD

(by Fiona Watt et al., Usborne $39.95 ○○○○○) A stunning collection of more than 400 art activities that invite kids to try paper sculpture, collage, chalk, rubbings, embossing, resist painting, and so many more art forms. The book itself is both handsome and inspiring! You'll enjoy dipping into this with your whole family. 10 & up.

■ Seen Art? *2006*

(by Jon Scieszka and Lane Smith, Viking $16.99 ○○○○) One boy is looking for his friend Art and ends up on tour at the new MOMA in New York. For those who have seen the collection, the reproductions here might lend some recall. This is a one-joke book with small reproductions of a major collection. Good, not great. 7 & up.

■ Imagine *2006*

(by Norman Messenger, Candlewick $17.99 ○○○○ ½) As an object, this is a book designed to engage children in looking, and looking again to discover more than a quick glance will reveal. It's a visual romp for older children—not the very young who may find some of the images frightening. 8 & up.

Easy-to-Read Books

Many of the books in this section are from series designed especially for young readers and are available in paperback. Keep in mind that many regular trade books listed elsewhere may also be easy to read.

 BLUE CHIP BOOKS
EVERY BEGINNING READER SHOULD KNOW

✓**Amelia Bedelia,** by Peggy Parish
✓**Are You My Mother?** by P. D. Eastman
✓**Frog and Toad,** by Arnold Lobel
✓**Go, Dog, Go!** by P. D. Eastman
✓**Green Eggs and Ham,** by Dr. Seuss
✓**Henry and Mudge** and **Poppleton series,** by Cynthia Rylant
✓**Little Bear,** by Else H. Minarik
✓**My Father's Dragon,** by Ruth S. Gannett
✓**Polk Street series,** by Patricia R. Giff
✓**The Stories Julian Tells,** by Ann Cameron
✓**Fluffy Series,** by Kate McMullan
✓**Let's Read and Find Out Series** (HarperCollins)

To help your beginner:

📖 Choose books that are not a struggle. Easy does it!

📖 If every other word is too hard, you've got the wrong book for now.

📖 If your child gets stuck on a word, say the word. Some words can't be sounded out.

📖 A bookmark under the line your child is reading can help to keep the place.

Just Beginning Books: Easy to Read
■ Fish and Frog *2006*

(by Michelle Knudsen, Candlewick $14.99 ●●●●) New to the *Brand New Readers*, a collection of four small stories—one line to a page—about Fish and Frog. Illustrations help the begin-

ner with sight words that may be new but are obvious in context. Funny little stories with plenty of repetition, position words, and opposites. First grade.

■ Moving Day *2006*

(by Anthony G. Brandon/illus. by Wong H. Yee, Harcourt $12.95 **oooo**½) This tackles a tough problem with a short but snappy ending. Annie doesn't want to move until a new member of the family (a puppy) arrives and is moving with her. Part of the excellent *Green Light Readers* series.

■ Termite Trouble *2006*

(by Kathy Caple, Candlewick $14.99 **oooo**½) Four funny stories featuring a termite who eats his friends' houses; bounces on a trampoline; makes a piece of sculpture; and helps an ostrich to fly. These are like short comic strips with enough action in the images to tell the story. The text is repetitive and one line long per page, so it's a happy magic key to sight reading from the *Brand New Readers*. First grade.

■ Rose and Riley *2006*

(by Jane Cutler/illus. by Thomas F. Yezerski, Farrar Straus $15 **oooo**) Three predictable stories about Rose, a youngish vole, and Riley, an older and wiser groundhog; one about wanting to use new umbrellas in the rain, another about un-birthdays, and a last one about nighttime fears with a clever solution that might satisfy young worriers. Also amusing, **Rose and Riley Come and Go.**

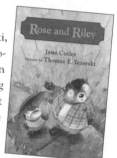

Intermediate Readers

■ Babe Ruth Saves Baseball! *2006*

(by Frank Murphy/illus. by Richard Walz, Random House $3.99 paper **oooo**) Baseball fans are going to love every moment of this story, which traces Babe Ruth's career from being both batter and pitcher for the Red Sox to his days at Yankee Stadium—where he hit the first home run! Illustrations have the same lively spark that the text does. Also: **Let's Go to the Ballpark** (by James Buckley, Jr. DK $3.99 ❍❍❍❍) Two kids go to their first major league game at Dodger Stadium.

■ Big Bugs 2006

(by Seymour Simon, SeaStar/Chronicle $3.95 paper ❍❍❍❍) Vivid photographs and clear language make this a good choice for bug lovers. Simon, who writes some the best science books for upper grade readers, has switched gears for beginners and created new *See More Readers*. He uses concrete examples to make connections between what children know and what they are learning. Marked Level 1, there is not a lot on each page, but the language makes a better fit for the next level up. Also recommended, his **Amazing Bats** and a handsome book, **Bridges.** 2nd & 3rd grade.

■ From Slave to Soldier 2006

(by Deborah Hopkinson/illus. by Brian Floca, Atheneum $14.95 ❍❍❍❍) When Union Soldiers arrive at the farm where Johnny is a slave, they ask him to come along with them. Based on a true life story of a boy who served in the Union army.

■ Mercy Watson to the Rescue 2006

(by Kate DiCamillo/illus. by Chris Van Dusen, Candlewick $12.99 ❍❍❍❍) Mercy, an indulged "porcine wonder" to her owners, is nothing but a pig to her cranky neighbors. This is the first of a series and Mercy will no doubt continue to pull the wool over the Watsons' loving eyes. 2nd, 3rd grade.

■ Sniffles, Sneezes, Hiccups, and Coughs 2006

(by Penny Durant, DK $3.99 paper ❍❍❍❍) Young readers are often more curious about real things than the usual fiction stories written for beginners. This informative book has simple explanations and clear photos.

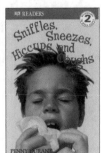

Transition Chapter Books for Advanced Beginners and Beyond

Kids at this stage often love reading books in series with continuing characters and familiar settings. Reading every book in a series may seem boring to adults, but satisfies young readers and helps them gain fluidity in their reading. Among our top-rated series to consider are:

Polk Street series, by Patricia Reily Giff; **Sports series,** by Matt Christopher; **Boxcar Children,** by Gertrude C. Warner; **Amber Brown** series, by Paula Danziger; **Ramona** and **Henry Huggins** series, by Beverly Cleary; **Arthur** chapter books, by Marc Brown; **Song Lee** and **Horrible Harry** series, by Suzy Kline; **The Zack Files,** by Dan Greenburg; **Junie B.** series, by Barbara Park; **Magic Treehouse** series, by Mary Pope Osborne; and the **Star Wars Jedi** series, by Jude Watson.

■ Spy Force Series 2006

(by Deborah Abela/illus. by George O'Connor, Simon & Schuster $9.95 ○○○○) Eleven-year-old Max looks like your everyday kid, but she is a superspy involved in an international agency, Spy Force. **In Search of Time and Space** is the first in the series and our eleven-year-old reader found it exciting and suspenseful.

True Readers

Editors' Note: Better than a flashlight under the covers, the **Harry Potter LUMOS Book Light** 2006 Platinum Award (Lightwedge $34.95 ○○○○○) comes with an acrylic lens that you place over the book page and it lights the page evenly. Truly amazing! Also comes sans Harry Potter motif and in smaller versions. You'll want your own. (877) 777-9334.

Non-fiction

■ Code Talker 2006

(by Joseph Bruchac, Dial $16.99 ○○○○½) Based on true events during WWII, Joseph Bruchac tells the once-secret story of the Navaho soldiers who served in the Marine Corps using the language of their culture to send messages that were impossible for the enemy to read. Opening with the narrator's days in an Indian school where his native language was outlawed, there is more than a little irony in this story of courage that saved the lives of scores of GIs in the Pacific. 9 & up.

■ A Friend Called Anne 2006

(retold by Carol Ann Lee, Viking $15.99 ●●●●½) Anne Frank's diary has inspired movies, plays, and a wealth of books. This latest is about Anne and her "best" friend, "Jopie." This is a book for those who have read the diary. The two girls meet at the Jewish school they must now attend. Their brief, intense friendship and Jacqueline's own story give readers a fuller sense of their lives. 10 & up.

Fiction

We have more fantasy in this section than realistic fiction. Much of the reality fiction that arrived this season was so soap opera-ish that we had trouble finding titles we wanted to pass on to young readers. If you are looking for books for your fourth, fifth, or sixth grader, better read the synopses, first.

■ Eldest 2006 PLATINUM AWARD

(by Christopher Paolini, Knopf $21 ●●●●●) The much-anticipated Book Two in *The Inheritance Trilogy*. Eragon and his dragon are off to pursue Eragon's skills as a Dragon Rider and meet new adventures at every turn. Meanwhile, at home, Eragon's cousin Roran is battling the Ra'zac, and fighting for his life. For fans of fantasy, created by a teenager, this is a page turner. 10 & up.

■ Gregor and the Curse of the Warmbloods 2006

(by Suzanne Collins, Scholastic $16.95 ●●●●½) Collins has created an entire world of creatures (giant cockroaches, bats) and violet-eyed humans that inhabit the "underland" beneath New York City. Book Three continues with the story of the threat of a plague to the underworld that only Gregor can prevent. 10 & up.

■ Harry Potter and the Half-Blood Prince 2006 PLATINUM AWARD

(by J.K. Rowling, Scholastic $29.99 ●●●●●) The sixth in the best-selling series about Harry Potter and his adventures at Hogwart's School of Magic. Darker than earlier titles, some of our tween readers were even more disturbed by the amount of kissing in this book. While some found the ending crushingly sad, it has elicited great speculation about what will happen in the final book.

■ Inkspell *2006* PLATINUM AWARD

(by Cornelia Funke, Scholastic $19.99 ●●●●●) "Even better than *Inkheart!*" was the report from our 11-year old reader. A year has passed since Meggie first encountered the book, *Inkheart*, where the characters came to life. Now Dustfinger seeks a way back to the tale. Meggie and Farid find a way to get into the book themselves. Also wonderful, **The Thief Lord.** 9 & up.

■ Kitty and Mr. Kipling *2006*

(by Lenore Blegvad, McElderry Books, $16.95 ●●●●½) Those who know *The Jungle Book* may be surprised to know it was written not in India but in Vermont! Kitty, a fictional character who lives on a neighboring farm, tells the story of the four years when Rudyard Kipling and his American-born wife build a dream house that they must abandon. 7–10.

■ Operation Red Jericho *2006*

(by Joshua Mowll, Candlewick $15.99 ●●●●½) Pull-out pages of imaginative art add to the incredible mystery adventure told in the form of a diary with sidebars, codes, and made-up photographs. Our readers found the story of two young people in search of their parents grisly at times and suspenseful at every turn, and the graphic quality of the book itself, a treasure of visual surprises. 10 & up.

■ The Search for Belle Prater *2006*

(by Ruth White, Farrar Straus $16 ●●●●½) When Woodrow's birthday arrives on New Year's Eve the phone rings, but the person on the other end hangs up. Woodrow is certain it is his mother, Belle Prater, who disappeared a year ago. A sequel to the award-winning **Belle Prater's Boy,** this beautifully crafted novel is about young people who not only suffer losses, but have the grit to go on to do something about them. White has also drawn some strong adults that the young people in the story can rely upon. 9–12.

■ Shakespeare's Secret *2006*

(by Elise Broach, Holt $16.95 ●●●●½) Hero has just moved and her elderly neighbor tells her that there might be a million-dollar, historically significant diamond hidden in her house. The sheriff's son, who has his own reasons for finding the missing gem, befriends Hero. Just enough history here to add interest with a feel-good (if slightly unbelievable) ending. You don't have to know the Bard to enjoy this one. Plenty of suspense and a dollop of history! 10 & up.

■ **The Sisters Grimm** **2006** PLATINUM AWARD

(by Michael Buckley, Amulet/Abrams $14.95 ❍❍❍❍❍) Two sisters, Sabrina and Daphne, are sent to live with their grandmother, Relda Grimm. They discover that Grimm's fairy tales are really a work of history, not fiction, as they quickly meet an assortment of villains and heroes from the fairy tales (Jack, Puck, Prince Charming, the Three Little Pigs). Buckley, a television writer, has imagined a fast-moving tale—you can already see where the special effects will go! 9 & up.

Read-Aloud or Read-Alone Chapter Books

Long before school-age kids can tackle big chapter books on their own, they enjoy the more fully drawn characters, richer language, and multilayered plots found in storybooks. These first novels, with more words than pictures, push children to imagine with the mind's eye—something they will need to do as they grow into reading. In time these books may be reread independently. For now, the best way to motivate the next level of readership is to continue reading good books to your child. Among the most beautiful and collectible for the family library are the Books of Wonder editions. After seeing films such as *The Borrowers* and *Charlotte's Web*, try reading the originals and do a little comparative literature with young listeners.

- 📖 **The Black Stallion,** by Walter Farley
- 📖 **The Borrowers,** by Mary Norton
- 📖 **Catwings,** by Ursula LeGuin
- 📖 **Charlie and the Chocolate Factory,** by Roald Dahl
- 📖 **Charlotte's Web** and **Stuart Little,** by E. B. White
- 📖 **Freddy the Pig Series** by Walter R. Brooks

- 📖 **Harry Potter series** by J. K. Rowling
- 📖 **The House at Pooh Corner,** by A. A. Milne
- 📖 **James and the Giant Peach,** by Roald Dahl
- 📖 **Lassie Come-Home,** by Eric Knight
- 📖 **Little House series,** by Laura Ingalls Wilder
- 📖 **The Littles,** by John Peterson
- 📖 **Mary Poppins,** by P. L. Travers
- 📖 **My Father's Dragon,** by Ruth S. Gannett
- 📖 **The Real Thief,** by William Steig
- 📖 **Sarah, Plain and Tall; Skylark;** and **Caleb's Story** by Patricia MacLachlan
- 📖 **Wizard of Oz series,** by L. Frank Baum

Resource/Activity Books

■ Ballerina for a Day *2006*

(by Dawn Sirett et al., DK $12.99 ●●●●) Here's a combination pop-up, paper doll, and try-this-stretching-and-these-positions book. Not a lot of text, but a variety of activities for the beginning dancer. 5 & up.

■ How to Make Monstrous, Huge, Unbelievably Big Bubbles *2006*

(by David Stein et al., Klutz $16.95 ●●●●½) David Stein's "Bubble Thing" does make monstrous, 10-20 foot big, amazing bubbles. An updated classic, with full-color photos and clear tips on how to get results. Our 9-year-old tester and her dad gave this a rave review! Still top rated, PLATINUM AWARD-winning **The Klutz Book of Paper Airplanes** ($16.95 ●●●●●) Instructions for ten different paper airplanes. 7 & up.

■ Spool Knit Jewelry

(by Anne Akers Johnson, Klutz $16.95 ●●●●) Our 11-year-old tester gave this book an "A++" and loved making bracelets with the old-fashioned knitting spool and crochet hook. Comes with elastic cord, and glass and plastic beads. Marked 8 & up, we'd say more like 10 with parental help. Still top rated from the same author, PLATINUM AWARD-winning **Origami** (Klutz $16.95 ●●●●●). Our in-house origami master says this is the best origami book for beginners. 6 & up.

Coping with Life's Ups and Downs: Books for Mixed Ages

Many of the books in this section are what we call *bridge books*—they span two age groups. Some are on the young side, others are for older kids, and many will do for both. Included are books that address problems that families often need to cope with.

Feelings

■ Courage

(by Bernard Waber, Houghton Mifflin $16 ●●●●●) Waber explores all the large and small everyday kinds of acts that can be thought of as courageous: doing tricks on skates, riding a two-wheeler, keeping a secret, trying new things, saying good-bye. Most important of all, "courage is what we give each other." A gem! PLATINUM AWARD '03. 4–8.

■ Froggy's Sleepover *2006* PLATINUM AWARD

(by Jonathan London/illus. by Frank Remkiewicz, Viking $15.99 ●●●●●) For anyone who has had to go pick up a child in the middle of the night, this latest Froggy tale would be a good story to share with your child. While Froggy is excited about his first sleepover, he and his friend Max end up in a nightlong tug of war over where they will sleep. For those with mixed feelings about overnights, this may be a reassuring story. 5–8

A New Baby

■ Little Brown Bear and the Bundle of Joy

(by Jane Dyer, Little, Brown $15.99 ●●●●●) Little Brown Bear wants to know what the "little bundle of joy" is that his parents are expecting. The neighboring animals show him their own new bundles of joy. When he returns home, he is introduced to his baby sister, and is reassured that he remains their "big" bundle of joy! 2½ & up.

■ Dear Baby: Letters from Your Big Brother 2006

(by Sarah Sullivan/illus. by Paul Meisel, Candlewick $15.99 ●●●● ½) A clever idea that may inspire others to write letters to the newest member of the family. Mike, who is excited about having a new baby, starts writing and drawing pictures for the baby even before she is born. His letters through the year become a collection that records some of the highlights of her first year and ends with a card for her first birthday. 5–7.

■ Hi New Baby!

(by Robie Harris/illus. by Michael Emberly, Candlewick $16.99 ●●●●) Although many big sibs have warm and positive feelings for the new baby, some feel genuinely displaced. No book can solve these feelings, but here's a useful story that helps kids know that other kids have felt the same way. 3 & up.

Adoption

■ I Love You Like Crazy Cakes

(by Rose Lewis/illus. by Jane Dyer, Little, Brown $14.95 ●●●●) Heart-melting art blends with prose in this moving celebration of love and adoption. Although the baby is from China, the feeling and mood make this a universal story. 4 & up.

■ The Red Blanket

(by Eliza Thomas/illus. by Joe Cepeda, Scholastic $15.95 ●●●●) A single woman tells her adopted child of her journey to get her in China and their first shaky days together. She brings a red blanket from home, which gives the baby comfort. 4 & up.

■ You're Not My Real Mother!

(by Molly Friedrich/illus. by Christy Hale, Little, Brown $15.99 ●●●●) A reassuring answer to an adopted child about what it means to be someone's mother. Addresses differences in appearance, birth mothers, and the bonds that truly make us family. 5 & up.

NOTABLE PREVIOUS WINNERS: **Tell Me Again About the Night I Was Born** BLUE CHIP (by Jamie Lee Curtis/illus. by Laura Cornell, HarperCollins ●●●●●); **Happy Adoption Day!** (by John McCutcheon/illus. by Julie Paschkis, Little, Brown ●●●●●)

PLATINUM AWARD '97; **Mommy Far, Mommy Near** (by Carol A. Peacock/illus. by Shawn C. Brownell, Whitman ●●●●).

Moving
■ Absolutely Positively Alexander BLUE CHIP

(by Judith Viorst/illus. by Robin P. Glasser, Atheneum $20 ●●●●●) Now in one volume, three well loved stories about Alexander, including **Alexander, Who's Not (Do you hear me? I mean it!) Going to Move.** 5 & up.

■ Good-Bye, House

(by Robin Ballard, Greenwillow $14 ●●●●) Room by room, a child says good-bye to the house she has always lived in. A tender book with an upbeat ending. 3 & up.

■ I Like Where I Am

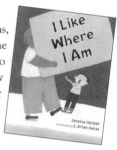

(by Jessica Harper/illus. by G. Brian Karas, Putnam $15.95 ●●●●) Moving is not what the six-year-old narrator of this sad tale wants to do. But moving day does come and the new home turns out to be not such a bad place after all. A gentle mix of anger and humor with a reassuring ending. Also see **My Best Friend Moved Away** by Nancy Carlson, Viking) 5 & up.

Divorce, Separation, and New Families
■ Mama and Daddy Bear's Divorce

(by Cornelia M. Spelman/illus. by Kathy Parkinson, Whitman $13.95 ●●●●) Dinah Bear is frightened when she learns that the two people she loves best are getting divorced. A reassuring story that says important things stay the same. 3–6.

■ Two Homes

(by Claire Masurel/illus. by Kady M. Denton, Candlewick $14.99 ●●●● ½) Alex has different things at Mommy's and Daddy's. But the one thing that is the same in both places is the love that continues between parents and child. A reassuring book for young listeners. 2 & up. For older preschoolers, **A New Room for William** (by Sally Grindley/illus. by Carol Thompson, Candlewick $15.99 ●●●●). Moving is tough, but moving because of a divorce is a double whammy! 4 & up.

NOTABLE PREVIOUS WINNERS: **Amber Brown series** BLUE CHIP (by Paula Danziger, Putnam ●●●●●) 7 & up; **On the Day His Daddy Left** (by Eric & Kathleen Adams, Whitman ●●●●); **I Live with Daddy** (by Judith Vigna, Whitman ●●●●) 7 & up; **Stepfamilies** (by Fred Rogers, Putnam ●●●●). 5–8.

Staying Healthy

■ Froggy Goes to the Doctor

(by Jonathan London/illus. by Frank Remkiewicz, Viking $15.99 ●●●● ½) Going to the doctor is not a laughing matter, unless you go along with Froggy! Silly Froggy forgets to wear underpants or brush his teeth. Like some of the earlier books in this series, this has pace and laugh-out-loud fun! 3–7.

■ How Do Dinosaurs Get Well Soon?

(by Jane Yolen/illus. by Mark Teague, Scholastic $15.95 ●●●●) No whining, or tossing tissues on the floor, or refusing to swallow his pills. Kids who might be feeling sorry for themselves will see the humor of this great big dino with the flu who does what he should. A fine sequel to **How Do Dinosaurs Say Good Night?** 4–7.

■ Mabel the Tooth Fairy

(by Katie Davis, Harcourt $16 ●●●●) Aptly subtitled "and How She Got Her Job," there's a lot of tongue-in-cheek humor that also builds on the idea that brushing is important. 4–8.

NOTABLE PREVIOUS WINNERS: **Going to the Doctor** and **Going to the Dentist** (by Fred Rogers, Putnam ●●●●); **Don't You Feel Well, Sam?** (by Amy Hest/illus. by Anita Jeram, Candlewick ●●●●).

Illness

■ What's Happening to Grandpa?

(by Maria Shriver/illus. by Sandra Speidel, Little Brown $15.95 ●●●●) Kate recognizes that something is not right with her beloved Grandpa. Drawing on her own life experiences with her own father, Shriver gives parents the language for speaking intelligently and, most importantly, truthfully with our children about Alzheimer's disease. 7 & up. For two more traditional picture books about Alzheimer's: **Faraway Grandpa** (by Roberta Karim/illus. by Ted Rand, Henry Holt) and **Remember, Grandma?** (by Laura Langston/illus. by Lindsey Gardiner, Viking).

Death
■ Lighthouse, A Story of Remembrance

(by Robert Munsch/illus. by Janet Wilson, Scholastic $13.95 ●●●● ½) From the moment you see Sarah with a flower in her hair, waking her dad, you know it's a flower left from her grandfather's funeral. Going to their favorite place, the lighthouse, Sarah and her dad know this was the right night and the right place to share their loss—and love. 5–9.

■ Grandpa's Angel 2006

(by Jutta Bauer, Candlewick $12.99 ●●●●) Grandpa's reminiscences about his adventures through his long life are all the more outrageous as one sees his guardian angel protecting him from all sorts of danger, including the Nazis during WWII. Bauer's view of the world is decidedly cup-more-full-than-empty—a joy in the adventure that is being passed along to his fortunate grandson. 7 & up.

NOTABLE PREVIOUS WINNERS : **Annie and the Old One** BLUE CHIP (by Miska Miles/illus. by Peter Parnall, Little, Brown ●●●●●); **Flamingo Dream** (by Donna Jo Napoli/illus. Cathie Felstead, Greenwillow ●●●●).

Death of a Pet
■ Saying Goodbye to Lulu

(by Corinne Demas/illus. by Ard Hoyt, Little, Brown $ 15.95 ●●●●) If you've ever lost a pet, this book is going to make you cry. Lulu the dog is in failing health; in this tender story her owner, a little girl, is coping with Lulu's inevitable death. Some aspects may be too much for your child; the little girl is brought to say good-bye to Lulu after she's died and then they bury the dog in the back yard. 5 & up.

■ The Tenth Good Thing About Barney

(by Judith Viorst/illus. by Eric Blegvad, Atheneum $12.95 **oooo**) When his cat Barney dies, a young boy deals with his loss by remembering the good things about him. This bittersweet classic says it all. 4–8.

■ When a Pet Dies

(by Fred Rogers, Putnam $5.95 **oooo**) Mr. Rogers talks in clear language about what happens when a pet dies because it is hurt or ill. 4–8.

Holiday Books

Thanksgiving

■ Thanks for Thanksgiving

(by Julie Markes/illus. by Doris Barrette, HarperCollins $12.99 **oooo**) With a warm autumnal feel, Markes chronicles all the things a brother and sister are thankful for in this retro-feeling ode to a traditional family at Thanksgiving. 4 & up.

■ We Gather Together . . .
Now Please Get Lost! **2006**

(by Diane deGroat, Chronicle $6.95 paper **oooo** ½) Gilbert is none too happy to be partners with Phillip on the class trip to Pilgrim Town. But when he tries to hide and lose Phillip, he gets stuck in the bathroom, and it's Phillip who finds and saves him. A lively book about being thankful and friendship. 6 & up.

Kwanzaa

■ Seven Spools of Thread

(by Angela S. Medearis/illus. by Daniel Minter, Whitman $15.95 **ooooo**) In a village in Ghana, seven brothers quarrel from morning to night. Their father says he will leave his possessions to them only if by sundown they can turn seven spools of colored thread into gold. Although this is called a Kwanzaa story, it is a timeless tale about working together for a common good. A memorable *pour quoi*-style tale with striking woodcuts filled with the symbols of Kwanzaa. PLATINUM AWARD '01. 5 & up.

Chinese New Year

■ My First Chinese New Year

(by Karen Katz, Henry Holt $14.95 oooo) With festive illustrations, Katz highlights all the traditions of celebrating the Chinese New Year from a child's point of view. 4–8.

Christmas

■ Dear Santa Claus 2006

(by Alan Durant/illus. by Vanessa Cabban, Candlewick $14.99 oooo½) What child hasn't got a million questions for Santa? In a series of letters to and from Santa, this is something of a novelty book, like *The Jolly Postman*. It has a special magical quality as Holly and Santa get to know each other. 4–7.

■ The Miracle of the Poinsettia

(by Joanne Oppenheim/illus. by Fabian Negrin, Barefoot Books $16.99 ooooo) Inspired by an old Mexican folktale and our own family's love of Mexico. With nothing to bring to the baby Jesus, Juanita gives from her heart with a miraculous outcome. Understandably one of our favorite titles, available in English and Spanish, and in paperback. 6 & up.

■ Santa Claus the World's Number One Toy Expert
2006 PLATINUM AWARD

(by Marla Frazee, Harcourt $16 ooooo) Here at the Toy Portfolio we understand just what it is that Santa goes through in finding just the right toy for just the right child. We do it the year 'round. So our hat's off to the busy old fellow. We relate to his post-its and like his wardrobe, too. He often consults us, you know.

■ Snowmen at Christmas 2006

(by Caralyn Buehner/illus. by Mark Buehner, Dial $16.99 oooo½) Once again the Buehners give us a fantasy about those magical snowpeople who come alive when night falls. This time it's the Christmas season, so, there's little surprise that such a lively group would want to have a joyful celebration! 4 & up.

Our Favorite Classic Christmas Picture Books

Dream Snow (by Eric Carle, Philomel) PLATINUM AWARD '01. 2½ & up.

If You Take a Mouse to the Movies (by Laura Numeroff/illus. by Felicia Bond, HarperCollins) PLATINUM AWARD '01.

Carl's Christmas (by Alexandra Day, Farrar, Straus & Giroux) 4 & up.

The Jolly Christmas Postman (by Janet and Allan Ahlberg, Little, Brown) 4 & up.

Mim's Christmas Jam (by Andrea Davis Pinkney/illus. by Brian Pinkney, Harcourt) 4–8.

The Polar Express (by Chris Van Allsburg, Houghton Mifflin) 5 & up.

Santa Calls (by William Joyce, HarperCollins) 6–10.

The Night Before Christmas, PLATINUM '03 and **The Twelve Days of Christmas** (by Robert Sabuda, Simon & Schuster) 6 & up.

Who'll Pull Santa's Sleigh Tonight? (by Laura Rader, HarperCollins) PLATINUM AWARD '04. 4–8.

Hanukkah

■ Chanukah Bugs

(by David A. Carter, Little Simon $10.95 ●●●●●) Each of the eight nights of Chanukah is represented with an amusing and amazing gift box that opens to a twirling dreidel, sizzling latkes, sparkling menorah, and others. PLATINUM AWARD '03. 3–7.

■ Latkes, Latkes, Good to Eat

(by Naomi Howland, Clarion $15 ●●●●) Borrowing the old folktale device of a bountiful pot that won't stop giving, Howland has spun a tale that's as delicious as a plate full of latkes with sugar on top! 4 & up.

■ Three French Hens 2006 PLATINUM AWARD

(by Margie Palatini/illus. by Richard Egielski, Hyperion $15.99 ●●●●●) Three French hens are shipped from Paris to Philippe Renard, but the address is smudged! So the three deliver themselves to the address of Phil the Fox. In this merry mix-up, the generosity of the three saves them from a dreadful fate. When Phil the Fox tries to give his feathered friends Christmas gifts, they announce that they celebrate Hanukkah . . . so they celebrate both holidays. 4 & up.

Reference Books for Mixed Ages

Dictionaries

Preschool: Very young children don't really need a dictionary, but their love of words and their exploding vocabulary make books with tons of pictures and labels great for looking at. Most are arranged in categories rather than alphabetical order.

■ First Picture Dictionary 2006 PLATINUM AWARD

(Scholastic $14.95 ●●●●●) Eight-hundred-word "pictionary" with words and pictures organized thematically. Has "magic" transparent pages at start of each section showing objects in home, school, supermarket, farm, and other familiar settings. 3 & up.

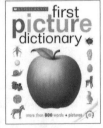

Early School Years—First to Third

Grades: Beginning readers and writers start to use dictionaries with A-to-Z listings and pictures to find words they need. Too big a book will be hard to sift through, so less is best!

■ Scholastic First Dictionary

(Scholastic $14.95 ●●●●) Easy-to-read definitions with pictures, and the words are used in sentences. 6–9.

■ Macmillan First Dictionary

(Macmillan $14 ●●●●) Illustrated with photos and drawings. Gives plurals of nouns, past tenses of verbs, and defines words with multiple meanings. 6–9.

■ Merriam-Webster's Primary Dictionary 2006

(Merriam-Webster $16.95 ●●●● ½) This is for advanced readers who are interested in knowing the origin of words as well as how they are used in sentences, and their multiple meanings. Long entries make this less friendly looking.

Later School Years–Fourth Grade and Up: These dictionaries are more complex, with syllabification, pronunciation, and often word histories. They have fewer illustrations and many more words. Both also include maps and biographical and other historical data. For 9 & up.

■ Macmillan Dictionary for Children

(Macmillan $16.95 ●●●●) Updated in 2002 with more color photos. 8–12.

■ Scholastic Children's Dictionary

(Scholastic $17.95 ●●●●) With new and updated entries, this edition has more photos and uses phonetic pronunciation instead of traditional symbols; includes Braille and American Sign Language alphabets and 100 high-tech terms. Also **Scholastic Student Thesaurus** ($15.95 ●●●●). 8 & up.

Encyclopedias

Before making a big investment in an encyclopedia, go to the public library or your child's school. Look at several sets without pressure from a salesperson. Keep in mind:

> Most kids won't regularly use an encyclopedia before fourth grade, so don't rush.

> Look up the same entry in each set—for example, look at the presentation for "dogs" or "dinosaurs" in each encyclopedia and compare content, style, and illustrations.

> Visuals such as photos, charts, and drawings will be very important to your child.

> A used edition costs less, but statistics, maps, and other information may be dated.

Following are the best choices:

■ Compton's Encyclopedia or World Book

(Compton's/World Book $420 & up ●●●●) Either of these sets will be used by students from fourth grade through high school. The entries are not super-easy to read, but they are clear and well written, with attractive, colorful illustrations and photos. Both sets are of equal value and the choice is one of personal preference.

Single-Volume Resource Books

■ e.guides Human Body 2006

(by Richard Walker et al., DK $17.99 ●●●●) One of a series of single-volume encyclopedias with solid information, illustrations, and a link to fuller information online that has been produced by DK and Google. Others in the series include **Insects, Mammals,** and **Rocks & Minerals.** Each book has dedicated pages with more information and downloadable images that would spruce up a school project.

■ The Atlas of Ancient Egypt 2006

(by Delia Pemberton, Abrams $19.95 ●●●●½) Chock full of information, this is a splendid resource with artworks and photographs from the British Museum. Pemberton includes information about the history and geography, maps, and archeological history, as well. 10 & up.

■ National Audubon Society First Field Guides

(Scholastic $11.95 each ●●●●) Designed to be used in the field or as a resource at home, each of these handsome books has hundreds of photos, clear information, and a "spotter's card"—a quick reference card to identify an animal or plant. Titles include **Birds, Insects, Reptiles, Rocks,** and **Trees.**

■ National Geographic World Atlas for Young Explorers

(National Geographic Society $24.95 ●●●●) Stunning images from space, photos, and handsome physical maps introduce each continent and its people with political maps that zoom in on countries and states. This book could not have existed when today's parents were in school, but it could turn kids into map lovers instead of map phobics!

■ Smithsonian Children's Encyclopedia of American History

(by David C. King, DK $29.99 ●●●●½) This is like a coffee-table book for young history buffs. Visually exciting with photos, art, and photographs all explained with captions and short, crisply written passages. Fun to dive into rather than to read from front to back. 8 & up.

■ State-By-State Atlas

(by Beth Sutinis et al., DK $19.99 ●●●●) Organized by region, this state-by-state atlas presents information about geography, population, industry, famous people, and landmarks. 8 & up.

■ The White House

(by Catherine O'Neill Grace, Scholastic $19.95 ●●●●) An illustrated history of the White House with handsome photos, behind-the-scenes information, and firsthand accounts from many people who work in the "People's House," the 132-room mansion that is a museum, home, office, and setting for so many occasions that live in history. Includes an introduction by First Lady Laura Bush. For those who have visited and the many others who will do so one day. 8 & up.

III • DVDs

What's new in videos? Not a lot. But that may be a blessing. Most of the best videos we saw this season are digitized versions of old videos that we originally reviewed in the VHS format. Be forewarned: don't judge a DVD by its title. The lead story may be the same, but other stories on the same disk are often totally different. By mixing them up this way they appear to be "new"—but once again, "new" is not always better.

The old VHS format usually had four stories max, while the new DVDs may have six, ten, or even more stories. True, you are getting more for your money, but a DVD that runs the length of a feature film adds up to more than 100 minutes of your child's time. In effect, you are bringing home a library of stories that can gobble up a lot of your child's day in a passive way. If you brought home a library of books you would not be likely to read them all in one sitting.

With the new media it's more likely that you will slide the disk in and let it play from one end to another. If you are traveling cross-country these long DVDs might make the miles fly by. But at home, they can be seductive and hard to turn off— another example of too much of a good thing. We've also found that they are harder to navigate, so it's sometimes hard to skip ahead and kids are unlikely to push the pause button. Parents will need to monitor the length of time spent. Nor are all the stories equally worthwhile. Some of the choices are better than others and often there are too many "properties" that are downright forgettable. Ideally, you would be able to select a trio of films and then the DVD would shut down. But that is not possible. So, the new bigger and better DVDs are a mixed blessing that once again require parental management.

What's in a Name? As we've said before, the golden age of children's videos has passed. Many of our past award winners have new entries that have taken dramatically wrong turns, leaving us with the overall warning that name recognition and past performances are not enough to go by when selecting new videos for your kids. Series still need to be viewed one title at a time, otherwise you are apt to come home with a video for toddlers with story lines about aliens, witches, and ghosts (Kipper); or how about a "legend" for 2- and 3-year-olds told by a fairy who comes from a blue moon (Blue's Clues).? We even received a preschool video about a boy who has good parents, nice toys . . . everything . . . except a body.

Why No Baby Videos? Developmentally, babies learn from active, real-life experiences rather than from being "plugged in" to passively watching others at such an early age. We believe that a mirror would be more interactive and age-appropriate than a video screen. Reading books and talking about the pictures, or interacting as you sing songs and recite rhymes, will do more to build language than plugging babies into the TV to look at pretty pictures with music. For kids under 2 (and beyond), less is more! We are delighted that the American Pediatric Association has agreed with our position.

More Scare for Your Video Dollar. Entertainment that looks like children's fare sometimes comes laced with a heavy dose of adult-sized violence. While many of us remember watching the Wicked Witch of the West from behind a blanket, most of us were school-age, not three. Some filmmakers seem to forget that young children are still working on the distinction between real and make-believe. Given that many parents use videos as a better alternative to television, it's important to know that videos are not a safe haven.

Positive Choices. What you will find in this chapter are quality music, story, information, and how-to videos that involve kids in active doing. These are arranged from choices for the very young to those for older viewers. Some DVDs span a broad age range, from preschool to early school years. If you have a child between 4 and 8, look at the choices in Toddlers, Preschoolers, and Early School Years.

A Word of Warning. Like many products directed at children, age labels are often marked too broadly. Parents who fondly remember feature films from their childhood often hurry home with classics, only to find that these are too scary for young children. DVDs, like toys, are not "one size fits all."

Screen Your DVDs. Whenever possible, take the time to preview videos, or at least watch with your children the first time around. You may be surprised at the number of videos you choose not to watch to the end. Teaching kids to turn off a film because it's just not worth watching is also not a bad lesson to pass on.

Music and Activities

Preschoolers and Early-School-Years Kids

■ **Barney Movin' and Groovin'** *2006*

(HIT Entertainment $16.95 **oooo**) This Barney video is meant to encourage your kids to get up off the sofa and dance along. Nothing groundbreaking here, but a classic-style Barney video about making your own music that will appeal to fans of the purple dino. Or, if your child has ever been to or dreamed of going to a Barney show, the Barney's Colorful World (**oooo**)! will be the next best thing. We have to be honest—we had to mute part of it. Seventy minutes is just too much Barney. New for *2006*, **Just Imagine** (**ooo**), an attempt to introduce kids to transportation. It's really long and takes too long to get to the more interesting live-action clips. These DVDs may be a preschooler's dream come true, or your 9-year-old's worst nightmare. 2–6. (800) 791-8093.

■ **Blue Talks**

(Paramount $12.95 **ooo**) It would have been better for Blue to remain speechless. More importantly, the stories about "moon fairies" and far-out fantasy are way beyond the understanding of young preschoolers. The strength of the original Blue concept was right on the mark for preschoolers who loved the magic of helping the host finding the clues. Those episodes empowered kids, making them feel very smart. We find a disconnect between the new stories and the audience, who are still sorting out real and make-believe. We also have trouble with **Blue's Clues: Blue Takes You to School** (**ooo**). Our problem is that the featured color is chartreuse, and the shape of the day, a pentagon. How about starting with green and a triangle? A much better choice is **Blue's Clues Shapes and Colors (●●●●**½**)**. Joe and Blue play a lot of shape-hunting games with some licks of color thrown in. The new **Blue's Room: Alphabet Power** was not available for review, but the title leads us to believe that it too will be beyond the age group. 3 & up.

■ Be a Hula Girl

(Kuleana Prod. $14.95 **●●●●●**) We were testing a luau craft kit when this wonderful dancing video arrived from Hawaii. Our 8-year-old testers followed every motion and learned how to dance and move to the traditional music. We liked how the instructor kept reminding them to smile! You can buy the video alone, or with a raffia skirt and beads ($24.95). This would be fun to use for a luau party. 5–9. PLATINUM AWARD '02. (866) 367-4852.

■ Happy Healthy Monsters *2006* PLATINUM AWARD

(Sony $14.98 **●●●●●**) This is so much better than most of the piles of videos we reviewed this season. It delivers the information in a lively format that encourages kids to get up and move along with their friends from Sesame Street. Getting exercise, eating healthy—all important messages that are presented with humor that is age appropriate and not condescending in tone. Still top rated, **Fiesta!** BLUE CHIP (Sony $12.98 **●●●●●**) introduces kids to counting, colors, and familiar music with a Latin beat. Also top rated: **Get Up & Dance (●●●●●)** and PLATINUM AWARD '97 winner **Elmocize (●●●●●)**. We have found the *Elmo's World* series to be inconsistent. Our viewers enjoyed **Birthday Games & More (●●●)** (once they got past the first frenetic 10 minutes), but found **Elmo's Magic Cookbook (●●)** to fall below the usual high standards set by Sesame Street. We found the dumbed-down content was more irritating than inspiring. 2½ & up.

■ How to Be a Ballerina

(Sony $12.95 **●●●●**) Now on DVD, young ballerinas can join along with a children's class at the Royal Academy of Dance. From warmups, to rehearsing, to a charming performance of scenes from *Sleeping Beauty*, viewers are invited to dance along. A short version of *Sleeping Beauty* is told as film clips show adult ballerinas dancing, but it is the children's performance of the story that will inspire viewers. DVD also includes "How to Be a Ballet Dancer." 5–9.

■ Nursery Tap, Hip to Toe *2006*

(Nursery Tap $21.95 **oooo**) Here's a curious DVD that you will either love or hate (we couldn't stop watching it). Dressed in charming costumes, one or two dancers in toe or tap shoes dance while familiar nursery rhymes are chanted. Here's the innovative wrinkle—you never see the whole dancer—only their lower bodies. This may be offputting for some, but it is truly a fresh take. They say 1–7, we'd suggest the upper range—maybe more like 4 & up.

A brand new way of looking at and listening to nursery rhymes!

■ What's the Name of That Song?

(Sony Wonder $12.95 **ooooo**) A hit parade of favorite Sesame Street songs, but our favorite moments are Wayne Brady singing "Between," and Patti LaBelle singing the alphabet! Closer in spirit to the original show (with a sense of humor that isn't condescending to kids). PLATINUM AWARD '05. 2 & up.

■ Raffi on Broadway BLUE CHIP

(Rounder $19.95 **ooooo**) A real musical experience with the "eco-troubadour" singing many old favorites such as "Baby Beluga." We could have done without the pessimism of "Will I Ever Grow Up?" but kids probably hear it as a song of longing rather than doubt. 4 & up. Also classic: **Raffi in Concert (oooo)**. (800) 768-6337.

■ Sing Along Songs BLUE CHIP

(Disney $12.99) Over the years we have found some of the "Sing Along" series a better alternative for preschoolers than the feature-length films that are too scary for young viewers. However, these are uneven and sometimes include clips that are not for all ages (our tip: rent before you buy). For example, **Home on the Range (oo)** was not particularly engaging for our viewers. (The movie wasn't that great either.) **Winnie the Pooh Sing a Song with Tigger (oooo)** got much higher ratings. We do like the way the words to the songs bounce along the bottom of the screen so kids who can read can sing along. 4 & up.

BLUE CHIP Folk Music Videos

Three Favorites: **Ella Jenkins Live at the Smithsonian** (Smithsonian Folkways $14.98 ●●●●) Without gimmicks, here's a master teacher involving kids in sing-, clap-, snap-, and tap-along fun! All ages. (800) 410-9815. **Peter, Paul, and Mommy, Too** (Warner $19.98 ●●●●) From the opening bars of "Puff," the magic is still here! All ages. **This Pretty Planet: Tom Chapin Live in Concert** (Sony $14.98 ●●●●) Thirteen of his best-loved songs, such as "The Wheel of the Water," "Good Garbage," and others with an ecology theme. All ages.

Picturebook Videos

Many wonderful picture books have been brought to life as videos. Unfortunately, some video makers take the names of well known books and turn them into Saturday-morning-style programs. Be sure to look at the **Information, Please** (p. 232) and **Coping** (p. 236) sections for other toddlers' and preschoolers' videos.

Toddlers and Preschoolers

■ **Angelina Ballerina The Big Performance**
2006 PLATINUM AWARD

(HIT Entertainment $16.99 ●●●●●) Based on the Angelina Ballerina books, this year's entry has four original stories and two live-action sequences with young dancers. Unlike in some previous videos, there are no scary scenes in any of the stories—though there is some suspense. Miss Lily takes Angelina to dance for her friend the Queen and they have a transportation adventure on the way; Angelina's baby sister stirs up some expected unhappiness—but all's well that ends well. There are several other stories. This lasts 150 minutes, so you'll want to watch it in several sittings unless you are going cross country with an Angelina fan. 4 & up. Still top rated, **Angelina Ballerina Friends Forever** and **Rose Fairy Princess,** both PLATINUM winners. (866) 587-1778.

■ Bob the Builder 2006

(HIT Entertainment $14.99/$16.99 ●●●●) If "yes, we can" is big in your house, then **The Live Show** from this live-action stage show will be a hit. When the talking trucks first make an appearance, it is pretty neat. It's a lot like Barney—if you're four, it's really great fun; if you're forty, you'll want to bang your head against the wall. New for 2006, **Bob's Big Plan** (●●●) is about saving a little town from being urbanized—a pretty big concept for the preschool crowd. Also, **Help is on the Way!** (●●●) includes a story about a movie, "The Invasion of the Giant Bug." We guess this was designed to explain scary things away as Bob assures Spud it's just special effects and nothing to worry about. But the images of a giant bug on top of a skyscraper may override the verbal message. We'd pass on this one. Still top rated, **Building Friendships** (●●●●½): Bob and his crew of talking building machines are featured in four little stories that focus on cooperation, have a small dose of tension, and are not scary. 3 & up.

■ Caillou's Family Fun 2006

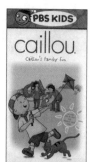

(Warner Bros. $12.95 ●●●●) Caillou is older than Maisy, less noisy than Elmo, and paced just right for young viewers. This year's new entry centers on Caillou's learning to take photos with his dad's old camera and seeing photos of the family from the past. It also includes a story about meeting new people. Still recommended are **Caillou at Play** (●●●●) —playground and friendship issues such as sharing and getting along are center stage here—as well as **Caillou's Neighborhood** (●●●●) and **Caillou the Explorer** (●●●●●) PLATINUM AWARD '02, which explored transportation from a child's point of view.

■ Click, Clack, Moo: Cows That Type

(Scholastic $14.95 ●●●●½) Farmer Brown's cows and hens are on strike. They want electric blankets, or else: no milk or eggs! A prize-winning story translated to the screen, narrated by Randy Travis with down-home music. Still top rated from this series: **Good Night Gorilla** (●●●●) and **Chrysanthemum** (●●●●●), PLATINUM AWARD '03. Meryl Streep, Sarah Jessica Parker, and Mary Beth Hurt narrate three wonderful picture books by Kevin Henkes. 4–7.

■ Discover Spot BLUE CHIP

(Disney $19.99 ●●●●●) A creative blend of short animated stories featuring Spot and his friends and live action showing real kids doing similar things. For example, when Spot and his friends see a band in the park, they go home to make their own music. Video then features real-life kids trying different instruments. PLATINUM AWARD '01. 3 & up.

■ Hi! I'm Todd *2006*

(HIT Entertainment $12.99 ●●●½) Based on the Todd Parr books, this made-for-TV series features lots of the issues kids face with their friends (e.g., a sense of belonging, feeling different). We found the friendly alien somewhat odd for a series intended for preschoolers. What does that mean to a 3 year old? These are not scary stories, but may be confusing to young viewers who have not got a firm grip on real and make believe. While we are usually fans of the books, the stories are not extremely compelling; not bad . . . but not great either. 3 & up.

■ Make Way for Ducklings

(Scholastic $14.95 ●●●●½) Parents, and even grandparents, have grown up with Robert McCloskey's three beloved Caldecott Award winners on this video. "Make Way for Ducklings" tells the jolly tale of Mr. & Mrs. Mallard, who find a home for their ducklings Jack, Kack, Lack, Mack, Nack, Ouack, Pack, and Quack. McCloskey's drawings have not been animated, but they retain superb vitality as the camera pans and zooms in on his jaunty ducklings and their world. There's delicious suspense in "Blueberries for Sal," and summer in Maine is beautifully encapsulated in "Time of Wonder." You'll find two more favorites, "Lentil" and "Burt Dow," plus a Spanish version of "Ducklings" and read-along features on the DVD version, making it worth the higher price. 4–8.

■ Miffy's Springtime Adventures

(Sony $12.98 ●●●●●) Based on Dick Bruna's picture books, the video includes more than a dozen small stories featuring Miffy and friends. Springtime focuses on the discoveries of the season. These are low-key stories, without nervous hype or tension, and include some simple counting games. Just right for older toddlers and young preschoolers. PLATINUM AWARD '05.

■ New Friends: Clifford's Puppy Days

(Scholastic $14.98 **oooo**) There are lots of stories and activities on this DVD based on Norman Bridwell's storybooks. This animated cartoon show has plenty of positive messages packed into the mix. We could have done without the suspense of a story called the "Monster in 3B." Of course there is no monster, but why present the possibility to threes? That said, this is otherwise a pretty good video for preschoolers. 3 & up.

■ JoJo's Circus Take a Bow! 2006

(Disney $19.99 **oooo**) Designed as a think-and-move show for preschoolers, this lively DVD does get kids up on their feet and interacting, rather than just sitting there and watching—at least a bit. In each of the episodes, JoJo, a circus clown, and her friends learn some small but important lesson. In Story One, JoJo is told not to touch the button of the Clown machine, but she can't resist and the robot clown throws pies that JoJo must clean up. She confesses, rather than lying, and learns that listening to directions is important. Each episode is followed with JoJo restating what she has learned. The pace of these stories is slow enough for the young viewer and the lessons are not so didactic as to spoil the fun. 2½ & up.

■ Kipper Fun in the Sun

(HIT Entertainment $9.99 **oooo**) This series seems to be back on track for the two-and-up crowd with the simple stories and adventures of Kipper the dog and his friends, Tiger and Arnold. Seven short stories include "The Rescue," "Clouds," "The Farm," and "Crazy Golf." We'd pass on **Kipper Imagine That!** (**ooo**), which included a hunt for scary creatures and other more Saturday-morning-ish cartoon clichés. 2 & up.

■ Little Bear's Rainy Day Tales 2006

(Paramount $16.99 **oooo**) Most of the tales in this collection are age appropriate with a dose of scary Perils-of-Pauline moments mixed in. Preschoolers may not get some of the "imaginative" moments, however; for example, there is a dream sequence in which only little Bear

(and child viewer) get to see a mermaid in the lake. How do they know he dreamed her up? They don't. Similarly, in "Follow the Leader," the player's imagination allows the characters to climb a grassy hillside, which then suddenly turns into craggy cliffs and a journey on the back of a sea serpent. For threes and many fours, this sort of fantasy is far-flung and not in the spirit of the classic Else Minarik stories that Maurice Sendak illustrated. There are only two solutions: look at the author's name on the stories. Some of the new ones are better than others and are fine fare for preschoolers, but you will also need to preview these before you walk away from the DVD player. Also reformatted with a mix of good and not so good stories, **Little Bear's Band (oooo)**.

■ Madeline at the Ballet BLUE CHIP

(Sony $9.95 **ooooo**) Once more they've come up with a new story based on the original characters. This one will have special meaning to the many little ballerinas who long to get their first toe shoes and worry about living up to their dreams of becoming prima ballerinas. Narrated by Christopher Plummer, this one talks to the importance of practice and believing in oneself. PLATINUM AWARD '00. 4 & up.

■ Play with Maisy BLUE CHIP

(Universal $14.98 **ooooo**) Maisy's little slice-of-life adventures with her friends are very slow-paced and are just right for young video viewers. Play with Maisy includes time at the playground and the fair. 2½ & up.

■ Swimmy 2006 PLATINUM AWARD

(Scholastic $14.95 **ooooo**) Many of Leo Lionni's stories not only tell a good tale, they say something meaningful without being overly didactic. **Swimmy** is a delightful story about cooperation. **Frederick** speaks to the importance of dreaming as well as planning ahead. There are three more Lionni books and, as a bonus, there are two other delightful books: **Each Peach Pear Plum** by the Ahlbergs and **Hush Little Baby** by Aliki. 4 & up.

■ The Very Hungry Caterpillar BLUE CHIP

(Disney $12.99 **ooooo**) The story of that very well loved, hungry caterpillar has been transformed into a totally magical video!

Animation and music have enhanced Eric Carle's beautiful illustrations and given them another dimension while retaining their original beauty. A delicate blend of imagination and information illuminated with great artistry. Closed-captioned. 2–6.

■ Winnie the Pooh Series

(Disney $12.99) In the past we have recommended this series as "kinder and gentler animated cartoons than most of Saturday morning fare." Unfortunately, all recent Pooh videos have gone in another direction with story lines that are too intense for young viewers. For example, in **Tigger-ific Tales (o)**, Tigger's so-called friends give him a bath and his stripes disappear—for preschoolers, who typically worry about body integrity, this video is developmentally inappropriate. We still recommend the original videos: **A Blustery Day (oooo)** and **The Honey Tree (oooo)**. Closed-captioned. 2 & up.

Story Videos for Early School Years

Some of the videos in this section have pieces that may be enjoyed by older preschoolers, but for the most part these are stories for 5 and up.

■ Dear America Series

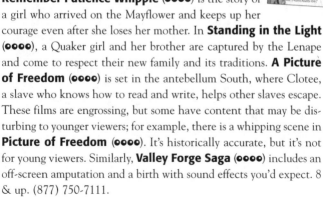

(Scholastic $12.95) Based on the award-winning *Dear America* diaries that we have recommended for school-age readers, this series combines history with story in live-action dramas. In **So Far from Home (oooo)**, Mary flees Ireland and the potato famine only to struggle for humane work conditions in the textile mills. **Remember Patience Whipple (oooo)** is the story of a girl who arrived on the Mayflower and keeps up her courage even after she loses her mother. In **Standing in the Light (oooo)**, a Quaker girl and her brother are captured by the Lenape and come to respect their new family and its traditions. **A Picture of Freedom (oooo)** is set in the antebellum South, where Clotee, a slave who knows how to read and write, helps other slaves escape. These films are engrossing, but some have content that may be disturbing to younger viewers; for example, there is a whipping scene in **Picture of Freedom (oooo)**. It's historically accurate, but it's not for young viewers. Similarly, **Valley Forge Saga (oooo)** includes an off-screen amputation and a birth with sound effects you'd expect. 8 & up. (877) 750-7111.

■ The Emperor's New Clothes
🏆2006 Platinum Award

(Scholastic $9.95 ●●●●●) This collection of Hans Christian Andersen tales is a study in contrasts. It opens with Nadine Bernard Westcott's zany illustrations, with the added charm of animation. It is followed with Jerry Pinkney's gossamer watercolors that are so perfect for the watery world of "The Ugly Duckling." These are followed by Bjorn Winblad's bold images that light up "The Swineherd," a tale of a clever prince, and Michael Sporn's delightful images for "The Nightingale." 65 mins. 5 & up.

■ Goodbye, Mr. Chips

(Masterpiece Theatre/WGBH $19.95 ●●●● ½) Based on James Hilton's novel, this video features Martin Clunes playing the endearing Latin master at an English boarding school. His inept style is transformed by the woman he loves (Victoria Hamilton) and tragically loses. A glimpse into the past and a life that will seem very foreign to young viewers. Also recommended, Platinum Award-winning **The Railway Children** (●●●●●). 8 & up. (800) 949-8670.

■ Parents Are From Pluto

(Sony $12.98 ●●● ½) Three new Arthur stories address school-aged kids' sometimes mixed emotions about their parents. The title story centers on wanting parents to make a good impression at "Parents' Open House," something older kids are more apt to worry over than kids in early grades; in "My Dad, the Garbage Man," Francine is not sure she wants classmates to know what her father does. This is well done and good food for talking. "Mom and Dad Have a Big Fight" talks to the big idea that grown-ups sometimes argue and kids often fear their family will fall apart. It's an important idea, but the video slips from real to imaginary situations so glibly that parents may need to help kids sort out the real from make believe in both video and life. **Arthur's Eyes** (●●●●), reissued in DVD format, includes several themes that are meaningful to school-age kids. Poor Arthur can't see the chalkboard and he must come to terms with wearing glasses. "Francine's Bad Hair Day" centers on wanting to look like someone else instead of oneself. "Draw" is an extra story that was not on the original video. Here Francine calls Fern a "mouse" and discovers that name-calling can backfire. These stories stay truer to the original storybooks. 5–8.

■ Pollyanna 　2006　 PLATINUM AWARD

(WGBH/Masterpiece Theatre $19.95 ●●●●●) Anytime you need a good old-fashioned three-hanky movie, **Pollyanna** awaits! A Masterpiece Theater production starring Amanda Burton as Aunt Polly and Georgina Terry as her orphaned niece. Taught as a child that one can always find a good side to any adversity, Pollyanna teaches everyone the "glad game" and manages to cheer just about everyone but her dour aunt who has been unhappy in love. But when disaster befalls Pollyanna, a silver lining does appear! Beautiful to look at with a fine supporting cast! 100 min. 8 & up.

■ Sylvester and the Magic Pebble 　2006　

(Scholastic $14.95 ●●●½) **Sylvester** is one of our all-time favorite tales by William Steig, about a small donkey who makes one wish too many with a magic pebble. This part of the video is well animated and would have been a PLATINUM winner, but we felt less enthusiastic about the other lead stories on this DVD, which center on "magic." **Possum Magic** and **Princess Furball** just don't match the magic of Sylvester! Too bad they didn't keep this an all-Steig collection!

■ Tikki Tikki Tembo…and More Favorite Tales 　2006　

(Scholastic $14.95 ●●●●) You probably grew up chanting this boy's name, Tikki, Tikki Tembo–No Sa Rembo–Chari Bari Ruchi–Pip Peri Pembo! Based on an old Chinese folktale, it explains why boys—not even first sons—are no longer given such long names. There is not much animation on this classic, but it is a well loved story. The most terrific story on this DVD, "The Tender Tale of Cinderella Penguin," is a wordless telling of the Cinderella story featuring an amusing cast of penguins. Obviously, this is intended for kids who already know the original and will enjoy seeing it played out in pantomime. DVD also includes, "The Happy Lion," and "The Magic of Anansi," but you might want to skip the bonus,"Little Red Riding Hood" in which Red and Granny are gobbled up, but magically saved when the woodsman chops up the big bad wolf! 5 & up.

■ The Day Jimmy's Boa Ate the Wash
2006 PLATINUM AWARD

 (Scholastic $14.95 ○○○○○) This collection might have been subtitled, "Tales out of School." Steven Kellogg's illustrations come to life in this lightly animated version of one of the zaniest class trips in children's books. It's one of those tall tale stories that grows as the narrator goes on and on. Other stories on the video include "Shrinking Violet," narrated by Calista Flockhart, and "Will I Have a Friend?" which is much younger than the other stories. DVD bonus stories are "Wings: A Tale of Two Chickens" and the marvelous Canadian film, "The Sweater," about a boy who receives the wrong sweater through a mail order mix-up and is an outcast on his hockey team. 6 & up.

■ The Snowman BLUE CHIP

(Miramax/Buena Vista $12.99 ○○○○○) An enchanting fantasy of a snowman who takes a small boy on a flying adventure. A word of warning: one three-year-old dissolved in tears when the snowman melted. A better choice for 4 & up.

■ Why Mosquitoes Buzz in People's Ears 2006

(Scholastic $14.95 ○○○○½) This collection of African folktales includes two Caldecott winners. The title story is a tall tale that explains how mosquitoes came to buzz; "A Story, A Story" is an Anansi the Spider Man story; plus "Who's in Rabbit's House?" James Earl Jones narrates the two stories with illustrations by Leo and Diane Dillon. This DVD includes two other stories, "The Village of Round and Square Houses," and "Hot Hippo." 5 & up.

Feature-Length Films

■ Charlie and the Chocolate Factory
2006 PLATINUM AWARD

(Warner Brothers $TBA ○○○○○) In the interest of full disclosure, one of us is devoted to the original movie and approached the Tim Burton/Johnny Depp version with disdain. Unfortunately, from the opening credits onward, it was clear that the new adaptation of the Dahl's classic story was truly inventive, entertaining, and hit that difficult chord of appealing to all ages. While some found Depp's Willy Wonka a bit odd or creepy, we never had the sense that he went too far (maybe having young children at home gave him a different sensibility). With nods to pop culture of yesteryear (Busby Berkeley,

Esther Williams musicals, "2001: A Space Odyssey," The Beatles, Kiss, etc.)—there's something delicious for everyone. 7 & up.

■ Herbie Fully Loaded *2006*

(Disney $TBA **oooo**) There's absolutely nothing objectionable about this adaptation of the '68 film, "The Love Bug." Lindsay Lohan stars as the new owner of Herbie. While you won't wince watching this movie with your kids, there's nothing surprising about it, either. There are no plot twists, not a one (but also no profanity or bathroom jokes). Will appeal to NASCAR fans (there are cameo appearances by Jeff Gordon and Jimmie Johnson). It's nice to see Michael Keaton and Matt Dillon back on the big screen (although we hope their next films will be more substantial). 5 & up.

■ Ice Princess *2006* PLATINUM AWARD

(Disney $29.99 **ooooo**) How about a movie about a super-smart math and science student who becomes a great skater applying what she knows about physics to her own skating? While it may take a leap of faith to get the same girl to the Nationals, it is a fun leap. Michelle Trachtenberg (of "Harriet the Spy") is allowed to be smart and beautiful. Kim Cattrall plays her coach and Joan Cusack plays her mother (and they make her look upsettingly matronly). The behind-the-scenes look at the cutthroat world of figure skating may be eye-opening to many young skaters. 6 & up.

■ The Incredibles *2006* PLATINUM AWARD

(Disney $29.99 **ooooo**) We first reviewed "The Incredibles" in a packed New York City movie theater. Parents and kids found aspects of the movie that especially appealed to them. Kids loved the fast-paced adventure and were big fans of Dash's speed. While siblings could identify with the tension between Dash and his big sister Violet, parents identified with the everyday problems and frustrations of the middle-aged former superheroes. Unlike many family films that are tolerated by adults, "The Incredibles" is truly family entertainment. The adult humor is there but not in an over-the-top way that would make you or your 10-year-old uncomfortable. The DVD's extras are worth a look.

■ Lemony Snicket's A Series of Unfortunate Events *2006*

(Paramount $29.99 **ooo**½) Combining the first three books in the series, the film version of this well known tale of three orphans is visually amazing. While the sets are first rate, the rest of the movie, unfortunately, is not. Jim Carrey plays the orphans' wicked uncle, Count Olaf. His performance is so over-the-top "Carrey" that you can't forget that you're watching the actor playing a part. Even with Meryl Streep and a cameo appearance by Dustin Hoffman, there's something missing here, allowing the film to fall flat—much to the disappointment of the loyal readers.

■ Madagascar 2006

(Dreamworks $TBA ○○○) We really looked forward to what we hoped would be the next great family film à la "Shrek" or "Finding Nemo." The premise sounded great—animals that break out of the Central Park Zoo end up being shipped back to Africa only to find themselves shipwrecked on Madagascar. Add to that a great cast of voices including Chris Rock, Ben Stiller, and David Schwimmer. Unfortunately, that's where all the good news ends. The screenplay, not as zippy as we had hoped, seems to be stranded in the wild. We were equally disappointed with the poor script and unpleasant look of "Shark Tale" (our viewers kept teasing, "Do you think Nemo's going to show up?" and "Could we just watch Nemo instead?").

■ The Pacifier 2006

(Disney $29.99 ○○○) A decade ago this would have been an Arnold role. But now that he's busy, these roles have landed on Vin Diesel. A Navy Seal assigned to protect the children of an assassinated scientist, Vin Diesel approaches his babysitting job with a take-no-prisoners attitude that just isn't funny for the first half of the movie, and the second half is way too predictable.

■ Pooh's Heffalump Movie 2006

(Disney $29.99 ○○○○) The gang from the 100 Acre Wood go in search of the dangerous Heffalump. Roo is told that he's too small to go along. So of course that means, in Disney terms, that Roo goes anyway on his own and finds the dreaded lavender creature. They become quick friends. Moral: embrace difference. Good concept with a low dose of safe scare for young viewers. 4 & up.

■ Samantha: An American Girl Holiday
2006 PLATINUM AWARD

(Warner $19.95 ○○○○○) A charming story of friendship between Samantha, a wealthy young girl who lives in New York with her

Grandmary, and Nellie O'Malley, the servant girl next door. We were concerned that this was just marketing for the American Girl Dolls by the same names, but, indeed, there's a moving and meaningful story here, as well as a beautifully old-fashioned film with the look of Masterpiece Theatre, and with Mia Farrow. 7 & up.

BLUE CHIP and Notable Past Winners: Feature-Length Films

These are widely available films that you'll find in the video store or library. They also are shown frequently on TV, but the video versions lack interrupting commercials—a real plus! Most of these are for early school years and beyond.

- Anne of Green Gables
- Apollo 13
- Babe
- Beauty and the Beast
- Beethoven Lives Upstairs
- The Borrowers
- Cinderella and Cinderella II
- Charlotte's Web
- Chicken Run
- Chitty Chitty Bang Bang
- E.T.
- Finding Nemo
- Fly Away Home
- Freaky Friday
- Gulliver's Travels
- Harriet the Spy
- Harry Potter series
- Holes
- Homeward Bound and Homeward Bound II
- Honey, We Shrunk Ourselves
- The Indian in the Cupboard
- The Lion King and The Lion King II
- The Little Mermaid
- Madeline
- Mary Poppins
- The Miracle
- Mulan
- My Dog Skip
- The Nutcracker (with Baryshnikov)
- October Sky
- Peter Pan (Mary Martin version)
- The Red Balloon
- Remember the Titans
- The Rookie
- The Santa Clause
- Sarah, Plain and Tall
- The Secret Garden
- Shrek and Shrek 2
- The Sound of Music
- Snow White
- Sounder
- Stuart Little and Stuart Little 2
- Tarzan
- To Kill a Mockingbird
- Willy Wonka and the Chocolate Factory
- The Wizard of Oz

Information, Please

Toddlers and Preschoolers

■ A Day at the Circus 2006

(Universal $17.98 ●●●○) If you grew up with Mr. Rogers you may be happy to share some of his old shows with your children. So far two have been released. We found **A Day at the Circus** more entertaining than **Adventures in Friendship**. Our favorite segments are the live-action films at the circus. This DVD also has a music adventure with instruments from around the world, a bass fiddle festival, and a visit to a pretzel factory, among other segments. In other words, you will want to select episodes rather than just running all 58 mins. 3 & up.

■ Cleared for Takeoff BLUE CHIP

(Fred Levine Productions $14.95 ●●●●●) Fasten your seat belt and get ready for a fast-paced look at commercial aviation that follows a mother and three kids on a trip from start to finish. Interesting information and film footage takes kids behind the scenes at the airport. From the maker of the granddaddy of construction videos, **Road and House Construction Ahead** (●●●●●). BLUE CHIP '96. 2½ & up. (800) 843-3686.

■ Doing Things BLUE CHIP

(Bo-Peep Productions $14.95 ●●●●●) Every video library should have **Doing Things**! With almost no talking or cutesy narrative, it presents kids and familiar barnyard animals going through the routines of the day—eating, washing, and playing. There's something new to see each time you watch. The cast of kids is multiethnic and the music is fun but not intrusive. **Doing Things** leaves the talking to you and your kids. 2 & up. (800) 532-0420.

■ Elmo's World: Families, Mail & Bath Time!

(Sony Wonder $12.95 ●●●○) Elmo, Mr. Noodle, and the rest of his gang give information about how different families can look, how to mail a letter, and how to take a bath. High marks for inclusion of multicultural families and children with special needs. We question why the mailbox needed to fly for "air mail" delivery. As cloying as Mr. Noodle may be to adult viewers, he has big-time appeal with kids. Also recommended,

Wake Up With Elmo (●●●● ½) with tips on sleep, getting dressed, and taking care of teeth. Live-action film of a first visit to the dentist is especially useful. 2 & up.

■ Peep and the Big Wide World
2006 PLATINUM AWARD

(WGBH $29.95 ●●●●●) A set of three DVDs from the young science show that introduces children to big science concepts, first through a cartoon and then with live-action film. For example, **Peep's New Friends** focuses on the metamorphosis of a butterfly, told through a cartoon story and followed by a visit to a real butterfly pavilion. Other concepts include things that hatch, making boats that float, and a follow-your-nose smelling adventure. "Nova" for the preschool set. 2½ & up.

Early & Later School Years
■ Firefighter George and Amazing Airplanes 2006

(Starts Smarter $14.99 ●●●●) From private planes to huge jets, this gives children an inside view of how planes are piloted and maintained. Without getting too technical, there is a fair amount of information here, and female as well as male pilots. The only downside to this video is host Firefighter George, who is a bit over the top in enthusiasm, but that did not bother our young viewers. They say 2–8, we'd say more like 3 & up.

(404) 944-1351.

■ Ken Burns American Lives Collection
2006 PLATINUM AWARD

(PBS $139.99 7DVD Set ●●●●●) Here is an outstanding set of seven biographies and stories of Americans and the historical events in which they played a leading role. Burns's stories begin with his memorable 1997 program "Thomas Jefferson" and conclude with his newest work, "Lewis and Clark," "Frank Lloyd Wright," "Not For Ourselves Alone: The Story of Elizabeth Cady Stanton and Susan B. Anthony," "Mark Twain," "Horatio's

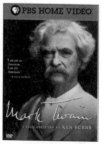

Drive," and "Unforgivable Blackness: The Rise and Fall of Jack Johnson." 24 hours, 40 mins. Titles are available separately. 10 & up.

■ Empires Collection: The Dynasties `2006`

(PBS $89.99 5 DVD Set oooo ½) Here is a rich resource for bringing history to life. For young people who are so visually attuned, this set (or individual titles) provides a library that introduces five great empires of the past. Set includes "The Greeks: Crucible of Civilization"; "The Roman Empire in the First Century"; "Egypt's Golden Empire"; "Japan: Memoirs of Secret Empire"; "The Medici: Godfathers of the Renaissance." 14 hours, 43 mins. 10 & up.

■ The Artists Specials

(Devine Entertainment $19.95 each ooooo) Rather than make biographies of an artist's entire life, these made-for-TV **Artists** series videos zoom in on a short but significant period in an artist's life. They weave fact and fiction in a relationship between an artist and a young person with very human and universal problems. **Mary Cassatt: American Impressionist,** PLATINUM AWARD '01, stars Amy Brenneman. In **Degas and the Dancer,** struggling with debt and his own self-doubt, Edgar Degas inspires a young dancer to believe in herself and her talent. In helping her, he helps himself. For those who love Degas, the ballet, or both, this is not to be missed! 8 & up. (877) 338-4633. devineentertainment.com

■ Rainy Day Art `2006` PLATINUM AWARD

(Jumby Bay $19.95 ooooo) It's like having an art teacher come to your house! These are great projects for a rainy day or play date or for just plain doing instead of simply sitting there and watching. Cheri Lynn shows kids how to do 30 projects. Some are made with tissue paper and modge podge glue, some with model magic and scissors and foam board, others with something as simple as weaving paper and turning it into a mask! Be forewarned, Lynn uses a hot glue

gun for some of her work where staples would do—especially with young kids. Our favorite was the Funky Line drawings done with pens and paper. You can print out directions and most projects will work well with 5 & up. For older kids, see her **World Art.** 10 & up. (800) 476-1991.

■ Building Skyscrapers BLUE CHIP

(David Alpert Assoc. $19.95 ●●●●●) Kaboom! Down with the old and up, up, up with a new skyscraper in New York City. Step by step from implosions to raising the steel, to concrete oozing out of hoses, here's a ringside seat for watching a building go from foundation to finish. Real construction people, both male and female, answer the questions of a 7-year-old child in a well paced, clearly written film that was shot from many perspectives, including from a helicopter.

■ Families of the World Series

(Master Communications $19.95 each ●●●●) Narrated by a child from the featured country (videos cover, among other places, China, Thailand, Mexico, India, Japan, Korea, Vietnam, and Israel), these are low-on-energy but high-on-information films about the food, work, school, and customs, told from a child's point of view. More like social studies films for school or libraries, they are nevertheless one way to introduce kids to far-away places. 30 min. 5–11. (800) 765-5885.

■ Look Mom! I Have Good Manners

(Thinkeroo $14.95 ●●●●½) Based on the title alone, we expected this would be a didactic thumbs down. But with its quiz-show format, the hyper-happy show host involves viewers as players with questions that center on table, good health, playground, and school manners. Kids featured are school-aged kids—the audience for this lively and non-preachy video. (800) 477-7811. 6–10.

■ The Magic School Bus Gets Planted

(Kid Vision $12.95 ●●●●) Phoebe gets transformed into a giant vine and needs to learn what she needs to grow. Still top rated: **Magic School Bus Greatest Adventures** ($12.95 ●●●●●), a compilation of best videos that includes **Busasaurus,** a journey back into the time of dinosaurs (PLATINUM AWARD '98); **. . . Gets Lost in Space** and **. . . In a Pickle.** The series features the wacky Ms. Frizzle (voice of Lily Tomlin) and her class. Recommended prior winners: **. . . Getting Energized,** a look at different types of energy; **. . . Gets Ants in Its Pants,** a trip into the social world of ants; and **The Magic Schoolbus for Lunch,** a journey through the digestive system. PLATINUM AWARD '96. 5 & up.

■ Popular Mechanics for Kids: Radical Rockets

(Koch Vision $12.98 **oooo**) Two teens take kids on a visit to NASA and get to try out all sorts of equipment used to train real astronauts. This is an interesting video for kids who are taken with the idea of exploring space. We didn't like **Slither & Slime** (**ooo**); it has too many moments that felt like "Fear Factor," with earthworms slithering over the kids' faces. 7 & up.

■ Really Wild Animals BLUE CHIP

(National Geographic/Columbia TriStar $14.95 each **oooo**) A lively blend of splendid film footage, information, and music have made this series a hit with kids. Dudley Moore narrates all three videos: **Monkey Business** looks at animal families, **Dinosaurs and Other Creature Features** explores the mysteries and characteristics of some of the weirdest wildlife, **Polar Prowl** travels from North to South Pole. Closed-captioned. 5–11.

Coping with Real Life and Death

■ Arthur: The Good Sport

(Sony Wonder $12.98 **oooo**) These are three stories that will appeal to sports-minded kids. In "The Good Sport," Francine has to get over not winning the Athlete of the Year Award. Champion figure skater Michele Kwan (our favorite!) helps Francine see her way to becoming a good sport. In "Muffy's Soccer Shocker," Muffy has to deal with her demanding coach—her dad! "Francine Frensky, Olympic Rider" is a funny story about dreaming of becoming an Olympic equestrienne. 5 & up.

■ When Someone Dies 2006

(Comical Sense $14.99 **oooo**½) Trevor Romain mixes live action with animation in a DVD that deals with a girl, Skye, who is grieving over the loss of her grandmother. It deals briefly but honestly with the memorial service, the cemetery, and typical questions about "Am I going to die?" "Is her death my fault?" In a dream sequence Grandma returns and takes Skye on a journey explaining the physical as well as spiritual aspects of death. Shared with a school-aged child, this may well be a helpful resource. It is not for young children who may not understand grandmother's return as temporary. They say 6 & up. We'd suggest more like 7 & 8. Also available as a book. 80 mins.

Bedtime Fears

■ Goodnight Moon and Other Sleepytime Tales

(HBO Kids $12.95 ●●●●●) Though toddlers might enjoy the title story, this is not a film for the very young. Through interviews with dozens of real kids, this refreshing film captures kids' typical feelings about dreams and bedtime. Viewers will find comfort in knowing that they are not alone in some of their fears. Laced throughout these wise remarks from kids are Natalie Cole narrating Faith Ringgold's *Tar Beach*, Billy Crystal's telling of Mercer Mayer's *There's a Nightmare in My Closet*, and familiar bedtime songs sung by Tony Bennett, Aaron Neville, Lauryn Hill, and Patti LaBelle. And, yes, *Goodnight Moon* comes to life faithfully with brilliant color and minimal animation, and is read just as it should be, with simplicity, by Susan Sarandon. Save this for kids from 4–7. PLATINUM AWARD '01.

New Baby in the House

■ Arthur's Baby

(Sony $12.95 ●●●●●) When Arthur learns that he's about to become a big brother, he has mixed emotions about the changes in his life. A second story, "D.W.'s Baby," features the arrival of Baby Kate. PLATINUM AWARD '98. Note: Unfortunately, this series has not been consistently solid. In **Arthur's Tooth** (●), there are monsters and spitting contests; in **Arthur Makes the Team** (●), the second story, "Meek for a Week," has a fantasy sequence in which Francine "blows her top" and her head actually comes off and lands on a lawn (still

talking). We find these images unnecessary for any age, but particularly inappropriate for Arthur's large preschool audience.

■ Three Bears and a New Baby

(Sony Wonder $12.95 ●●●●●) Baby Bear is freaked out when he discovers that the new baby on the way is going to actually live at his house. "But I'm the baby bear! That's my name, Baby Bear!" He reminds his parents that they are, after all, the storybook classic, "The Three Bears," not the four bears. A reassuring choice for older siblings who may be ambivalent about pending new arrivals. PLATINUM AWARD '04.

Going to School
■ Arthur's Famous Friends

(Sony $12.95 ●●●●●) This is one of our favorite Arthur videos. Each of the three stories features a guest visitor whose voice is used with animated images. In the first segment, Mr. Rogers comes to visit, but Arthur thinks Mr. Rogers is for babies and is surprised to discover that his friends want to meet their old friend. In the second story, poet Jack Prelutsky comes to the local library for a poetry contest and recites some of his own verse. There's some gratuitous grossout verse in this segment that we could have done without, but kids will find it funny. The third episode, with Yo-Yo Ma, centers on a debate about jazz vs. classical music. PLATINUM AWARD '01. 5 & up.

Potty Videos

There are no magic bullets, but these may be helpful reinforcements. Of course, don't be upset if your reluctant potty user leaves the room when you put these tapes on!

■ Potty Power

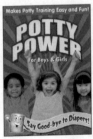

(Thinkeroo $14.95 ●●●● ½) Toddlers who are on the threshold of "potty power" will relate to the kids in this video who demonstrate all the things they as big kids can do—including "going potty." An amiable young woman sings and speaks along with an animated roll of toilet paper—sounds a bit hokie, but comes across as age-appropriate and not preachy. No miracles promised, but it couldn't hurt! (800) 477-7811. 2½ & up. Also recommended: **It's Potty Time** (A Vision $19.98 ●●●●). Developed by the Duke University Medical Center, this "story" features kids of many ages getting ready to go to a party.

Safety

■ Big Bird Gets Lost BLUE CHIP

(Sony $12.95 **ooooo**) In this episode of Sesame Street's *Kids' Guide to Life* series, Maria takes Big Bird shopping. The bad news is that Big Bird gets lost; the good news is that Maria has taught Big Bird and viewers a catchy song for remembering their phone numbers as well as how to find help in the store. A nonthreatening and valuable video with guest star Frances McDormand. 3–7.

Other Issues

Staying Healthy

■ Arthur Goes to the Doctor

(Sony $12.95 **ooooo**) There are several health-related stories in this excellent video. In the first story Arthur cuts his knee and is afraid to tell his parents. It's D.W. who helps him do the right thing. In the second story D.W. gets poison ivy; and the third story features Buster and his asthma. This informative film includes a live-action visit to a doctor about asthma. PLATINUM AWARD '02.

Still top rated: **Arthur's Eyes** ($12.95 **oooo**), a video that may help kids who are getting used to needing glasses. 4–8.

■ A Trip to the Dentist Through Pinatta's View

(Boggle-Goggle $14.95 **oooo**) Move over, Oprah! Pinatta, a lively talk show star/puppet, hosts a preschooler and her mom on the subject of going to the dentist. Practicing is one way to overcome fears about a first trip to the dentist, and this includes a nice blend of live-action footage with puppets. 3 & up. (978) 287-4628.

Honesty

■ Telling the Truth

(Sony $12.98 **oooo**) Telly makes the mistake of telling a lie to impress his friends and then has to live with the consequences. Dennis Quaid makes a guest appearance and helps Telly face up to the truth. An age-appropriate retelling of "The Boy Who Cried Wolf" parallels Telly's predicament. From the *Kids' Guide to Life* series. Also, **Learning to**

Share, with Katie Couric. Closed-captioned 4–8.

Science and Ecology

■ Earth Stories Paleontology Vol. #1

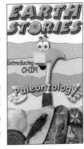

(Mazon Productions $19.95 ●●●●●) Chip, the talking rock hammer, is your animated host through this engaging introduction to paleontology. Really most appropriate for upper school (9+). Excellent graphics explain complicated concepts. Live action of digs in Argentina and Illinois are also included, and show the amazing process of fossil hunting. This is the type of film you only wish your Earth Science teacher had had! 30 mins. PLATINUM AWARD '04. (800) 332-4344.

■ The Inventors' Specials

(Devine Entertainment $19.95 each ●●●●●) An excellent series about famous scientists introduces young viewers to the past with an artful blend of fact and fiction. Each film pairs a well-known scientist with a young person—and both learn much from each other. **Marie Curie** (PLATINUM AWARD '01) is an exciting tale of two sisters whose lives cross paths with Madame Curie during World War I. **Edison** (PLATINUM AWARD '01) opens with a chase scene as a runaway orphan boy literally runs into the scientist's lab, where he becomes an apprentice. A wonderful period piece! Also top rated: **Einstein: Light to the Power of 2,** which portrays a bigoted teacher, a young black girl in the fifties, and the world-famous scientist who befriends her. 9 & up. (877) 338-4633.

■ March of the Penguins *2006* PLATINUM AWARD

(National Geographic $TBA ●●●●●) While we're not sure if your family shares our family's ongoing fascination with penguins, this stunning movie should intrigue you. The life of the Emperor penguins in the Antarctic is amazing to watch as they, without a director, jump out of the water and march single file to their breeding ground. The males watch over the eggs for two months (without eating), and cope with 100-mile-an-hour winds and temperatures well below zero—truly dedicated Dads! To make a good thing even better, the film is narrated by Morgan Freeman. 7 & up.

■ Nova: Welcome to Mars *2006* PLATINUM AWARD

(WGBH $19.95 ●●●●●) With all the attention
to Mars' recent close encounter with Earth, this
film gives you a chance to land with the Mars
rovers and get a look around. The drama of off-
again/on-again robotic communication gives us
a sense of the frustrations and triumphs of
those who explore the distant frontier of space.
10 & up.

■ Playtime With Ahpun & Oreo

(Alaska Postcards $19.95 ●●●●½) There's nothing
cutesie about this film featuring two bear cubs who
were orphaned in the wild and raised in the Alaska
Zoo. In the wild, one would never be able to see a
polar bear and brown bear playing together, but
these two playful cubs can be seen growing into
yearlings through the magic of video. The pace is
moderately slow, but the film footage is interesting
and likely to keep kids entertained and informed.
2½–7. (800) 248-2624.

Holidays

Christmas, Chanukah, & Kwanzaa

■ Angelina Ballerina, The Show Must Go On

(HIT Entertainment $12.99 ●●●●) It's Christmas
in Mouseland and Angelina wanted to be the star
of the show. But, alas, she dances better than she
sings and ends up cast as the mean old stepmother
in Cinderella. This is the first feature-length special (50 mins.) and was the best of last year's
Angelina videos. 4–8.

■ Elf

(New Line Home Entertainment $29.95 ●●●●●) Starring Will
Ferrell as the man who grew up at the North Pole, thinking he was
an elf. He heads to New York to seek out his father, a Scrooge-
inspired character played by James Caan. Ferrell is great at the physical humor that appeals to kids; adults also didn't mind this family
fare with a memorable performance by Bob Newhart as Papa Elf.

PLATINUM AWARD '05. 9 & up.

■ Bob the Builder: A Christmas to Remember

(HIT Entertainment $16.99 **oooo**½) Bob's brother Tom is coming home for the holidays and Bob is thrilled. But Bob is busier than ever getting the city lights, tree, and park ready for the Christmas concert. Tom misses the last boat, but all's well that ends well. Sir Elton John is a featured guest, appearing as an animated character in the show. 50 mins.

■ Sesame Street Celebrates Around the World

(Sony $14.95 **oooo**) If you lived in Portugal, you would celebrate the New Year by making wishes and eating 12 grapes, one for every month of the year. With music and humor, Big Bird and friends introduce viewers to children and customs in many parts of the world. Also, **Shalom Sesame Chanukah (oooo)**, **Jerusalem Jones and the Lost Afikoman(oooo)**, and **The Aleph-Bet Telethon (oooo)**. 4 & up.

Noteworthy Catalogs

Big Kids Productions (800) 477-7811
Music for Little People (800) 409-2457
PBS Home Video (800) 645-4727
WGBH (800) 949-8670

Noteworthy Websites

amazon.com
bigkidsvideo.com
ebay.com
musicforlittlepeople.com
reel.com
shopPBS.com

IV • Audio
Great Music & Stories

Music Exploration. CDs are a great way to introduce children to a broad range of music such as folk songs, marches, classics, and show tunes, that they might not hear on the radio. These musical explorations are opportunities for dancing, conducting, drawing while listening, and even daydreaming.

Story Power. Listening to stories can help beginning readers as they follow along in a book. Simply listening to longer books provides food for the imagination—to make one's own pictures from the spoken word. Children enjoy and understand stories well beyond their reading level and readily do so when no adult is available to read with them. For quiet or sit-down travel time, few take-alongs are as valuable as some well selected audio stories.

Criteria. In testing new products, we continue to reject "children's music" that is preachy, overproduced, and in many cases, condescending to young listeners. Our ultimate test is still whether we can stand being in a car with it or whether someone in the driver's seat or car seat screams, "Turn it off!"

Shopping Tips. We also recommend that you share your favorite music, whether it be contemporary, folk, jazz, classical, or show tunes. If you're enjoying the music, chances are it will be contagious.

Large music stores carry products of major companies such as Disney and Sony Wonder. We have provided phone numbers and websites to help you locate titles from smaller recording companies that sell directly or through catalogs.

Music

Lullabies and Songs for the Very Young

■ All the Pretty Little Horses

(Randa Records $15.95 ●●●●½) A very traditional collection of 14 lullabies from Gershwin to "Rock-a-bye Baby." Miranda Russell's voice is as smooth as satin and the variety of instuments—flutes, guitars, harpsichord, and bass—all add to the richness of this recording. www.mirandarussell.com.

■ American Lullaby

(Ellipsis Arts $15.98 ●●●●●) A special collection of lullabies from American folk, country, and gospel traditions, sung by the best in children's music including Maria Muldaur, Bill Staines, Cathy Fink and Marcy Marxer, Sweet Honey in the Rock, and Susie Tallman. Songs include "Prairie Lullaby," "Hush Little Baby," and "My Creole Belle." PLATINUM AWARD '04. (800) 788-6670.

■ At Quiet O'Clock BLUE CHIP

(Sally Rogers, Rounder $8.98 ●●●●●) These lullabies are just the ticket for a quiet time—whatever the hour might be. With guitar, dulcimer, or piano as accompaniment, this wonderful collection of traditional and original lullabies by award-winning vocalist Sally Rogers is still our favorite! Trust us, this is a must-have for all new babies (and their parents). (800) 768-6337.

■ Baby Einstein: Lullaby Classics

(Buena Vista $9.98 ●●●●) We're not usually big fans of synthesized music, but this is a pleasing collection that includes selections by Mozart, Beethoven, Chopin, Dvorak, and others. Also, **Baby Vivaldi (●●●●)** and **Baby Galileo: Concert for Little Ears (●●●●)**.

■ Wings of Slumber *2006*

(Banana Slug String Band $14.98 ●●●●½) If you like your lullaby with a country western twang, this is for you! Soothing voices with dulcimer, mandolin, banjo, bass, and guitar all blend as they celebrate the many beauties of nature—from sunsets to swimming whales to singing to the moon. All ages.

■ Dreamland

(Putumayo $15.98 ○○○○○) Soothing lulla-bies from many lands sung with authentic instruments in the language of each land. Songs from Brazil, Madagascar, Canada, Scotland, Japan, Argentina, and more. Perfect for snuggle-down time. All ages. PLATINUM AWARD '04.

■ Dream with Me Tonight

(Sandman Records $12.98 ○○○○○) Melodie Crittenden's beautiful voice makes you want to find your blankie and get cozy. The original music com-posed by Lanny Sherwin is lovely and right on tar-get for setting the mood for bedtime. From the title song "Dream with Me Tonight" to the instrumen-tals at the end of the recording, this will do the trick for naptime (just be careful that you don't fall asleep too!). PLATINUM AWARD '03. Also, **Dream With Me Tonight (Volume 2)** features Gene Miller. The title song is our favorite. Miller's voice is calming but one song sounds too much like the last. www.echomusic.com.

■ Goodmorning Guitar

(Homesong Media $14.98 ○○○○○) The reissue of the PLATINUM AWARD-winning Ray Penney's classical guitar recording is just right for danc-ing, painting, reading, or just plain daydream-ing. Pure and pleasant mix of classic and folk-tunes to enjoy—sing along if you like, but most of the selections are simply for your lis-tening pleasure. (631) 728-4483.

■ Lovely Sleepy Baby 2006

(Lovely Baby Music $17.95 ○○○○) To us this music reminds us most of going to a spa. Not quite Enya, but still very calming. Composer Raimond Lap encourages parents to use this music to soothe your baby (we think it may soothe you, too!).

Pleasant in a very mellow kind of way. All instrumental. (877) 695-2229.

■ Pocket Full of Stardust

(Rounder $12.99 ●●●●○) Consistently, Cathy Fink and Marcy Marxer can be counted on for humor and musicality that you and your child will enjoy. This entry opens with some pretty lively fare for sleep time, but it calms down as the tracks proceed, almost mirroring the way we unwind slowly at the end of the day. Save this for older kids, not toddlers. PLATINUM AWARD '03. Still top rated, **Pillow Full of Wishes.** (800) 768-6337.

■ The Sun Upon the Lake Is Low BLUE CHIP

(Mae Robertson & Don Jackson, Lyric Partners $16 ●●●●●) A collection of glorious traditional and contemporary folk songs—a soothing way to end any day. Includes, among others, "Circle Game," "Michael Row Your Boat Ashore," and "Gaelic Lullaby." Also top rated, **All Through the Night.** (800) 490-8875.

Music for Moving, Singing, and Dancing
■ Best of the Muppets *2006*

(Disney $15 ●●●○) If you want to share some classic songs from your own childhood, here's a collection of Muppet hits including "Rainbow Connection" (makes us cry everytime) and "It's Not Easy Bein' Green." To update their sound, Ashanti sings with the gang on several songs. May appeal more to you than your kids, but hey, that's okay.

■ Celebration of America

(Music for Little People $15.98 ●●●○) A blend of folk songs, patriotic marches, and traditional patriotic music performed by a wide range of well known artists including Linda Ronstadt ("Back in the USA"), the Weavers ("This Land is Your Land"), and the American Philharmonic Orchestra ("America the Beautiful"). A feel-good collection just right for a 4th of July celebration! (800) 409-2457.

■ Classic Nursery Rhymes

(Rock Me Baby Records $16.99 ●●●●○)
"Skidamarink," "I'm a Little Teapot," and "All
Around the Mulberry Bush" are among the 37 clas-
sics Susie Tallman performs with stylish wit and
energy. PLATINUM AWARD '03. Also appealing,
Children's Songs (●●●○), a collection of 38

best-loved traditional songs and rhymes in English, Spanish, and
French. (505) 254-7744.

■ Don't Blink 2006

(Parachute Express $15 ●●●●○) Parachute
Express is a talented trio that has been per-
forming and recording music for kids since the
'80s. There's a time when "I Like Trucks" will
be just the best song in your child's life. You
won't mind watching your kids dance and sing
along to this one. Other songs include "Gotta
Lotta Love" and "Clean Up Crew." 2 & up.

■ Come and Make a Circle

(Peachhead Productions $15.99 ●●●○) Susan Salidor combines eight
previously released songs with twelve new songs and fingerplays that
are sure to be favorites for home and cirlce time fun. Lyrics include
playful suggestions for moving to the music using fingers, toes, and
whole bodies with a variety of multicultural songs. 3 & up.

■ Disney Wishes! 2006 PLATINUM AWARD

(Disney $13.99 ●●●●○) If you're looking for good old-
fashioned Disney schmaltz sung by some of biggest
names (Sting, Elton John, Barbra Streisand, Phil
Collins, Bette Midler, Peabo Bryson, Olivia Newton
John), look no further. Singing a range of movie hits
from "A Whole New World" and "Can You Feel the
Love Tonight," to old classics such as "When You

Wish Upon a Star" and "Someday My Prince Will Come." If you are a
closet Disney singer (you know who you are!),
go ahead and enjoy this compilation that benefits the Make a Wish Foundation.

■ I Sang it Just for You

(Music by Mary Kaye $15 ●●●○) A collec-
tion of refreshingly original music sung by
the composer. Her songs have humor, a vari-

ety of styles, and don't talk down to kids. You won't mind listening to this—with or without them.

■ Hey, Picasso *2006* PLATINUM AWARD

(Rounder $15.98 ●●●●●) Inspired by the work of Picasso, Degas, Cassatt, and other great artists, Jessica Harper brings another bright collection of music that will be enjoyed by the preschool set. She is among the few artists to create music for kids that is smart and entertaining without resorting to condescending or ridiculous lyrics. Still top rated, for getting kids up and moving to samba, rap, swing, and reggae beats, **Inside Out.** 2½ & up. (800) 768-6337.

■ Raffi: Let's Play

(Rounder $12.98 ●●●●●) This celebrated children's composer and performer hasn't lost his touch. This collection includes both original music and well known songs, including "Yellow Submarine" and "The Eensy Weensy Spider." Jane Goodall contributes sound effects of chimp sounds in Raffi's tribute song to her work. PLATINUM AWARD '03. (800) 768-6337.

■ Nancy Cassidy's Kids' Songs

(Klutz $21.95 ●●●●●) This is a strong collection of classics, including "She'll Be Coming 'Round the Mountain," "Apples and Bananas," "Day-o," and "This Little Light of Mine." This two-CD set comes with a sing-along songbook (a real plus when you don't remember all the words!). Platinum Award '05. 2 & up.

■ Ragtime Romp

(Music for Little People $15.98 ●●●●●) Put on Ric Louchard's collection of Scott Joplin and watch your child's eyes open wide. From "Elite Syncopations" to "The Ragtime Dance" to "The Entertainer"—it's never too early to introduce kids to this part of America's musical heritage. PLATINUM AWARD '02. (800) 409-2457.

■ Scat Like That: A Musical Word Odyssey
2006 PLATINUM AWARD

(Rounder $14.98 ●●●●●) Cathy Fink and Marcy Marxer are back with another lively collection of music that your kids will enjoy dancing to. They begin with scat singing in the style of big band music. But they don't get stuck in one groove—they move on to swing, polka, blues, Latin, and old-time country music. This duo consistently delivers fun music that is affirmatively written with kids in mind without being preachy or sappy. (800) 768-6337.

■ Sing Along with Putumayo

(Putumayo Kids $15.98 ●●●●●) What a spirited collection of folk and blues classics! Arlo Guthrie opens the festivities with "Bling-Blang," and the quality of the singers and selections never lets up! You'll hear Taj Mahal with "Don't You Push Me Down"; Dan Zane doing "Bushel and a Peck"; Rosie Flores singing "Red, Red Robin"; and so many more. PLATINUM AWARD '05. We found the new **Swing** collection too esoteric for kids. (888) 788-8629.

■ Songs from the Street

(Sony $49.98 ●●●●●) The Street is Sesame. Need we say more? Parents, themselves old Sesame Streeters, will relish hearing their old favorites in this three-CD box set featuring over 63 remastered tracks with performances from the past 35 years PLATINUM AWARD '04. All ages.

■ That's What Kids Do!

(Building Block Music $15 ●●●●●) Here's an original musical with the feel of a kids' version of "A Chorus Line." Players from 4 to 14 sing their stories in a sassy variety of musical styles with lyrics that are often funny, sometimes wistful, and always entertaining. We saw the show live and are proud to say this was composed, produced, and played by five members of our family! PLATINUM AWARD '02. (800) 842-7664.

■ Under a Shady Tree

(Two Tomatoes Records $14.99 ●●●●●) Laurie Berkner is back with

a happy collection of original music and a bright voice to match. Berkner strikes just the right balance of creating music for children, and displaying a strong musical quality that will appeal to parents as well. PLATINUM AWARD '04. All ages.

Folk Tunes for All Ages

■ Bill Staines' One More River

(Red House Records $17.98 oooo) If you are a folk music person, you'll need no introduction to Bill Staines. This isn't a collection of cutesie songs chosen for the kiddies. It's honest-to-goodness music— some somber, some classic, some less familiar, and all joyful. Accompanied by everything from banjoes to violins, congas to penny whistles, guitars to bass. (800) 695-4687.

■ Bright Spaces

(Rounder $15.95 ooooo) A must-have collection of wonderful songs sung by the best in children's music. The voices of Arlo Guthrie, Woody Guthrie, Jessica Harper, Dave Mallett, Cathy and Marcy, and Sweet Honey in the Rock are brought together for this collection to benefit homeless children. Between Woody Guthrie's "This Land Is Your Land" and Dave Mallett's "Garden Song," all seems right with the world! PLATINUM AWARD '02. (800) 768-6337.

■ Family Fare: Folk Songs for Children and Their Families

(Elm Hill $15 ooooo) You're going to love this lively collection of songs by Woody Guthrie, Pete Seeger, and other traditional favorites plus many original songs with catchy lyrics and a sense of humor. Accompanied by guitar, banjo, autoharp, dulcimer, and harmonium, and all played and sung by the talented Ellen Edson. A gem that's destined to be a sing-along hit! PLATINUM AWARD '02. (603) 336-7796.

■ Folksongs and Bluegrass for Children

(Rounder $15.98 oooo) From the minute this disc starts spinning, you'll be singing along and tapping your foot! Phil Rosenthal's collection starts with "The Train Song" rolling down the track, on to "In the Jungle," followed by such well loved songs as "Six Little Ducks," "The Paw Paw Patch," "Mama Don't Allow," and "Aiken Drum," among others. A winner! (800) 768-6337.

■ Kids, Cars & Campfires

(Red House Records $15 ●●●●●) If you are going to buy one recent collection of folk tunes, this is it. Bill Staines, Tom Paxton, Sally Rogers, the Chenille Sisters, and other great singers combine forces—the only thing missing is the marshmallows! Songs include "Froggie Went a Courtin'," "Little Brown Dog," and "Your Shoes, My Shoes." PLATINUM AWARD '02. (800) 695-4687.

■ Little Johnny Brown

(Smithsonian Folkways $15 ●●●●) With this reissue of a collection from the early '70s, a new generation will enjoy Ella Jenkins, the ultimate songsmith for the young. Features Ms. Jenkins interacting with her young audience with such songs as "Miss Mary Mack" and "Head, Shoulders, Knees and Toes." These are classic folk songs with plenty of repetition and easy sing-, clap-, and tap-along fun. (800) 410-9815.

■ Pete Seeger American Folk, Game & Activity Songs for Children BLUE CHIP

(Smithsonian Folkways $15 ●●●●●) Roll up the carpet and get ready to dance! You'll have a library of the best-loved folksongs and games with this reissue of Seeger's classic *American Folk Songs for Children* and his *American Game and Activity Songs for Children*. Accompanied by his banjo, Seeger sings 22 well loved tunes such as "Bought Me a Cat," "Shoo Fly," "This Old Man," "Skip to My Lou," and "Clap Your Hands." 3–7. PLATINUM AWARD '01. (800) 410-9815.

■ Sweet Dreams of Home BLUE CHIP

(Magnolia Music/Lyric Partners $16 ●●●●●) Mae Robertson and Eric Garrison's eclectic collection of contemporary folk music in appreciation of the concept of "home" includes songs ranging from Graham Nash's "Our House" to David Byrnes' "This Must Be the Place." PLATINUM AWARD '00. (800) 490-8875.

■ This Land Is Your Land BLUE CHIP

(Rounder $15.98 ●●●●●) Introduce your kids to the music of Woody and Arlo Guthrie as they sing such classics as the title song, "So

Long, It's Been Good to Know Yuh," and "Riding in My Car. " (800) 768-6337.

Multicultural Music

■ Cajun

(Putumayo $15.98 ●●●●●) From the first note, you're transported to the bayous of southwest Louisiana. It's almost impossible to sit still while this collection of Cajun music is on—fun for kids to move to! PLATINUM AWARD '02. (888) 788-8629. Also top rated, **Le Hoogie Boogie: Louisiana French Music for Children** BLUE CHIP (Michael "Beausoleil" Doucet et al., Rounder $10.98/$15.98). (800) 768-6337.

■ Still the Same Me

(Sweet Honey in the Rock, Rounder $15.98 ●●●●●) Once again this superb African American ensemble gives us an inspired collection of songs and improvisations. Featuring only their voices and percussion instruments, this is a listening treat for the whole family that will move your spirit and your whole being! PLATINUM AWARD '02. (800) 768-6337.

Introducing the Classics

While there has been a great deal written about the "Mozart effect," you should know that even the researchers who did the original study did not work with babies—and are generally dismayed at the marketing that has been spun around their research with college students. That said, listening to classical music is a treat. If you have your own collection, experiment and see what your child enjoys at different times of the day. Here are some collections:

■ Beethoven's Wig 2

(Rounder Kids $12.98 ●●●●●) Bravo! Bravo! Lighthearted LOL lyrics are set to classics by Bach, Schubert, Vivaldi, Strauss, Brahms, Grieg, and others. Richard Perlmutter has done it again— linking familiar music with witty ditties and each composer's name! Like the original **Beethoven's Wig,** PLATINUM AWARD '03, this is an amusing symphonic romp in the spirit of PDQ Bach for young audiences. PLATINUM AWARD '05. (800) 768-6337.

■ The Best of Mozart 2006

(The Children's Group $15 ●●●○) While the Mozart effect has been debunked and there is no longer a guarantee that listening to this music will make children smarter, it will enrich their lives. Put it on while they paint, draw, or dance—and enjoy. If you have your own Mozart library, no need to bring this home, but it's a good introduction if you're looking to get started. Also, **The Best of Beethoven.** All ages. www.childrensgroup.com

■ Classical Child at the Opera BLUE CHIP

(MetroMusic $15.95 ●●●●●) Selections are by turns as playful as "Papagena!" from *The Magic Flute*, as powerful as the "Anvil Chorus" from *Il Trovatore*, and as heavenly as the "Flower Duet" from *Lakme*. What a splendid way to introduce young listeners to the opera! PLATINUM AWARD '01.

■ H.M.S. Pinafore BLUE CHIP

(London $14.96 ●●●●●) Part of every child's musical experience should include the sparkling music of Gilbert and Sullivan. *H.M.S. Pinafore* is always a good place to start.

Stories: Audio/Book Sets

Most storybooks published in audio form already have been well received as stand-alone books. Add music, sound effects, and a well known narrator, and a good thing just gets better! These combined forms of media can do a lot to promote kids' positive attitudes and appetites for books and reading. Here are some of the best tickets to pleasurable and independent storytimes. Some are just audio; others are packaged with CD and book.

Preschool Stories

■ A Hen, A Chick and A String Guitar 2006

(by Margaret Read MacDonald/illus. by Sophie Fatus, Barefoot $17.99 ●●●● ½) Based on a Chilean folktale, this is a cumulative tale with names of animals and their babies built into the telling, along with simple counting. Best of all is the Andean look to the art and that, as the story grows, so does the pace of the music with its Latino beat. 4 & up.

■ Blueberries for Sal

(by Robert McCloskey, Puffin $7.99 ●●●●) In this classic mix-up, a mother bear and cub get separated, as do a human mother-and-child duo. All's well that ends well. This no-frills set has no big-name stars, but beginning readers can follow the text or flip the tape for lively activity songs related to bears and berries. This series includes many other classics. 3–7.

■ If You Take a Mouse to the Movies

(by Laura Joffe Numeroff/illus. by Felicia Bond, HarperFestival $11.95 book & tape ●●●●●) The amusing circular story of what happens if you take a mouse to the movies is now available in a book-and-audio set. Narrated by Jason Alexander. The story is followed by "Mouse's 12 Days of Christmas" and other mouse Christmas carols. PLATINUM AWARD '02. 3–7.

■ Marsupial Sue Presents The Runaway Pancake *2006*

(retold by John Lithgow/illus. by Jack E. Davis, Simon & Schuster $17.95 ●●●● ½) As the Runaway Pancake chants his repetitive line, kids soon will be singing along with narrator John Lithgow in this lively version of a classic. Davis' illustrations are anything but classic and Lithgow doesn't exactly say the words as they are printed on the page. Still, this is a keeper! 4 & up.

■ Tell Me a Story Series BLUE CHIP

(HarperChildren's Audio $7.95 ●●●●) Many best-loved classics are available in inexpensive paperback-and-audio sets. These make good take-along travel treats and great gifts, and are an excellent way to build your child's listening ability and personal library. Bring home a mix of classics such as **Caps for Sale,** by Esphyr Slobodkina, **Dr. DeSoto Goes to Africa,** by William Steig, and **Dinner at the Panda Palace,** by Stephanie Calmenson.

Early School Years

Not all story tapes are equal. A solo narrator holding a listener's attention for several hours is no small feat! Here are the best new and BLUE CHIP choices:

■ The Chronicles of Narnia BLUE CHIP

(by C. S. Lewis, HarperChildren's Audio $11.95 each/$50 set ●●●●●)
There are seven tapes in this notable collection—each can stand
alone. Narrated by Ian Richardson, Claire Bloom, Anthony Quayle,
and Michael York. Together, they tell the whole story of the magic land
of Narnia. 9 & up.

■ Some Friends to Feed:
The Story of Stone Soup 2006

(retold by Pete Seeger & Paul D. Jacobs/ illus by
Michael Hays, Putman $16.99 ●●●● ½) Here's
an old favorite tale of hungry soldiers and hungry
villagers who learn that with a little bit of cooperation they can stir up a powerfully good-tasting
soup. With a CD and sing-along music in the
text, this is a new turn on a story that never grows old. 5 & up.

■ Stories in Music:
Mike Mulligan and his Steam Shovel

(Simon & Simon $16.98 ●●●●●) More than a recording of a beloved
storybook, this is a musical happening with original symphonic
music, á la Peter and the Wolf, plus some jazz and ways of listening
for the whole family to enjoy. 6–9. PLATINUM AWARD '05. (800) 419-
2409.

■ Harry Potter and the Half-Blood Prince
2006 PLATINUM AWARD

(Listening Library $75 CDs 17 disks ●●●●●) We
wish Jim Dale would record all our favorite titles.
He doesn't just read them, really, he performs
them with such artistry that our testers looked forward to getting back into the car to hear the next
installment! For kids who find a 600+ page book
a little daunting, or who want to experience the
world of Harry Potter in another way, here is a
bravura performance!

■ The Opal Deception,
Artemis Fowl 2006

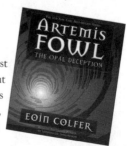

(Listening Library $34 ●●●●) In this newest
of the series, Artemis Fowl returns without
his memory and is scheming to steal a famous
painting. His long-term enemy, Opal Koboi,
is up to her evil ways. Fans of this series will

find plenty of action and suspense as Nathaniel Parker narrates what some say is the best of the books so far! 10 & up.

■ The Wonderful Wizard of Oz 2006

(Ear Twiggles $14.99 ♥♥♥♥) A dramatization of this classic story in an abridged musical version. OK, it's not Judy, but it is another take on the familiar story. It's like listening to the radio in the olden days when Grandma was growing up. 80 min. (858) 756-8644.

Online Resources

- **amazon.com**
- **cdbaby.com**
- **ebay.com**
- **itunes.com**
- **musicforlittlepeople.com**
- **rounder.com**

V • Using Ordinary Toys for Kids with Special Needs

Our continuing goal is to suggest products that are entertaining and to provide useful tips for getting the most play and learning value out of toys. We also know that children enjoy playing with products that are like their siblings', cousins', or neighbors'. By adapting ordinary toys, we can help put special needs kids' play lives into the mainstream.

Most toys have more than one use and will provide various kinds of feedback for children with different kinds of disabilities. Although we have used the headings *infants, toddlers,* and *preschoolers,* age guidelines are blurred, since conventional age labels will be less meaningful for children with significant developmental delays. For children with visual or hearing impairments, learning to make effective use of other senses is essential. Similarly, those with motor impairment need products that are easy to activate and that motivate exploration. Many toys are chosen because they are especially easy to activate physically and because they provide interesting sensory feedback.

While all the new products here are highly recommended,

the most outstanding products selected for these pages have received our SPECIAL NEEDS ADAPTABLE PRODUCT (SNAP) AWARD for 2006. It's our hope that bringing attention to these products will serve kids and motivate manufacturers and publishers to become more aware of children with disabilities who, like all children, need quality products.

Be sure to check out our database! We've put our database of SNAP AWARD winners from past years on our website at www.toyportfolio.com.

Infants and Toddlers

All the toys in this section were selected because they provide plenty of sensory feedback. Some of the best toys for infants and toddlers need little or no adapting.

Note: Reviews of top-rated basics are in the Infants and Toddlers chapters and also will be of interest. Here we have focused on products that are adaptable, easy to activate, or loaded with sound, light, texture, or motion.

☼ BASIC GEAR CHECKLIST FOR INFANTS AND TODDLERS

✓Mobile	✓Fabric blocks	✓Teethers
✓Musical toys	✓Soft huggables	✓Floor toys
✓Crib mirror	✓Manipulatives	✓Balls
✓Fabric rattles	✓Bath toys	✓Infant seat

■ Gymini Total Playground Kick & Play
2006 SNAP AWARD

(Tiny Love $69 ●●●●●) This company continues to be the leader in activity mats for young babies. We'd put this mat on the "must have" list for the baby shower. The new feature this year is a kick-and-play aspect that babies can activate with their feet, or bat at from their tummies as they get older. The key difference between this mat and so many others we tested is that the lights and music are soothing and not over-the-top loud or jarring. Comes with a mirror that babies will enjoy. (800) 843-6292.

■ Me in the Mirror

(Sassy $14.95 ●●●●) This wedge-shaped mirror (9½")
has no music, but does have a place for adding your
own photo. Can also be used as a tummy-time floor
toy. (800) 323-6336.

■ Symphony in Motion Deluxe

(Tiny Love $45 ●●●●●) This award-winning mobile now
comes with a remote control so you can turn the music on from a distance. Unlike most mobiles, this innovative offering has more visual
interest of several kinds: it tips as it spins, causing objects to shift their
positions in interesting ways; it also pauses, and the start-and-stop
motion adds another kind of interest; small shapes slide on the arms of
the mobile and make small clicking sounds as the musical mobile turns.
The sound quality on this mobile is better than most, and it plays several classical music selections. (800) 843-6292.

Making Things Happen

■ Classical Stacker

(Fisher-Price $10 ●●●●●) This prior SNAP Award-
winning stacker is reintroduced in new colors. Star
rings fit on the post in any order (a plus). Post has
magical lights that wink and play music when top is
pressed. Sound quality is not excellent, but it is a
long-term favorite. (800) 432-5437.

■ Earlyears Soft Busy Blocks

(International Playthings $15 ●●●●½) These have
been scaled down in size and are easier to grab than the originals. The
set of four fabric blocks has interesting textures and patterns and a
quiet sound in each block. **Activity:** Sit on
the floor, put one or more blocks on your
head or shoulder, and encourage your tot
to knock 'em off! (800) 445-8347.

■ Lamaze Whirl & Twirl Jungle *2006* SNAP AWARD

(RC2/Learning Curve $19.99 ●●●●●) One of our all
time favorite toys in this category. Three jolly creatures, a lion, elephant, and monkey, spin when
placed on the colorful musical platform. A
single big button activates the music and
motion, providing a little lesson in cause
and effect. This innovative toy develops motor

skills, visual tracking, and a powerful sense of being in charge. Unlike the overly frenetic Fisher-Price's **Jungle Friends Treehouse,** the animals here spin at a reasonable rate. (800) 704-8697.

■ Neurosmith Music Blocks 🎖️*2006* SNAP AWARD

(Small World Toys $45 ●●●●●) Welcome back! Comes with five colored plastic blocks, each side making a different sound. Match the shapes on the blocks or play them in random order—there's no right or wrong way. The "composer" allows you to record and play back your composition. Comes with one jazz cartridge; we'd suggest bringing home the Mozart cartridge, too. (800) 220-3669.

■ Roll-a-Rounds Swirlin' Surprise Gumballs 🎖️*2006*

(Fisher-Price $17.99 ●●●●½) Drop the gumball in the top, push the lever, and out comes the gumball. Play with sound off or on, this is a fun cause-and-effect toy with four gumballs. There's a ratchet-sounding dial on the front, but only the lever on the side releases the balls. You may need to hold the toy or secure it so that it doesn't tip over. Also, see **Drop & Roar Dinosaur,** p. 21. (800) 432-5437.

■ Poppin' Push Car

(Sassy $6 ●●●●½) Push this little car forward and the popping beads (safely enclosed in the dome roof) make a pleasing sound. Pull the car back and when you let go, the car zooms forward. One of the best toys in its category! Just right for floor-time play. (800) 323-6336.

Manipulatives

■ Ambi Pounding Apple 🎖️*2006*

(Brio $11.99 ●●●●½) Knock down one of four colorful caterpillars and another one with a happy face pops up. Tots can hit them with the apple core hammer or by hand. Caterpillars do not come out of the apple base. **Adaptation:** Hammer toys are sometimes a problem for kids who cannot grip or control movements. This is a gem of a pounding toy that operates without the hammer. **Activity:** With an older child, talk about the colors they hit or try playing a game of sequence: "Hit the red one and then the orange one." (888) 274-6869.

■ Lamaze Stack 'n Nest Birds *2006*

(RC2/Learning Curve $14.99 ●●●● ½) Four birds that can be stacked in a tower or nested one over the other. Three are fabric with zippy patterns, touchy-feely textures, and interesting sounds. The littlest bird is a funny-faced squeeze toy that can hide under all the others. Size order is built into the fun for peek-a-boo games of "Where's the birdie?" Designed for parent-child interaction. (800) 704-8697.

■ Learn-Around Playground *2006* SNAP AWARD

(LeapFrog $59.99 ●●●●●) This innovative table invites kids to explore and make things happen. Sitting down, tots can play the ball drop and tap the shape tabs and textures. On their feet, they can cruise around the sturdy table, test the pop-up and spinning shapes, press the letter that says their names, and activate the keyboard. The ball drop has jazzy percussion sounds and says the color of each ball as it falls. Has volume control and can be enjoyed with sound off. (800) 701-5327.

■ Lego Quatro

(Lego Systems $9.99 & up ●●●●●) Now there's a bigger brick (twice the size of Duplos and four times the size of standard Legos!). Made of a softer, easier-to-grasp material, we suggest that more *is* better, so start with the **Large Quatro Bucket** ($19.99/75 pieces; $14.99/50 pieces ●●●●●). SNAP AWARD '05. **Activity:** Sort the blocks by color, building towers or trains of red, yellow, or green. Which tower is taller? (800) 233-8756.

■ Musical Stack & Play

(Tiny Love $19.95 ●●●●●) An elephant-shaped stacking toy with a place for dropping balls in its top. The balls come out at the base with some fanfare (lights/sound) but not too loud. Testers liked the soft fabric rings for stacking, but really spent most of the time playing with the plastic balls. SNAP AWARD '05. (800) 843-6292.

Preschool and Early School Years

As children grow, they need a rich variety of playthings to match their expanding interests and abilities.

⚙️ BASIC GEAR CHECKLIST
FOR PRESCHOOL AND EARLY SCHOOL YEARS

✓ **Construction toys**
✓ **Sand and water toys**
✓ **Musical toys**
✓ **Toys for pretend**
  (dolls, trucks, puppets)
✓ **Tape player and tapes**

✓ **Art materials**
✓ **Big-muscle toys**
✓ **Electronic toys**
✓ **Puzzles, games,**
  and manipulatives

Age ranges are purposely broad; products need to be selected on the basis of your child's particular needs. Many basic toys reviewed in the Preschool and Early School Years chapters will be of interest and need no special adaptation. Here we have focused on products that lend themselves to adaptation.

Manipulatives, Puzzles, and Tracking Games
■ Puzzle Totes

(Lauri $8.99 ●●●●) Rather than having the traditional puzzle tray, these double-thick seven- and eight-piece puzzles have a handle just right for travel and carrying about. Two-toned pieces are able to stand up for dramatic play. Past favorites: **Big Shapes, Marine Life, Earthmovers, Dinosaurs,** and **Work & Play.** (800) 451-0520.

■ Beginner Pattern Blocks

(Melissa & Doug $19.99 ●●●●●) Ten wooden scenes are ready to fill with triangles, circles, squares, rectangles, and ovals. Part puzzle, part shape sorter, all beautifully crafted with wooden storage box. A good talking toy for developing language and visual discrimination. This company sells great sound puzzles, but with tiny handles that are harder to lift. **Activity:** Put all 30

shapes in a bag. Player One calls the shape that Player Two needs to find by touch—no looking! Winner is first to feel and find five pieces. SNAP AWARD '05. (800) 284-3948.

■ Fridge Farm Magnetic Animal Set

(LeapFrog $14.95 ooooo) Comes with five animals, each in two pieces; match them up and put them on the farm-board, and you'll hear the names of each animal. But what's really fun is if you put a horse head with a pig back, it will say, "horsepig." We love an electronic toy with a sense of humor! SNAP AWARD '05. (800) 701- 5327.

■ Puzzibilities Sound Puzzles 2006

(Small World Toys $15.95 each ooooo) Six raised pieces are easy to lift, and when they are put back in the puzzle board each makes a rip-roaring sound. Choose **Wild Animals, Dinosaurs,** or **Under**

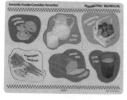

Construction. 2½ & up. SNAP AWARD '05. New for 2006, **Counting Out Loud Talking Puzzles** ($25 each oooo), with either numbers or the alphabet. (800) 421-4153. **Activity:** Use the animals to play a memory game. Put three or four in a row. Have child close eyes and take one away. What is missing? **Variation:** Rearrange the placement of two. Play "Guess what I moved?" (800) 421-4153.

Lacing Games 2006

Kids dive right into lacing activities without knowing they're a great way to develop the fine-motor skills they'll need for writing. While stringing beads, they can also sort by color and make patterns, learning to see likenesses and differences. New for 2006, **Seven Pets to Lace and Trace** (Lauri $6.99 oooo) are made of sturdy chipboard punched with holes that kids "sew" with colorful laces. Also recommended, **Lace & Link Numbers** ($14.99 oooo). 4 & up. (800) 451-0520. **VersaPegs** (Educational Insights $12 oooo) are 56 colorful pegs that can fit into a **VersaPeg mat** ($4) or be strung in patterns with the 8 laces. Good for dexterity, patterns, and color sorting/counting games. (800) 933-3277.

Tracking Toys

■ Rollipop Starter & Advanced Sets

(Edushape $19.95 & $24.95 ●●●●●) These are among our favorite toddler toys. Toddlers love to drop the oversized colorful plastic balls into the starter set, a tower, and track them as they go down. The balls also travel slowly down the advanced set, a bridge, making it an ideal toy for developing visual tracking. SNAP AWARD '04. (800) 404-4744.

■ Super Spiral Play Tower 2006

(International Playthings $32 ●●●●½) Toddlers love this marvelous toy that they can quickly take charge of operating. Two weighted balls and a little penguin twist down the spiral and slide into different slots. A green froggy slides down a chute and makes a funny sound that ends with the ping of a bell. Repetitive action provides the kind of predictable cause-and-effect results toddlers love. Develops eye-hand skills as well as visual tracking. 18 mos.& up. (800) 445-8347.

Games:
Matching, Memory, and Language Games

Games are entertaining ways for kids to develop social skills as well as counting, matching, and color concepts. You'll find other good choices in the Preschool, Early School, and Computer chapters.

■ 4-Way Countdown

(Cadaco $19.95 ●●●●●) This PLATINUM AWARD-winner just got more interesting. Now designed for 2–4 players, each player has 10 wooden pegs that flip. The object is to be the first player to turn over all your pegs by rolling dice. Players may add, subtract, multiply, or divide the numbers they roll in order to get the number they need. 6 & up. (800) 621-5426.

■ Talking Clever Clock

(Learning Resources $34.95 ●●●● ½) Here's a wonderful tool for teaching kids how to tell time. Our nine-year-old tester had given up on ever learning how to tell time—but within minutes he was having fun using the clock that has self-checking features with both digital and analog clock faces. He liked moving the hands of the clock to match the digital read-out. There are buttons that will tell you the time out loud, along with quiz and answer buttons. The same company's nonelectronic clock is still a great choice, but hearing the time out loud is a plus. **Activity**: Set the clock for typical times when you eat, rise, go to bed, leave for school. (800) 222-3909.

ABCs and 1, 2, 3s and Colors

Most kids learn to read with a mix of approaches; these products give kids playful practice with sounds and letters and things to count.

■ Balloon Lagoon

(Cranium $19.99 ●●●●●) Turn on the musical merry-go-round timer as players take turns fishing for magnetized letters to spell a word, spin wheels to get four parts of an animal lined up, collect matching dice as they fall through the roof of the snack hut, or "tiddly-wink" four frogs into the pond. The first to collect 15 mini-balloons is the winner. A lively game that's fun and develops sequencing, dexterity, matching, and simple spelling skills. SNAP AWARD '05. Also top rated, **Cranium Hullabaloo**—shapes, colors, letters and active play all in one! SNAP AWARD '04. (877) 272-6486.

■ Design & Drill Activity Center

(Educational Insights $39.95 ●●●●●) Here's a new spin on a "working" drill with colorful pegs. Several bits fit into the battery-operated "drill," which works in forward and reverse. Bits can also fit in a hand-powered screwdriver handle when the batteries go dry. **Activity:** Give kids a few days to experiment with making open-ended original designs before they move on to the patterns. Use these to work on counting or color names. Did you use more red or blue pegs? Can you make an all-red row? How many yellow pegs did you use? SNAP AWARD '04. (800) 933-3277.

■ Fridge Phonics Magnetic Letter Set

(LeapFrog $17.99 **ooooo**) A set of uppercase letters that not only stick to the fridge, but can be felt, heard, and seen—a lot of sensory opportunities here! Put the "magnetic phonics reader" onto the fridge and play one capital letter at a time. They say and sing the letter's name and sing the sound they say. Letters are raised to give kids the feel for their shapes. Also top rated, **Fridge Farm Magnetic Animal Set** ($14.95), see p. 265. (800) 701-5327.

■ "Peg"gy Back Game 2006

(Lauri $14.99 **oooo**) It's often hard to find a true beginner's color naming game that is not too complex. This simple color cube game involves moving pegs on the pegboard forward to the color thrown. If you land on the same space as your opponent, you get a Peggy back ride! Nothing hard here. The graphics are not great, but the game is a good place to start with one concept instead of three. (800) 451-0520.

■ IQ Preschool Around the Blocks

(Small World Toys $26.99 **oooo**½) A high-quality set of 26 blocks with upper- and lowercase letters, plus images to match. All store in a big cloth bag. **Activity:** Use these blocks for playing sound games. Put blocks with three distinctive sounds in sight. Ask child to find the block that has the same sound as the word you say. (800) 421-4153.

■ WonderFoam Big Letters 2006

(Chenille Kraft $11.50 **oooo**) Twenty-six big colorful foam letters. These are fun to trace and stick to the wet wall of the tub to spell out names and words. These have an interesting texture, as well, that make them an even better sensory learning tool. **Activity:** Because these letters have a textured finish they can be used for crayon rubs. Put a sheet of paper on top of a letter and use the side of a crayon to rub over the letter. Make a name sign with rubbings. Also, **WonderFoam Magnetic Letters and Numbers** ($10.50 ●●●●)—unlike old-time plastic magnetic letters with tiny magnets that can be a choking hazard, these foam letters are completely backed with magnetic material that mirrors their shape. Also, new **WonderFoam Dominoes** *2006* **SNAP AWARD** ($15.50 ●●●●●) Twenty-eight big  dominoes with colorful dots that are color-coded to match. One can feel some sensory information in the cut-out form of the dots. They are not raised, but you can feel their outline. A great matching game. (800) 621-1261.

Electronic Games

■ The Big Brain Book Interactive Dictionary *2006*

(Oregon Scientific $34.99 ●●●●) We don't love the cartoonish illustrations in this big book of words, but that said, it has a stylus that reads the definitions on the oversized pages. Children will need to learn how to click the stylus each time they change pages, but once learned they can enjoy this independently. This is a better choice than the **Encyclopedia** from the same maker, with information that seems more appropriate for middle school. 5–8. (949) 608-2848.

■ ION *2006*

(Hasbro $119.99/additional catridges $19.99) ION hooks up to the TV and projects not just the game, but the players! Kids see themselves on-screen along with the bubbles they must "break" as they move in front of the screen. So this is an active game that gets them on their feet instead of keeping them sitting on a couch and moving only their fingers. The prototype looked great, but it was not ready for testing. (888) 836-7025.

■ Candy Land DVD Game *2006* SNAP AWARD

(Milton Bradley $29.99 ●●●●●) Put the play mats on the floor, plug this into your DVD player, and kids are ready for an active but not-too-fast-moving game that gets them up off the couch. Players move from one of 24 color

playmats to another, collecting tokens. 2–4 players. (888) 836-7025.

■ Leap Pad Plus Writing Learning System

(LeapFrog $39.99 ooooo) We were delighted with the many Dr. Seuss classics such as *Fox In Socks* and *One Fish Two Fish* that have been adapted for this platform for the Leap Pad. In addition, kids who are learning to write their letters and numbers will like this electronic workbook with stylus that really writes. For beginning readers and writers. For younger kids working on letters and phonics, see review of **My First Leap Pad Bus** in Preschool chapter, p. 96. (800) 701-5327.

■ Story Reader 2006

(Publications International $19.99 ooooo
) New for 2006, the only new additions to this collection are more licensed characters—Sponge Bob, My Little Pony and more Dora. Last year we were happy to find that we could hear and read along with a set of Beatrix Potter's classics: *The Tale of Peter Rabbit, Jemima Puddle-Duck,* and *Tom Kitten.* The original art has been used, as well as the language. This platform is less complex than other electronic book readers on the market. Simply plug in the cartridge, and no touching or stylus is needed. The "reader" turns the pages and follows along. Other books for the series are more licensed properties such as **Dora, Scooby Doo,** and **Bambi.** Still recommended, 2004 SNAP AWARD winner, **Active Pad** ($24.95 ooooo). This looks a lot like so many talking book platforms. Touch the pictures with a stylus and it says the name of the object. It's a knowing-and-naming book with lots of familiar objects to talk about. Look for the shape and counting book version of this, too. (800) 454-9006.

Construction Toys

Building invites creative thinking and decision making. Color, counting, and size concepts are built in (we couldn't resist). Best of all, blocks offer a win-win opportunity because there is no right or wrong way for them to be used. Kids with visual challenges can learn their shapes by rubbing the textured blocks on cheeks or hands. For shopping info about classic and new blocks sets, see the Toddlers, Preschool, and Early School Years chapters.

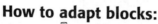

How to adapt blocks:

Add strips of sticky-backed Velcro tape to standard wooden unit blocks or Mega Blocks for a more stable base for building. To increase two-handed skills, have child play at pulling blocks apart and putting them together.

Use colorful plastic Lego Quatro, Duplo, and standard Lego building blocks for developing color-matching, counting, and size-discrimination concepts for a child with learning disabilities. **Activities:** Provide containers and play size-, shape-, and color-sorting games to reinforce concepts. Put the toys away by playing a singing color game: To the tune of "Where Is Thumbkin?" Sing, "Where is red? Where is red? Here it is! Here it is!"

■ Gears! Gears! Gears!

(Learning Resources $20/$40 ooooo) Fitting gears together not only develops dexterity; it's a challenging way to promote problem-solving skills as kids make moving "machines." Motors can be added, but start with hand power. SNAP AWARD '99. Stick with the open-ended sets—most of the theme machines get in the way of the play. **Activity:** Play a game of "Keep It Going!" Players take turns adding one gear at a time, but every gear added must connect and keep the motion going. (800) 222-3909.

■ Magneatos 2006 SNAP AWARD

(Guidecraft $30 & up ooooo) Jumbo-sized magnetic balls and rods are covered in primary colors and designed for ease of handling. Unlike the typical magnetic building sets, this is a child-friendly building toy with showy results! Great for-three-dimensional building, dexterity, and imagination. Sets come with 36, 72, or 144 pieces. (800) 544-6526.

Pretend Play

Pretend play is not just great fun, it's the way kids develop imagination and creative thinking skills, and try out being big and powerful. Pretending also brings the world down to the child's size and understanding. It's a way to develop communication skills and is an outlet for expressing feelings and fears.

Housekeeping Equipment

Playing with replicas of real household equipment is a safe way for kids to step into new roles. Add real ingredients to play kitchens, such as water for pouring, playdough, and dry cereal. Kids love the messiness of it all, which motivates ample touching and exploration that strengthen fingers and hands as well as encouraging language and motivating curiosity. For descriptions of toy kitchens, plates, and other pretend props, see reviews in the Toddlers and Preschool chapters.

■ YOUniverse ATM Machine 2006

(Summit Inc. $39.95 ●●●●½) After setting the ATM with your name and PIN, you can make deposits and withdrawals, and check your balance. Comes with an ATM card and will take both coins and bills. The machine recognizes the coins and adds them to your total automatically. For younger kids we prefer the less complicated **Amazing Money Jar** ($12.99 ●●●●); it tallies up coins only—but still very neat. **Activity:** Learning to count money and exchange coins is a process that takes time. Playing store or restaurant with real money is a good way to start. Also allowing children to pay for small items in the course of an outing gives them a hands-on way to understand the give and take of money. (205) 661-1174.

■ Teaching Cash Register

(Learning Resources $44.95 ●●●●●) A marvelous tool for pretend and math skills for kids. Kids can use built-in calculator, make change, use coupons and charge cards, and even check the customer's credit! You can even use real coins—very useful for teaching money concepts. The screen tallies, and kids press "Enter" to self-correct. SNAP AWARD '04. Still recommended, the quiz-free, solar-powered **Pretend & Play Calculator Cash Register** ($39.95). (800) 222-3909.

■ Pretend & Play Teaching Telephone

(Learning Resources $39.95 ○○○○○) For learning functional use of a phone, important numbers, and the concept of 911, this is a gem! Even the concept of taking messages is built into the play. You can program in any phone number and leave a message. When your child calls that number she hears your message. SNAP AWARD '00. (800) 222-3909.

■ Plan Toys Fruit & Vegetable Play Set

(Brio $15.99 ○○○○) Wooden fruits and veggies can be "cut" apart with wooden knife that seems to cut the Velcro-ed segments. Comes with lemon, orange, pear, mushroom, carrot, and tomato, plus board and wooden knife. **Activity:** Use fraction words when you ask child to cut you a half of one fruit or a quarter of something else. (888) 274-6869.

■ My First Stove *2006*

(Alex $19.99 ○○○○) Most of the big kitchens are in the toddler chapter, but this mini-kitchen (12" x 11" x 11") fits on a table top; ideal for tight spaces or for a child who cannot stand. A painted wooden stovetop with colorful knobs that turn, plus a drawer that opens to store pots, pans, and utensils. Companion to **My First Sink.** Don't be fooled by the picture on the box—no pots or dishes in the package! 3 & up. (800) 666-2539. **Activity:** For sniffing, tasting, and touching, present real fruits in parts or wholes. Put pieces in a bag. Child must name fruit without visual cues.

COMPARISON SHOPPER
Doctor's & Vet's Kits

For kids who visit the doctor more frequently than most, playing doctor gives them a chance to take charge, even if it is only pretend. Almost all kits come with cases that are hard to re-pack. Learning Resources' **Doctor Kit** SNAP AWARD '04 ($24.95 ○○○○○), is the exception to the rule, with tons of props and roomy case. (800) 222-3909. Also, for playing veterinarian, **Let's Pretend**

Veterinarian (Small Miracles $29.99 ○○○○½) has a child-sized jacket, puppy, and stethoscope and other medical tools. Also from the same maker, a **Doctor** kit with white coat and stethoscope. (888) 281-1798.

Sounds and Sights Toys

■ Lollipop Drum

(Remo $25 ○○○○○) This lollipop-shaped drum makes a pleasing sound and is ideal for games. **Adaptation:** For kids who can't grasp the handle, tape the handle to a tabletop with drumhead hanging off. **Activity:** One person hits the drum and the other person must change positions with every beat. When you are moving, use exaggerated goofy motions and freeze into funny poses. Switch roles—kids love the power of making you move. Also top rated, **Chick-itas Maracas** ($6.50 ○○○○), small maracas that have a great sound and a perfect fit for little hands. (800) 525-5134.

■ Lynn Kleiner Rhythm Sets

(Remo $34.95 & up ○○○○○) Many instruments for young kids make noise instead of music. Strike up the rhythm band with these kits that are well crafted with sound in mind. **Babies Make Music** includes jingle shaker, wrist jingle, and a small drum and scarf (safe enough for kids who still mouth their toys); **Kids Make Music** includes a 7" tambourine, triangle, wrist bell (with big jingles), rhythm sticks, and one maraca. SNAP AWARD '00. **Activity:** Use drum or rhythm sticks for a math game. Make a stack of cards labeled with numbers 1–10. Put them face down. As a player, you draw a card and tap that number. The other player must guess the number on your card. If she gets it, give her the card. At the end of the game, switch parts. Now the other player does the reading and tapping. (800) 525-5134.

Transportation Toys

Trains

See Preschool chapter for the latest wooden train sets. For kids who can't fit tracks together, adapt by mounting to a play board. A tabletop makes this toy accessible to a child in a wheelchair.

■ Duplo

(Lego Systems $10 & up ●●●●●) Chunky
plastic BLUE CHIP **Duplo** building bricks are
basic gear for working on developing fine
motor skills. The idea is to have a plentiful supply for original creations. Bringing home a themed
set is also a good idea. **Activity Tip:** Sort the Duplo bricks by color
and line them up. How many yellow do you have? Blue? This is a
hands-on experience with color. (800) 233-8756.

■ Little People Beep the School Bus

(Fisher-Price $14.99 ●●●●½) Like so many new toys, this classic now
comes with lights, sound, and action. Four Little People bounce up
and down as this jaunty yellow bus with googly eyes rolls along. It has
a wheelchair ramp and a talking bus driver; it also plays "The Wheels
on the Bus." We think kids could have done with less talk, but this is
likely to make a hit. **Activities:** Play "Who Got Off?" Have child
look at the four Little People. She closes her eyes and you remove one
passenger. Can she tell who got off the bus? (800) 432-5437

■ Little People Ramps Around Garage

(Fisher-Price $37.95 ●●●●●) Updated with
electronic sounds, this two-story garage
has ramps, elevator, car wash, and lots of
gateways and surprises. It closes for com-
pact storage. This type of toy gives you
plenty of opportunities for developing
language: colors and position words (*up, down, into* the car wash)—
all important concepts that are best understood when experienced.
See Preschool and Early School Years chapters for other pretend settings. SNAP AWARD '04. (800) 432-5437.

■ Bendos My First RC Buggies ★*2006*★ SNAP AWARD

(Kid Galaxy $19.95 each ●●●●●) Our testers loved this new line of
remotes designed with simplified remote controllers to operate.
Choose a **Bumble Bee** or a spotted **Ladybug** with simple one
button control. These have plenty
of action; even when the remote is
not pressed they spin. Still top rated,
Old Tyme R/C Bumper Cars
($49.99 ●●●●½) **Activity:** Two kids
can set up a racetrack and run their
two bumper cars. (800) 816-1135.

Puppets

Few toys provide a better way to get kids to express their feelings. Without the need to move themselves, kids in wheelchairs or beds can take on pleasingly active roles through the use of puppets. For top-rated puppets and stages, see the Preschool and Early School Years chapters.

How to Adapt a Puppet

Fill the puppet with a Styrofoam cone. Push a wooden dowel into the cone, and your puppet is ready for action!

Place puppets over big plastic soda bottles that can be moved around like dolls.

Attach a magnet to stuffed finger puppets or Little People-type figures and use them on a metal cookie sheet.

For a kid who can't grasp a rod, attach the puppet to the child's arm with Velcro straps. Her hand may not go inside the puppet, but the child can activate the whole puppet by moving her arm.

Dolls, Dollhouses, and Garages

Many wonderful dolls, soft animals, and dollhouses are described in the Toddlers, Preschool, and Early School Years chapters.

■ Check-up Time Elmo
2006 SNAP AWARD

(Fisher-Price $19.99 ●●●●●) This year Elmo is fitted out with stethoscope and thermometer and a little book on going to the doctor. Another good choice for role playing and rehearsing going to the doctor. (800) 432-5437.

Mail Order Dolls

The dolls below will be especially interesting for children with special needs, since they are available with adaptive equipment such as walkers, wheelchairs, and braces. All collections include boy and girl dolls, and are also available in multiethnic variations. We suggest requesting catalogs from several before you buy:

- Lakeshore ($30) 16" vinyl dolls and various special needs equipment. (800) 421-5354.

- Pleasant Company ($84 doll/$30 wheelchair only). (800) 845-0005.

Other Notable Dolls

■ Bendos

(Kid Galaxy $6 & up ●●●●●) Bendable action figures are perfect for dramatic play. Available as athletes, community workers, and nonlicensed male and female action figures, they stand up with blocks, fit into vehicles, and satisfy young collectors. The latest additions are zany-looking **Safari** and **Farm** animals with skinny legs. A *word of warning:* Remove hats and other small details that may be a choking hazard for kids who are still mouthing their toys. (800) 816-1135.

■ Groovy Girls/Boys & Supersize Groovy Girls

(Manhattan Toy $15 & $50 ●●●●●) These all-fabric 13" multi-ethnic dolls continue to be a big hit. Still top rated, **Supersize Groovy Girls** ($50 each ●●●●●), a 40" child-sized fabric doll that's like a pretend play pal. **Activity Tip:** Give kids real clothing with buttons and zippers that they can dress Supersize Groovy in. Helps develop dressing skills needed for independence. SNAP AWARD '02.(800) 541-1345.

> **ADAPTATION IDEA FOR FABRIC TOYS:** Make your own play board by gluing colored felt on the lid and sides of a sturdy box. Use board for sticking on cutout shapes, letters, and animals. Box can be used to store pieces.

■ Woodkins

(Pamela Drake $11.95–$25 ●●●●●) For kids who don't have the dexterity to sew, cut, or paste, this wooden doll frame has fabric choices that stay in place with a "frame" that closes over the edges of the doll.

Dolls have four faces for changing moods. SNAP AWARD '00. Available as a boy or a girl, and in several ethnic variations. Also top rated: a **Fairy** collection with glittery fabric choices. SNAP AWARD '05. (800) 966-3762.

■ **Magna Morphs** 🏷️*2006*

(Wild Republic $11.99 ●●●●½) These dinosaurs have interchangeable heads, feet, and tails that hold together with magnets buried inside the bodies and parts. There are three dinosaurs to a set and no end to the ways kids can put them together. A playful way to learn the names of the most familiar dinosaurs while developing part-whole relationships, dexterity, and dramatic play. (800) 800-9678.

> **ADAPTATION IDEA FOR MAGNETIC TOYS:** Put pieces on a cookie sheet so that players can see the choices and reach for a change easily.

Art Supplies

Art materials are more than fun. They provide a great way to motivate kids to develop dexterity and express feelings without words, and they give tons of sensory feedback. Creative exploration without lots of rights, wrongs, or rules also gives kids a wonderful sense of "can do" power.

Special Art Tools

✴: **Crayon Sticks** (Elmer's $2.99 ●●●●) These oversized crayons are softer than most and will be easier to grasp. These will be fine for encouraging big sweeping arm motions and tracing or free-form drawing. (888) 435-6377.

✴: **Crayola Window Mega Markers** (Binney & Smith $4.99 ●●●●), washable wide markers that kids can use to draw on windows. (800) 272-9652.

✴: **Chubby Colored Pencils** (Alex $10 ●●●●●) These pencils have thicker "lead" and an easier-to-grasp hexagonal shape, and they are especially wonderful for kids who cannot grasp traditional pencils. (800) 666-2539.

Beginner Paintbrushes (Alex 3 for $6 ooooo) Extra-large brushes with handles shaped like bulbs help kids with fine-motor difficulties to paint. Also, **Sponge Painters** now come with color-changing wands. (800) 666-2539.

Chunkie Markers (Bluepath $10 & up oooo) Bypass brushes altogether! Washable paint in easy-to-grasp bottles with sponge applicators. (800) 463-2388.

Stamp Kits and Stencil Kits. Although we like kids to create their own pictures, stampers and stencils can be extremely satisfying for older kids who want realistic results. To adapt stampers for kids with fine-motor difficulties, glue a dowel handle to the back of each stamp.

Crayola Dough (Binney and Smith $1.99 & up oooo) Super-soft modeling dough. Buy a six- or eight-pack. (800) 272-9652.

Modeling Dough Pattern Rollers (Alex $8 oooo) interchangeable patterned rollers snap between the rolling pin-style handles. (800) 666-2539.

ADAPTATION IDEA: Adapting Crayons, Markers, Glue Sticks, and Brushes. For an easier grip, use a foam hair curler over the drawing tool. Or wrap a crayon with a small piece of Velcro and then have the child wear a mitten. The Velcro will stick to the mitten, allowing the child to color without dropping the tool.

■ Aquadoodle 2006

(Spinmaster $24.99 oooo ½) Our four-year-old tester looked up and said, "Even if I get it on the floor—it won't show, will it?" Indeed, this is a mess-free and semi-magical oversized mat for drawing with water! Using the "water pen," blue drawings appear on the surface and disappear once they are dry. Great for developing hand and arm movements needed for writing without restrictive lines. A new travel version was not ready for testing. Marked 2 & up, but will be enjoyed by older kids as well. (800) 622-8339.

■ Crayola Color Wonder Paper, Markers & Learning Book: Opposites

(Binney & Smith $7.99 & up **oooo**) Spiral activity books have been added to this line of mess-free products. The **Opposite** book is the best and develops language skills while giving kids immediate self-correcting pay-offs. Pre-readers may need an adult to reinforce the pairs of opposites. They color the page with their no-mess markers and then can enjoy re-"reading" the pairs. Still recommended, **Color Wonder** blank paper and markers, ideal art materials because the markers are colorless and won't stain anything. They have a "magic" quality and turn color as kids draw on the special paper. **Activity:** Draw letters or a heart of dots and have your child connect them. SNAP AWARD '01. (800) 272-9652.

■ Fuzzy Pet Parlor Play-Doh 2006

(Hasbro $12.99 **oooo**) This is an update of a familiar theme for Play-Doh—a "barber shop" with three colors of dough plus a monkey, cat, dog and barber. Put snip of doh in their heads and press down—abracadabra, out comes hair to style with scissors and brush. Pretend play that develops dexterity. (800) 327-8264.

> **ACTIVITY TIP: Making Ropes, Snakes, and Other Shapes.** Dough and clay are ideal for developing hand and finger muscles. Save cookie cutters for last. Encourage kids to roll long ropes of dough and coil them into letters and shapes. Give them dull plastic knives for cutting and plastic forks for poking the dough. All of this fun and games develops dexterity.

Craft Kits

As always, we look for craft kits that are quick and easy and create satisfying results. For more kits see Preschool and Early School chapters. Here are our favorites:

■ Ceramic Allowance Bank

(Creativity for Kids $14.99 **oooo**) A chubby white ceramic pig ready to paint and hold spare change or allowance. It has an easy-to-pull-out rubber stopper, so kids don't need to break the bank when they want to spend some of their savings! Includes a "chores" booklet with star stickers . . . the idea being that they earn their allowance. We have mixed feelings about paying kids for chores, but we do like the idea of encouraging them to save their pennies, nickels, and dimes! 7 & up. (800) 311-8684.

■ Finger Painting Party

(Alex $20 ●●●●½) Finger paints allow kids to explore color directly with their whole hands and big sweeping arm movements. For reluctant explorers, this kit comes with chunky-handled tools that make squiggles, swirls, and other delicious patterns. Also ideal for open-ended art exploration, **Collage Party** ($20 ●●●●), a kit chockfull of buttons, pom-poms, wiggly eyes, scissors, stickers, feathers, and paper. (800) 666-2539.

ACTIVITY TIP: Smelly Art. Add a few drops of scented oil or spices to homemade dough for extra sensory stimulation. Play a "smelling matching" game: Make pairs of matching balls of putty in paper cups and cover with foil. Punch small holes in foil for sniffing. Players take turns smelling cups to make matching pairs. Add more pairs as child develops the ability to make matches.

Dab-a-Dab-a-Do Sponge Art: Sponges are easy to grab and they motivate artistic and messy art explorations. Cut your own sponges or buy a premade set.

Marble Painting: Place a piece of paper in a shallow box. Dip a spoonful of marbles in tempera paint and place them in the box. Tip box to produce a marvelous marble masterpiece. Great for kids with limited motor control.

Make a Slanted Play Board: For kids who need a slanted surface to work on, cut the sides of a cardboard box at a slant and it's all ready for coloring and other projects.

Easels

There are a number of great stand-alone or tabletop easels on the market. **Portable Easel** (Battat $21 ●●●○) is a double-sided magnetic easel that will fit easily on a tabletop. One surface can be used as a chalkboard, the other is a white wipe-off board. Storage holds magnetic letters, numerals, markers, and chalk and eraser. (800) 247-6144. **My Drawing Station** (Alex $40 ●●●○) has a chalkboard surfaced slant-board with a 100' roll of paper and three cup holders for supplies. Still top rated, Alex's **Tabletop Easel** ($40 ●●●●○) has a magnetic side to use with magnetic games. SNAP AWARD '00. (800) 666-2539.

Big Muscles/Physical Play

Toys that challenge children to use their big muscles help them develop gross motor coordination, a sense of their own place in space, independence, and self-esteem.

■ Crayon Balance Beam

(Artistic Coverings $199 ●●●●½) A pricey but neat piece of equipment that will be a hit with preschoolers and early school-age kids who love the challenge of walking on a beam (with the safety of knowing that they're only inches off the ground). The crayon is 6' long, 10" wide, and has a 4" beam surface. (877) 599-9343.

■ Crawl N Fun

(Playhut $25 ●●●○) Testers giggled their way through this 6'-long tunnel as they crawled along! Also top rated: longer and more spacious **Yellow School Bus** and **Red Fire Engine** and a blue **Deluxe Train** engine. These each easily accommodate two kids for pretend fun. 3 & up. (888) 752-9488.

■ Gertie Balls

(Small World Toys $6 & up ●●●●○) These gummy inflatable balls are soft enough for kids who may be scared of big heavy balls coming toward them. We particularly like the "magical" color-changing Gertie. Put in a cold place, it turns pink; toss it and your handprints show up in blue! SNAP AWARD '02. **Activity:** Start out with a cold ball and count how many catches back and forth it takes to turn the ball another color. An active counting game. Also top rated, **Jungle Gertie Balls** with fun zebra and tiger stripes; **Nobbie Gertie** with bumps that make it easier to catch; and **Loopies** ($7–$15 oooo), six loops of soft fabric-covered foam that are easy to catch. (800) 421-4153.

> **SHOPPING TIP:** Battery-operated ride-in cars that can be activated with a touch of a button may be a good choice for kids who are unable to pedal. Such toys, however, require constant supervision, regular battery recharges, and a hefty investment.

Trikes and Bikes

Your child may be able to ride a trike or bike with few or no adaptations. You'll find our guidelines for buying and descriptions of top-rated wheeled toys in the Preschool and Early School Years chapters.

How to Adapt a Wheel Toy

Adapting a bike may involve adding an easily made belt of Velcro. Other kids may need a trunk-support seating system or foot harnesses, or a hand-driven trike. Two companies that specialize in adapted riding toys and supplies are Sammons-Preston Corp. (800) 323-5547, and Flaghouse Inc. (800) 221-5185.

Sand Fun

For kids who can't get down on the ground to play in the sandbox, why not bring the sand up to them? Put a small sandbox on a picnic table and, voilá!, a child in a wheelchair can now dig in. Also great, see the **Naturally Playful Sand & Water Table** (Step Two) in the Preschool Chapter.

Books

For years, children with special needs were essentially invisible in picture books. Today publishers are issuing more books that reflect the feelings of, and issues faced by, children who are physically or mentally challenged.

Friends and Family

■ ABC for You and Me

(by Meg Girnis/photos by Shirley L. Green, Whitman $15.95 **oooo**) Full-color photos capture school-age kids with Down syndrome playing with familiar toys and each other. There's a lot to talk about as you look at the upbeat photos of this alphabet book with your child and perhaps make another book with A–Z photos of your child.

■ How About a Hug?

(by Tricia Taggart, Jason & Nordic $8.95 **oooo**) A sweet story that follows a girl with Down's syndrome from wake-up, to school, and home again. Each of the people in her world gives her encouragement as well as a loving hug. 4 & up. (814) 696-2920.

■ I Can't Stop!
A Story about Tourette Syndrome *2006*

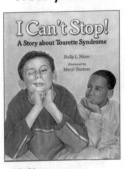

(by Holly L. Niner/illus. by Meryl Treatner, Albert Whitman $15.95 **oooo**) Nathan's problem began with a tick. In time, his tick went away, but was followed by other uncontrollable actions. At first Nathan is teased and his parents tells him to stop. Although there is no cure for TS, once they discover the reason for his actions, everyone is better able to cope.

Siblings

■ Big Brother Dustin

(by Alden R. Carter/photos by Dan Young with Carol Carter, Albert Whitman $14.95 **oooo**) Dustin, a boy with Down's syndrome, prepares with his parents and grandparents for the arrival of his baby sister. Beautifully told and marvelously illustrated with photos that capture the ups, downs, and wonder of expectanthood—across genera tions. 3 & up.

■ Ian's Walk: A Story About Autism

(by Laurie Lears/illus. by Karen Ritz, Albert Whitman $14.95 ●●●●)
Ian, who has autism, hears, tastes, and sees things differently from his
two sisters. So a simple walk to the park to feed the ducks is anything
but simple. Told in the first person by his sister, this tender tale cap-
tures the ambivalent feelings that a sibling must deal with as she also
deals with her brother's special ways of experiencing the world. A reas-
suring tale for siblings. 5 & up.

■ Way to Go, Alex!

(by Robin Pulver/illus. by Elizabeth Wolf, Albert Whitman $14.95
●●●●) When Carly helps her brother (who has mental retardation)
train for the Special Olympics she forgets to prepare him for running
through the blue ribbon at the finish line! This touching story
reflects the ache and the pride and affection siblings have for their
sibs with disabilities. 6–8.

Kids Coping in Mainstream Classrooms and the World

■ Let's Talk About It: Extraordinary Friends

(by Fred Rogers, Putnam $15.99 ●●●●) Newest in
an excellent series, this book is ideal for opening a
dialogue about how kids without disabilities feel
and interact with kids who have disabilities. Photos
and simple text raise issues about feeling shy, and
concerns about what to say and do. Mr. Rogers reinforces the idea that we are all special. 4–8.

■ Seeing Things My Way

(by Alden R. Carter/photos by Carol S. Carter, Albert Whitman
$14.95 ●●●●) Amanda goes to a mainstream class, but gets a lot of
extra help with her schooling with special equipment and teachers.
This firsthand account tells how the world looks to Amanda and
other kids with severe visual impairments but optimistic and deter-
mined outlooks. 6–9. Also by the same team, **Stretching
Ourselves: Kids with Cerebral Palsy,** about three kids with very
different degrees of cerebral palsy and how they "stretch" themselves
physically, socially, and intellectually. 5 & up.

Inspirational Books

■ The Boy Who Grew Flowers

(by Jen Wojtowicz/illus. by Steve Adams, Barefoot $17.99 ●●●●½)
Rink Bowagon is different from other boys. He doesn't grow flowers
in a garden, they bloom all over him when the moon is full. When
Angelina, a new girl who is also different, comes to his class, the two
discover a bond of friendship. Inspired by the author's brother, who
has autism.

■ Franklin Goes to the Hospital

(by Paulette Bourgeois/illus. by Brenda Clark, Scholastic $4.50 ●●●●)
Franklin is injured and needs an operation. He's very brave until he
has to have an x-ray. Then he fears people will be able to see that he's
not brave inside. A good story along with a glimpse at what it's like to
be a hospital patient. 4–7.

■ Howie Helps Himself

(by Joan Fassler/illus. by Joe Lasker, Albert Whitman $13.95 ●●●●)
Howie, a boy with cerebral palsy, wants to be able to move his wheelchair on his own. A book that reinforces a positive sense of "can do."
4–8.

Coping with Visual Challenges

■ Little Stevie Wonder *2006*

(Quincy Troupe/illus. by Lisa Cohen, Houghton Mifflin $18 ●●●●½)
Stevie Wonder's story is told in lyrical prose. It's a bit over the top,
but just may be an inspiring book for a child who is musical or blessed
with some other gift. There is a very short CD with this book—only
two songs on the disk—which might be disappointing to someone
who doesn't read the fine print!

■ The Night Search

(by Kate Chamberlin, Jason & Nordic $8.95 ●●●●) Heather, who i
blind, does not want to carry the white cane her teachers have taugh
her to use. On a camping trip she discovers how important it is to her
Available in Braille. ($24.95). (814) 696-2920.

■ Private and Confidential: A Story About Braille

(by Marion Ripley/illus. by Colin Backhouse, Dial $16.99 ●●●●
Laura discovers that her Australian pen pal is visually impaired. U-
for the challenge, Laura learns how to write in Braille so that he ca
read her letters by himself. The book comes with a Braille chart s

that kids can try their own hand at Braille writing.

■ The Right Dog for the Job

(by Dorothy Hinshaw Patent/photos by William Muñoz, Walker $16.95 ●●●●) Ever wonder how dogs are trained to become seeing eye dogs? Follow puppy Ira as he prepares for his special job. 5 & up.

SHOPPING TIP: A neat novelty for a child learning to read Braille is a plastic placemat with the Braille alphabet imprinted on it. From Straight Edge Products.

Coping with Hearing Impairments and Introducing Sign Language

Every day more than 500,000 Americans use American Sign Language to communicate. You'll find great choices here for kids of every age.

■ The Handmade Counting Book

(by Laura Rankin, Dial $15.99 ●●●●) Painterly images of toys, seashells, and flowers help readers learn to sign numbers 1–20, 25, 50, 75, and 100 in American Sign Language. All ages. Also: **The Handmade Alphabet.**

■ Moses Goes to School

(by Issac Millman, Farrar, Straus & Giroux $16 ●●●●) An upbeat slice-of-life book that follows Moses throughout the day in the special public school he attends, where all the kids are deaf or hard of hearing. This is a sequel to the even more remarkable **Moses Goes to a Concert,** which features a deaf percussionist and shows how Moses and his friends "feel" the music. SNAP AWARD '01.

Previously recommended signing books: Handsigns (by Kathleen Fain, Chronicle), all ages; **Handtalk Zoo** (by George Ancona & Mary Beth, Aladdin); **More Simple Signs** (by Cindy Wheeler, Viking); **Opposites** and **Happy Birthday!** (by Angela Bednarczyk & Janet Weinstock, Star Bright Books).

Audio

■ Alex, Ben & Co. BLUE CHIP

(Kid'n Together $9.98 tape/$14.98 CD ●●●●○)
Inspired to sing songs to help his son
Matthew (who has Down's syndrome) learn
concepts such as body parts, the ABCs, counting,
and more, Alex Meisel and his brother created
this collection of classics and original music with
dollops of humor and upbeat flavor. (800) 543-6386.

■ Come Outside to Play

(Makin' Music $14.99/$9.99 ●●●●○) A mix of 26 lively traditional
and original get-up-and-move songs designed for active participation.
Lyrics for action songs, finger play, and chants are included in the
booklet with entertaining ideas for enlarging upon the songs. Also
available separately, a set of rhythm sticks and egg-shaped shakers
with a wonderful feel and sound! 3 & up. SNAP AWARD '03. (877)
236-1984.

■ Ella Jenkins' Nursery Rhymes BLUE CHIP

(Smithsonian Folkways $9.50 ●●●●○) A good choice for working on
memory and language skills. Jenkins sings familiar rhymes and cues
kids to repeat and join in.

■ Songames for Sensory Integration

(Sensory Resources $24.95 ●●●●○) Here's a collection of playful musi-
cal activities for developing motor, language, and listening skills in
child-appealing ways. Two CDs and a booklet full of ideas for sensory
integration were developed by occupational therapists. SNAP AWARD
'01. (888) 357-5867.

■ Time to Sing

(Center for Creative Play $16.99 ●●●●○) Developed by Dave
Hammer, a speech-language pathologist from Children's Hospital of
Pittsburgh, this collection of traditional songs has been arranged at a
slower pace and sung with greater clarity to enable all children to sing
along. CD features musicians from the Pittsburgh Symphony as well
as adult and child singers. SNAP AWARD '02. 2–6. (800) 977-5708.

Resources

Books: Most bookstores will order any books listed here from major publishers. Here are the phone numbers for several smaller publishers they may not regularly deal with: Jason & Nordic (814) 696-2920; Albert Whitman (800) 255-7675; Woodbine House (800) 843-7323.

■ Healthy All Over

(Healthy All Over $24.95 each ●●●●○) These two tapes, made especially for kids with disabilities, feature 'tween/teens with Down syndrome doing exercises with a pleasant exercise coach leading the fun. In **Let's Have Fun,** the boys and girls do stretching and aerobic exercises. The video reinforces what the leader is saying with images. So when she suggests they are walking up steps, half the screen shows a flight of steps. On **Let's Get Strong,** the leader and kids use weights. SNAP AWARD '03. (631) 864-9173.

Additional resources: A number of useful catalogs are targeted directly for the special needs market. Many contain useful adaptation devices. Browsing the catalogs below can help you find some great products as well as ideas for adapting more widely available toys.

- Achievement Products (800) 373-4699
- Lighthouse, Inc. (800) 829-0500
- Crestwood Communication Aids (414) 352-5678
- Constructive Playthings (800) 832-0572
- Enabling Devices (800) 832-8697
- Environments (800) 342-4453
- Flaghouse Inc. (800) 221-5185
- Lakeshore (800) 421-5354

Online sites of interest:
- www.disabilityresources.org
- www.familyvillage.wisc.edu
- www.autism-resources.com
- www.geocities.com/heartland/plains/8950
- www.ericec.org

Two national organizations provide toy lending library services and play-centered programs for children with special needs and their families. To locate the center nearest you, contact:

- National Lekotek Center, 2100 Ridge Avenue, Evanston, IL 60201, or call (800) 366-7529.

- USA Toy Library Association, 2530 Crawford Avenue, Suite 111, Evanston, IL 60201, or call (847) 920-9030. usatla.deltacollege.org.

VI • DVD Plug Ins & Game Platforms

One of the hot trends in the toy industry is a whole new class of toys that plug into the television. While many of us grew up with Pong, there's a whole new generation of toys that even encourage kids to get up off the couch.

Microsoft, Sony, and Nintendo have all announced next-generation home gaming platforms. Microsoft's Xbox 360 will arrive first, in time for this holiday season, but has the least software for kids under ten years old. 2006 promises to bring the introduction of the multimedia marvel, the PS3, and Nintendo's Revolution (a product that is still top secret). Meanwhile, Sony's new PSP, and Nintendo's DS and Gameboy Mini continue to bring excitement to the portable marketplace.

For Preschool and Early School Years

■ ION *2006*

(Hasbro $119.99/additional cartridges $19.99) The goal of ION is to bring high tech game play to the preschool crowd through age appropriate game play. ION hooks up to the TV and projects not just the game, but the players! Kids see themselves onscreen along with the bubbles they must "break" as they move in front of the screen. So this is an active game that gets them on their feet instead of sitting on a couch and moving their fingers. Our impression from the prototype was positive, but the final product was not ready for testing. (888) 836-7025.

■ Candy Land DVD Game **2006** PLATINUM AWARD

(Milton Bradley $29.99 **ooooo**) Put the play mats on the floor and plug this into your DVD player and kids are ready for an active but not too fast moving game that gets them up off the couch. Players move from one of 24 color play mats to another collecting tokens. This type of game is ideal for developing listening skills and color concepts in a playful manner. A grown up will need to supervise. 2–4 players. (888) 836-7025.

■ Black Belts Karate Studio **2006**

(Spinmaster $24.99) Billed as a way to introduce preschoolers to Karate, this comes with DVD and mat. Not available for testing, but we suspect the directions on the video may be like last year's **Bella Dancerella** ($29.99 **ooo**), which did not impress our testers or their moms. One word: "Boring," said our 8-year-old testers who felt the intro took way too long. The references to using your left and right foot are going to be well beyond most 4, 5 and 6s. One tester liked the new **Tap Dance DVD** (**ooo**) but the adjustable tap dance shoes did not stay on—no matter what they tried. (800) 622-8339.

■ Wild Adventure Mini Golf **2006** PLATINUM AWARD

(Milton Bradley $49.99 **ooooo**) This is a plug-in-and-putt game for multigenerational fun! Better than a trip to the miniature golf course, it has six different settings that players can swing through with the plastic putter and a tee that you turn to change the direction of the ball. Can be played solo or with others. Another good choice for getting kids up on their feet and playing actively. 6 & up. (888) 836-7025.

Older School Years and Teens

Trend: Wireless Gaming *Preview 2006*

Last year brought the rise of inexpensive, non-expandable video games that plugged into the TV. Typically these contained anywhere from 20 to 40 vintage video games (or games based on those old designs). New this year, manufacturers are cutting the cable between the controller and the TV. Majesco and Jakks Pacific are each implementing wireless controllers with arcade themes. For the first time Jakks' platform will accept expansion cartridges that will add new games, while Majesco's approach has been to use a more sophisticated and potentially more responsive radio link between the TV and input device.

■ EyeToy

(Sony $49.99 ●●●●●) The EyeToy is a camera that acts a controller for the PS2. Originally bundled with **Play,** a series of arcade mini-games, the technology found its way into many games including Harry Potter for PS2. PLATINUM AWARD '04. **PREVIEW 2006:** Sony is introducing **Play 2,** with sports games as well as an arcade-style program: Monkey Mania, based on the Ape Escape series. There will also be a room security package (Eye Spy) for 'tweens—not an important item, in our opinion—and a fitness package for teens and adults (Kinetics). For younger players, see ION, p. 289.

■ Dance Dance Revolution Extreme

(Konami $50 ●●●●●) This series continues to pump out delightfully difficult dance challenges featuring hot, current songs. The new version will mix EyeToy and DancePad support. The difficulty factor makes this game better for kids 10 & up.

■ Groove

(Sony $29.99 ●●●●●) As in most dance games, you have to move to the beat, but here there are special bonuses since the camera can see you! Dance well and you'll actually begin to glow or leave trails of shimmering colors. Our favorite feature: the game takes still and video clips of the players that are great fun to watch in instant replay. Runs only a PS2.

■ Harry Potter Deluxe Edition Scene It? *2006*

(Screenlife $49.95 ●●●●) Chances are you've seen and even played Scene It? before. Players race to identify and answer questions from old films or TV shows. This one is especially for Harry Potter film aficionados, with images and questions from all the Harry Potter films including Harry Potter and the Goblet of Fire. (866) 383-4263.

■ Karaoke Revolution 2

(Konami $50 ●●●●●) Konami knows how to throw a good party-witness the popularity of the Dance Dance Revolution Series. Now they've take the Karaoke craze to the next level with a game that monitors how well you sing. (For some of us that's more painful than fun!) The closer to pitch and rhythm, the more the crowd cheers. 8 & up.

■ Play TV Baseball 3

(Radica $39.99 ●●●●) At first our tween and teen testers thought this simulation baseball game was too hard, but 30 minutes later they were having a great time taking turns at bat. They also liked the opportunity to work on pitching. The set comes with a tethered ball (that you don't actually throw-we had trouble with that concept, our testers did not) and a plastic bat that keeps track of how you're doing! Marked 8 & up, we'd say more like 10 to 45. (800) 803-9611.

■ Star Wars Game Saga Edition *2006*

(Tiger Games $49.99 ●●●●) Plug the training droid into your TV and players with wireless light saber are ready to become Jedi warriors. Testers had an aerobic workout swinging the light saber and ridding the galaxy of droids and other evildoers! We don't usually review zap-it games, but this is more fantasy than war, and multi-generational—may even get parents up and on their feet! May the Force be with you. 8 & up. (888) 836-7025.

■ Vex *2006*

(Radio Shack $299 & up) Pulling inspiration from old fashioned Erector sets and TV shows like Robot Wars, Radio Shack has designed a metal-and-rivet construction system that will have a mountain of add-ins. Robots will be controllable by radio frequency remote controls or with the optional computer programming module. As the price and subject matter suggests, this is a 'tween-and-up package. Looked interesting but was not ready for testing.

Educational Plug Ins. For reviews of **Read with Me DVD** (Fisher-Price), **V.Smile** (VTech) and **Leapster L-Max,** see pp. 96 and 159.

Gaming Platforms

If your family is like most, at some point your kids are likely to ask for a video gaming machine. There are strong opinions about when, if ever, to bring one of these machines home. On the one hand, video games are very much a part of our culture. Playing these games is part of belonging to your social group, of great importance to the school aged set. That said, you need to know the following is also true:

Time Machines. Once a video game platform is brought into the house, many other traditional types of play disappear. You'll probably see a dramatic decline in the dramatic play, construction building, and playing with boardgames and puzzles. Most kids find the allure of the graphics and sound much more compelling.

Your kids will lose some part of their ability to hear.

If you think your kids did not always respond to you prompt-
ly before, watch what happens when you ask them a question
while they are engrossed in a video game. Our suggestion if
you really need an answer, put yourself between your child and
the screen. That usually works, but not always.

Go outdoors, why? Your heretofore active child who
enjoyed a good bike ride or neighborhood kickball game, will
become hard pressed to find a reason to seek natural sunlight.

Our recommendation, clearly, is to delay this purchase for
as long as possible. If your neighbor has one, you're probably
safe for a couple of months. If you do purchase a game platform (we know you will!), here are our recommendations:

1. **Set the ground rules first.** Before the machine
   comes into your house, be clear with your kids as to
   what the time limits are for playing. It really is hard
   not to play for a long time. The games are designed so
   that there is always a next level and it's fun to try to get
   there. It's understandable why they seem in a trance
   (much like most adults playing solitaire at work).

2. **Monitor what they play.** You will probably be surprised that even games with "E" rating for everyone
   can be modified point and shoot games. We recommend sticking with racing games and sports games (but
   even many of the sports games can be overly aggressive
   and include trash talk).

3. **Values.** This year we got lots of email from parents
   that wanted to know if Sims City was appropriate for
   their 9 year olds. One of the game play scenarios is
   adultery. No kidding. Here's an opportunity to share
   your values with your kids. You may also want to dis-
   cuss what games are being played at your neighbor's
   house.

4. **Older gamers.** Be careful of games rated "T" or "M";
   these games tend to include violence, aggressive, and
   sexual material. No matter what your 10 year old
   argues, know that the labels are so loose on these

games to begin with that a game with an older rating is not for a younger child.

5. Be on the Same Page. For the sake of your relationship with the other adults in your house, present a united front on the use of the machines. You will otherwise be at odds with everyone in your house, young and old!

The main platforms are PS2, XBox, and Game Cube.

Here are the questions we are most often asked about these machines.

Which would be most appropriate for younger children?

Software, not hardware, tends to drive the choice in age-appropriate gaming platforms. Nintendo clearly has the lead in the younger market. Its core Mario, Donkey Kong, and Pokemon franchises are intended to be cross-generational, but are aimed squarely at children and 'tweens. Even when the same game is available on all three platforms, the Nintendo versions are often tamer. If you need a video game platform that will appeal to all ages, however, Sony may offer a better choice. Its library is larger and wider than the competition.

One of the positive trends in video gaming are programs that get kids to move more than their thumbs. These first started showing up on the Sony PS2 with dance games like Dance, Dance, Revolution (Konami) and Pump It Up (Mastiff). This year kids can dance to the beat on Nintendo's Game Cube with Dance, Dance, Revolution Mario Mix. Sony is bringing out four new EyeToy games for the PS2: Play2, Kenetic, Monkey Mania and Spy Toy—all activated and controlled by a camera that senses a player's movement.

What is the difference between a Gameboy and a PSP? Which one is better?

The Gameboy DS and PSP are power-packed portable entertainment platforms, whereas the Gameboy Mini takes the functionality of the old Gameboy and crams it into a device only slightly larger than a credit card. The differences are more than cosmetic: Games designed for the DS use two screens (one of which is touch sensitive). The PSP has an enormous 4.3" wide screen, wireless connectivity, optical drive and memory card support—and a price that is nearly two times that of the DS. The PSP is designed as a platform for teens and adults looking to take the gaming experience, together with music and movies, wherever they go. For most kids under 10, the Gameboy Mini will be more than enough, though the games on the DS—particularly NintenDogs—will be reason enough to upgrade to the more powerful (and expensive) dual-screen platform.

If I buy one of these platforms, will I need to buy a new one next year?

Of course, you don't "need" a game machine at all. That said, as with other forms of technology, there will always be a new version to entice you back into the store. Manufacturers force your hand a bit by making the new games only playable on the newest platforms.

Safety Guidelines

Many people assume that before toys reach the marketplace they are subjected to the same kind of governmental scrutiny as food and drugs. The fact is that although the government sets specific safety standards, there is no agency like the FDA that pretests and approves or disapproves products.

The toy industry is charged with the responsibility to comply with federal safety standards, but they are self-regulating, which means it's not until there are complaints or reports of accidents that the Consumer Product Safety Commission (CPSC) enters into the picture. The CPSC is the federal government agency charged with policing the toy industry—but not until the products are already on the shelf!

What does all this mean to you as a consumer? Basically it means "Let the buyer beware!" Both small and large manufacturers have run into problems with small parts, lead paint, strangulation hazards and projectile parts.

The CPSC releases useful recall warnings that are posted in most major toy stores, and manufacturers are required to release recalls to the wire services. The CPSC has a hotline if you want further information about a recalled product or want to report one that perhaps should be recalled; you can call (800) 638-CPSC. The CPSC also publishes a safety handbook that you can request.

To protect your child, here is a safety checklist to keep in mind when you're shopping for playthings:

For infants and toddlers:

- **Dolls and stuffed animals.** Select velour, terry or non-fuzzy fabrics. Remove any and all bows, bells and doo-dads that can be swallowed. Stick to dolls with stitched-on features rather than buttons and plastic parts that may be bitten or pulled off.

- **Crib toys.** Toys should never be attached to an infant's crib with any kind of ribbon, string, or elastic. Babies

and their clothing have been known to get entangled
and strangled by such toys.

- **Soft but safe.** Be sure that soft toys such as rattles,
  squeakers and small dolls are not small enough to be
  compressed and possibly jammed into a baby's mouth.

- **Heirlooms.** Antique rattles and other treasures often do
  not meet today's safety standards and can be a choking
  hazard.

- **Wall hangings and mobiles.** Decorative hangings near
  or on the crib are interesting for newborns to gaze at
  but pose a safety hazard once a child can reach out and
  touch. They need to be removed when an infant is able
  to touch them.

- **Foam toys.** Avoid foam toys that can be chewed on
  and swallowed and present a choking hazard.

- **Push-and-straddle toys.** If you're looking for your
  child's first push toy, make sure it's stable and your child
  can touch the ground when sitting on the toy.

- **Toy chests.** Old toy chests with lids that can fall do
  not meet today's safety standards. They can severely
  injure and even entrap small children. New chests have
  removable lids or safety latches. We recommend open
  shelves and containers for safe and easy access instead
  of the jumble of a deep toy chest.

- **Age labels and small parts.** When you see a toy labeled
  "Not for children under 3," that's a warning signal! It
  usually means there are small parts. Such products are
  unsafe for toddlers—no matter how smart they may be!
  They are also unsafe for some threes and fours who frequently put things in their mouths.

- **Batteries.** Toys that run on batteries should be designed
  so that kids cannot get to the batteries.

- **Quality control.** Run your fingers around edges of toys
  to be sure there are no rough, sharp or splintery, hidden
  thorns. Check for products that can entrap or pinch little fingers.

For older children:

- **Eye and ear injuries.** Avoid toys with flying projectiles. Many action figures come with a number of small projectile parts that can pose a safety hazard if pointed in the wrong direction and that certainly pose a danger if there are younger children in the house.

- **High-power water guns.** Doctors report many emergency room visits from children with eye and ear abrasions caused by the trendy high-powered water guns.

- **Burns.** Avoid toys that heat up when used. Many of the toy ovens and baking toys become hot enough to cause burns.

- **Safety limits.** Establish clear rules with kids for sports equipment, wheel toys, and chemistry sets.

- **Adult supervision.** Avoid toys labeled "Adult supervision required" if you don't have the time or patience to be there.

For mixed ages:

Families with children of mixed ages need to establish and maintain safety rules about toys with small parts.

- Older children need a place where they can work on projects that younger sibs can't get hurt by or destroy.

- Establishing a work space for the older sib gives your big child the privilege of privacy along with a sense of responsibility.

- Old toys need to be checked from time to time for broken parts, sharp edges, or open seams. Occasionally clearing out the clutter can foster heightened interest in playtime. It also brings old gems to the surface that may have been forgotten.

Safety Standard for Bike Helmets

We applaud the federal safety standard that all bike helmets had to meet by February 1999. Do little kids really need helmets? Look at the data and you decide:

About 900 people, including more than 200 children, are killed annually in bicycle-related incidents; about 60% of these deaths involve a head injury. Data shows that very young bike riders incur a higher proportion of head injuries! More than 500,000 people are treated annually in U.S. emergency rooms for bicycle-related injuries. Research indicates that a helmet can reduce the risk of head injury by up to 85%!

New helmets must adequately protect the head, and have chin straps strong enough to prevent the helmet from coming off in a crash, collision, or fall. Helmets for children up to age five will cover more of the head to provide added protection to the more fragile areas of a young child's skull. New helmets will carry a label stating that they meet CPSC's new standards, to eliminate confusion about which certification mark to look for on helmets.

CPSC offers the following tips on how to wear a helmet correctly:

- Wear the helmet flat atop your head, not tilted back at an angle.

- Make sure the helmet fits snugly and does not obstruct your field of vision.

- Make sure the chin strap fits securely and that the buckle stays fastened.

Noisy Toys

In addition to all the above criteria, we have always considered the noise level of products. Loud toys are more than just annoying—they can actually pose a risk to your child's hearing. Recently, with the generous assistance of Nancy Nadler of the League for the Hard of Hearing, we tested the sound level of many new toys. In doing so, we discovered that many ordinary rattles and squeakers produce sounds measured at 110 to 130 decibels. Yet experts say that sustained exposure, over time, to noise above 85 decibels will cause hearing damage. Because current regulations allow manufacturers to make toys which produce sounds up to 138 decibels at a distance of 25cm, parents must be informed consumers. We suggest that you:

- consider noise levels of toys before purchasing them.
- remember that musical toys, such as electric guitars, drums, and horns, emit sounds as loud as 120 decibels.
- stop and listen before purchasing a toy that makes a noise. If it sounds too loud for your ears, it probably is! Don't buy it.
- be very careful with toys designed to go next to the ear (such as toy phones and toys with headsets).
- remember that noisy floor toys are best listened to at a distance... teach your child not to place his ears on the speaker of the toy.

These guidelines have been prepared in conjunction with the League for the Hard of Hearing.

Subject Index

Subject Index

Brand Name and Title Index

NOTE: Toys and equipment are listed under manufacturer or distributor. The following codes are used for titles of works: (A) = Audio tape; (B) = Book; (D) = DVD and DVD Plug Ins.

Visit our website.

www.toyportfolio.com Updates, reviews of award winners, media listings, and parenting articles.

Don't miss our other great resources!

Reviews 50 classic storybooks every child from 3-8 should know and provides related activities to develop language, writing, math, and science skills. (ISBN 097210018; suggested retail $10). Available in bookstores, on-line, or by mail from the address below (add $3 for shipping and handling).

Are you in a parenting group or play group?

Contact us about special rates available for fundraisers and bulk orders.

Oppenheim Toy Portfolio, Inc.
40 East 9th St., Suite 14M
New York, New York 10003
(212) 598-0502
www.toyportfolio.com